Science
and
Its
Mirror
Image

Science and Its Mirror Image

A THEORY OF INQUIRY

Warren D. TenHouten
Charles D. Kaplan
University of California, Los Angeles

Harper & Row, Publishers
New York, Evanston, San Francisco, London

Science and Its Mirror Image: A Theory of Inquiry

Standard Book Number: 06-046589-1

Library of Congress Catalog Card Number: 73-1034

For David

Contents

Preface   **xi**

1. Introduction: An Approach to a Theory of Inquiry   1

PART ONE: THE MATERIALS   9

2. A Scientific Theory of the Brain   11
    The Left and Right Sides of the Brain   11
        The Split Brain   16
        Music and the Right Hemisphere   19
        Experiments in Sign Subception   21
        Culture, Nature, and Brain Asymmetry   22
        Psychological Manifestations of Cognitive Modes   24

3. Synthetic Inquiries: Three Case Studies—with Ronald DeZure   31
    The Tarot   33
        The Deck   33
        Arcanum 1: The Magician   34
        Arcanum 2: The High Priestess (Gnosis)   37
        Arcanum 3: The Empress (Venus)   39
        Manipulatory Techniques   40
    The I Ching   43
        The Lines   44
        The Trigrams   44
        The Hexagrams   45
        Hexagram 1: Ch'ien, the Creative   45
        Hexagram 2: K'un, the Receptive   46

Hexagram 11: **T'ai**, Peace   48
Hexagram 12: **P'i**, Stagnation   48
Manipulatory Techniques   50
The Vision Quest of Don Juan   51
The Practice: Sorcery and Seeing   53

4. **Concepts: Order and Mind; Form and Structure**   **65**
Order   66
Order and Measurement   67
Category Measurement   68
Ordinal Measurement   68
Interval Measurement   68
Ordinal Scaling   69
Mind and the Mental Order   77
Form and Structure   80
Culture and Nature   80

5. **Language in Inquiry**   **89**
English and Hopi Comparisons   90
Space and Hypermediation   100
Language as Tool   103

PART TWO: THE ANALYSIS   **109**

6. **Scientific and Synthetic Rationalities**   **111**
Scientific Rationalities   112
Synthetic Rationalities   115
Transformation C: Veiledness and Complexity "For Their
Own Sake"   116
Transformation B: Semantic Veiledness and Complexity   119
Transformation A: Layers of Structural Perception   126
Transformation D: Perception of the Situation   135

7. **Enemies in Scientific Inquiries**   **143**
Belief   144
Veiledness   146
Clarity Through Language   147
Veiledness and the Foundations of Logic   148
Weakness   152
Immaturity   154

8. **Synthetic Inquiry: Appositional Thought in the I Ching**   **157**
Layered Structures   159
Sign Particulars   162
Codes   166
Immediate Sensory Codes   167
Extended Ultracodes   173
Invariant Frames   184

9. **Dialectical Bases of Inquiry   193**
   On the Meaning of Dialectic   194
   The Laws of Dialectics in Inquiry   **202**
      Quality, Quantity, and Measure   202
      Measurement in Scientific Inquiries   204
      Measurement in Synthetic Inquiries   205
   The Unity and Struggle of Opposites   **207**
      Oppositions in Scientific Inquiries   207
      Oppositions in Synthetic Inquiries   208
   The Negation of the Negation   **214**
      Negation of the Negation in Scientific Inquiries   215
      Negation of the Negation in Synthetic Inquiries   217
   Conclusions   221
   References   226
   Index of Names   235
   Index of Subjects   237

Preface

Science is of practical concern to a civilization that relies on it as an instrument for solving technical problems and attaining political goals. And science is of personal concern to its practitioners and those college students who consider pursuing some scientific discipline as a vocation.

In the glow of its remarkable growth and capacity to answer questions that could never have been framed outside of it, however, science itself has been systematically portrayed in a one-sided way. It has been portrayed as logical, clear, precise, objective, and "value free." These admirable properties are contrasted with illogical, veiled, diffuse, subjective, and value-bound practices— including the work of sorcerers, necromancers, fortune-tellers, and "mystics." Such practices are not seen as offering truth in words, but illusion in perceptions; not the clear light of reason, but the veiled and shadowed regions of being that reach inward to the unconscious layers of awareness and outward to nature seen as a terrifying wilderness.

That science is objective and free of values—somehow detached from political struggle—is a myth that has been propounded with numbing intensity in scientific communities, in a philosophy of science that views the logic in science as its fundamental property, and in socioeconomic and political structures that control science and its inventions. Theodore Roszak writes:

> *As the spell of scientific or quasi-scientific thought has spread in our culture . . . the marked tendency has been to consign whatever is not available in the waking consciousness for empirical or mathematical manipulation, to a purely negative catch-all category (in effect, the cultural garbage can) called the "unconscious" . . . or the "irrational" . . . or the "mystical" . . . or the "purely subjective." Conversely, behavior that is normal, valuable, productive, mentally healthy, socially respectable, intellectually*

defensible, sane, decent, and practical is supposed to have nothing to do with subjectivity.[1]

This fragile myth is now coming apart at the seams. Youths who ten years ago could have sought careers as scientists now turn away from science in anger and are disillusioned. This response derives in part from the misuses of science in the name of rational decision making and "systems analysis."

If science is rejected, however, there is nothing left but to pick through the "cultural garbage can" in the hope that other practices may be discovered to replace the fallen idol. This "garbage can" has been an unexpected source of nourishment for it is lined with the alchemist's gold; and beyond that, the very act of abandoning one world of discourse and entering another is fraught with cultural and political implications. The nonscientific practices that have spread throughout the counterculture are not easily dismissed as the illusions of misguided fools. Many of these practices existed in ancient civilizations that did not produce truth in the form of propositions, but did produce a direct knowing in perception. These "left-handed" practices, along with their slightly more respectable companions—art, music, and poetry—attract a growing interest. It is recognized that the latest scientific instruments are not essential to phenomenological investigations of mind, and that useful instructions for pursuing these practices are available. An ancient Chinese book of divination is found to contain the wisdom of a philosophy that does not contradict the most recent advances in brain research. Shamans and sorcerers who use psychotropic plants or sensory deprivation to bring about nonordinary states of consciousness are found not to be mad, but to be disciplined in methods of constructing visions. These practices look irrational from a distance, but direct instruction can lead to the comprehension of strange rationalities. Moreover, while these rationalities are not part of the logic of science, they may be essential to the construction of theories and hypotheses.

In the midst of this changing situation, we decided to attempt a comparative analysis of scientific and nonscientific inquiries. If the practice of science contains rationalities that are not logical, and if nonscientific inquiries are not entirely illogical and irrational, then the rationalities and special enemies of scientific and nonscientific inquiries can be systematically compared. Almost immediately, it became possible to hypothesize the existence of a general class of nonscientific inquiries—to be called synthetic—in which the various nonscientific practices can be seen as disciplines. In this work we have been led to the view that the scientific and synthetic inquiries stand in a "mirror image" relationship, so that they are at the same time opposed and complementary. Our thesis is that scientific inquiries, though they involve perception, are primarily rooted in language and the clarification thereof, while synthetic inquiries, though they involve talk and can be written about, are primarily rooted in perception.

It is difficult to know just where ideas come from, but the notion that there are two such kinds of inquiry was in part motivated by exposure to a new neurological theory which shows that the two sides of the brain think in ways that are opposite—one being verbal and analytic, the other perceptual and syn-

---

1. Theodore Roszak, The Making of a Counter Culture, New York: McGraw-Hill, 1969, pp. 52-53.

thetic—but complementary. That things opposed to each other also complement each other is a dialectical notion, and consideration of this idea leads to a view that the two kinds of inquiry share a common basis in dialectical thought, in which the objective and the subjective, and the scientific and the synthetic, are in unity.

● ● ● ● ●

So many persons have contributed so much material, insight, and criticism to this book that the presence of our names as authors should not be taken too seriously. We do not claim to have possession of the ideas presented here; we only admit to having been possessed by them, and we hope that this book constitutes an exorcism of them. Sociologist Diana TenHouten has contributed innumerable ideas and thoughtful direction, and her grasp of the enterprise has contributed to its form and content. If it were not for the encouragement, advice, theoretical work, and professional skill of Dr. Joseph E. Bogen, the book could not have been written. Psychologist Ronald DeZure has helped all along, and he is the coauthor of Chapter 3.

Suzanna DeRooy read the entire manuscript and made innumerable critical suggestions that contributed to the internal consistency of the arguments. Ellen Neiman edited the book, rewriting numerous passages and sections with a sensitive touch that brought the ideas into clearer focus. Miss Françoise Kendall was much involved in the early planning and conceptualizing of the book; she contributed many stimulating ideas that found their way into the book, and through her editing, contributed to the overall coherence and clarity of the arguments. Additional editorial help was provided by Ellen Levine, Deanna Beeler, Faye Saben, and Gianetta TenHouten. We would also like to express our appreciation for the valuable contributions of Harper & Row Production Editor Robert Ginsberg and Designer Michel Craig.

Much of the content of the book has come about through informal conversation with June Don Batalla Kaplan, Ted Myers, Diane Dimperio Wright, Richard Beeson, Les Guliasi, Nora Harrington, Donna Seid, and David Coovert.

Among our professional colleagues, valuable help and innumerable suggestions came from Harold Garfinkel, Richard T. Morris, Charles W. Rusch, John F. Marsh, Jr., Peter Orleans, Melvin Pollner, and John Horton. For help of a more indirect nature, Santo F. Camilleri, Francis M. Sim, Arnold Brekke, and Richard P. Boyle are thanked.

The book was also stimulated by work on a research contract from the U.S. Office of Economic Opportunity, B00-5135, "Thought, Race, and Opportunity" (with John F. Marsh, Jr.). In connection with this study, helpful comment, information, and suggestions were provided by Robert Burns, Joan E. Laurence, Judith Parker, Sandra Marsh, Sharon Costello, David Listenbee, Carol Listenbee, Kirk Saunders, Thomas Banyacya, Jr., Laurel Hill, Ronald Watts, and innumerable others. Scholars who influenced the development of our thought through this study include Tommy M. Tomlinson, Barbara Williams, Paul Bakan, Elliott Liebow, Glenda Bogen, Barbara A. Henker, Richard Whitney, and Carol Whalen.

WARREN D. TENHOUTEN
CHARLES D. KAPLAN

Science
and
Its
Mirror
Image

Introduction: An Approach to a Theory of Inquiry

The aim of this book is to set forth the beginnings of a theory of inquiry. We have tried—while working toward the construction and formulation of the theory—to make the investigations scientific rather than philosophical. To this end an effort was made to avoid embedding the entire enterprise in any philosophical school of thought. Since inquiry—that disciplined activity that generates human knowledge—involves the mind, it will be necessary to deal explicitly with the concept of mind. At the outset, we want to specify two possible orientations that need to be avoided. The first of these philosophies is idealism: It will not be argued that mind is all there is, or that the physical world, including our own bodies, is illusion or is a manifestation of some Idea with soul, desire, and purpose.[1] The second is materialism: It will not be argued that mind is merely an artifact of brain mechanisms. It is possible that one of the two philosophies, idealism or materialism, captures the essence of reality, and one cannot exclude the possibility that scientists will some day settle the question within the context of their own practice; but this issue is beyond the scope of the book.

Much of modern science is grounded in materialistic philosophy, a doctrine maintaining that the physical world is ultimate reality, and that life and consciousness are manifestations of the physical world. Materialism suggests that biological and social sciences can eventually be reduced to physical laws. If this were so, then a theory of inquiry, and even a theory of consciousness, would be a physical theory. Accordingly, social and biological sciences would wither away; their topics would be explained on another level. After all, it **has** been proven that there is no essential difference between living and nonliving matter. And it seems inevitable that scientists will learn to constitute life from nonliving matter, and even constitute life with some sort of awareness or consciousness. Scientists speculate that computers will be invented that possess consciousness and emotions. This would show that even machines can have consciousness, leading to the view that mind is merely an incidental production of a machine that can be understood through a theory about machines.

The impressive advances in scientific understanding of higher brain functioning have so far produced little additional understanding of the structure of human knowledge. Consciousness itself remains a mystery; it stands as a hole in the mechanistic reality. Dean E. Wooldridge, an advocate of mechanistic reduction of consciousness to brain functioning, contends that research on brain mechanisms "may well be the only sound procedure for permanently plugging the hole in the logical structure of the mechanistic philosophy: to accept the sense of consciousness itself as a natural phenomenon suited to being described by and dealt with by the body of laws and methods of the physical sciences."[2] He goes on to describe the criteria for such a reduction: "All that is really required, for the sense of consciousness to constitute a reasonable candidate for admission into the structure of physics, is that it be orderly and lawful in its operation, and that techniques be conceivable for determining the relationships between its properties and the physical environment in which it occurs."[3]

Philosopher and scientist Michael Polanyi presents a critique of such efforts to reduce consciousness to physiochemical terms. He writes:

Neurology is based on the assumption that the nervous system—functioning automatically according to the known laws of physics and chemistry—determines all the working which we normally attribute to the mind of an individual. . . .

This raises the question whether in view of the logical analysis of "a machine in use" we can accept a neurological model (or an analogous psychological model) as the representation of an individual's mind. In answering this question we must take into account an obvious difference between an automatic neurological model and a machine operated for intelligent purposes; namely, that the neurological model is not supposed to operate for purposes of the neurologist, but for purposes attributed to its operations by the neurologist on behalf of the subject whose mind it represents. The tripartite system accordingly becomes:

I	II	III
Mind (of Neurologist)	Neurological model of subject	Intellectual purposes attributed to the subject by the neurologist.

But the informal mental functions briefly indicated under III are those of the neurologist's mind, since the informal and hence personal functions of the **subject's** mind are in fact not represented at all in the tripartite system. For the neurological model is—like a machine—strictly impersonal and can account for none of the unspecifiable propensities of the subject.

These personal powers include the capacity for understanding a meaning, for believing a factual statement, for interpreting a mechanism in relation to its purpose, and on a higher level, for reflecting on problems and exercising originality in solving them. They include, indeed, every manner of reaching convictions by an act of personal judgment. The neurologist exercises these powers to the highest degree in constructing the neurological model of a man—to whom he denies in this very act any similar powers.[4]

It is possible to be a practitioner of science without embracing the mechanistic doctrine. The mechanistic philosophy assumes that mind, being of the brain machinery, is not an independent level of reality. For example, Wooldridge suggests: "It is not clear that the behavior of any individual or the course of world history would have been affected in any way if awareness were non-existent."[5] We contend instead that the development of human knowledge, which is contained in awareness, has profoundly influenced history. Karl R. Popper argued that the impossibility of predicting the development of human knowledge rendered a theory of history impossible.[6] While Popper's argument may be exaggerated in the other direction, it is clear that a theory of history, if one is possible at all, presupposes a theory of knowledge.

We presume that society and mind can be understood on their own levels. The social order and the mental order are no less realities than the physical order. From this it follows that the study of inquiry is not a problem in physics and that a theory of inquiry cannot be produced within physics. To the extent that inquiry exists in social structure, a theory of inquiry must be produced within social science. Of course, scientific knowledge is physical in the sense that it consists largely of words printed on paper. But it is knowledge only because there are eyes that see these words and minds that grasp their meanings. While we cannot reduce inquiry to brain functioning, we **must** consider knowledge as a production of mind. While the study of the brain can never exhaust the study of the productions of inquirers, we can certainly hope to learn something about mind through studies of the brain, the autonomic nervous system, the senses, and the body in general.

The book begins with a recent scientific theory of the brain. There now exists impressive evidence that in most persons capacity for abstract logical thought is associated with the left side of the brain and capacity for perceptual and spatial thought with the right side of the brain. The kind of thinking associated with the left side of the brain seems to characterize thinking that scientists primarily use. The brain theory asserts that the thinking of the right side of the brain is not a "lower level" function; this kind of thought is nonscientific, but there is order in it. The right hemisphere is essentially involved in the construction of art, music, and poetry. It is associated with innumerable practices directed toward the attainment of knowledge that cannot be clearly stated in words. Neurosurgeon Joseph E. Bogen has chosen the words **propositional** and **appositional** as labels for those functions typically carried out by the left and right sides of the brain, respectively.[7]

We do not assume that all nonscientific ways of seeking knowledge fail.[8] Possibilities for attaining knowledge exist in either scientific or nonscientific inquiries. A scientific theory can be beautiful; a poem can lead a scientist to an insight, perhaps a new concept that he may employ in his scientific inquiries. But what is the difference between a theory and a poem? What is the difference between a scientific experiment and the operations of a sorcerer?

The findings that the left and right sides of the brain carry out two kinds of thought—propositional and appositional—suggest that a theory of inquiry that compares scientific and nonscientific ways of knowing might be possible. In this book we intend to present a theory that makes use of these concepts. It will be argued that there are two general kinds of inquiry: One is called scientific and uses propositional thought; the other is called synthetic and uses appositional thought.

A scientific theory requires empirical data. Since two kinds of inquiry are posited, scientific and synthetic inquiries must be used as case studies. Science has been expanded into such a vast enterprise and has been studied so intensely by philosophers that powerful analyses are at our disposal. The nonscientific ways of knowing, in contrast, have received almost no attention by scientists and only limited analysis by Western philosophers. The problem is compounded by the central role of perception and personal experience in these inquiries. There is no unified nonscientific method. This problem is dealt with by selecting a small number of nonscientific inquiries as case studies for the theory. While numerous synthetic inquiries are mentioned, three case studies are systematically pursued: the **I Ching** or **Book of Changes**, an ancient Chinese book of knowledge constituting the basis of both Taoism and Confucianism; the **Tarot**, a system of knowledge derived from medieval or ancient Western schools of occult thought, known today by a deck of fortune-telling cards; and the **vision quest**, a struggle to see, described by anthropologist Carlos Castaneda as a result of an apprenticeship to a Yaqui Indian sorcerer called don Juan. It will not be assumed that the reader has prior knowledge of these practices. Sufficient description of the inquiries will be provided so that a reader who has never heard of them can follow the analysis without difficulty.

We hope the book is of interest to practitioners of the **I Ching**, the **Tarot**, and related methods of inquiry; but be warned that while the topic includes nonscientific knowledge, the approach is totally biased: We are committed to carrying out an analysis as practitioners of science. In order to do this, we have also had to become practitioners of these nonscientific systems. Thus, the problem was approached by becoming practitioners of both scientific and nonscientific inquiries and making the topic of our scientific investigations the comparative analysis of the two kinds of inquiry. We feel that the study of nonscientific inquiries provides insight into the practice of science. But while these insights have contributed concepts to the theory and have led to a consideration of the logic in science as actually practiced, such insights are not themselves theoretical.

There are two tasks. First, it is necessary to analyze the ways in which scientific and synthetic inquiries are different. This involves the study of principles of reason that are peculiar to each method. To this end, use is made of sociologist Harold Garfinkel's four principles of reason, or rationalities, that are unique to science. It is argued that just as the two hemispheres of the brain are gross mirror images of one another, so there exist rationalities in all synthetic inquiries standing as "mirror images" of scientific rationalities. This analysis of the rationalities is reinforced by an analysis of the enemies of the scientific and synthetic ways of knowing. In explicating these negative factors, the enemies of scientific and synthetic inquiries are seen to stand in a mirror image relation.

Second, it is necessary to analyze the ways in which scientific and synthetic inquiries are the same. The last chapter argues that all advanced inquiries have laws of dialectics as their common basis. Hegel wrote that dialectics is the soul of all knowledge that is truly scientific. He did not claim dialectics to be the soul of all knowledge; this book advances such an argument. Since Marx, Engels, Lenin, and others propounded their theory of political history, dialectics has been associated with radical thought. While these scholars replaced Hegel's idealism with their own materialism, the study of dialectics itself has been given little attention. We shall attempt to show that nonscientific methods share with science a **basis** in dialectical thought, and we shall suggest that the practice of these systems develops dialectical consciousness.

The problem of duality haunts every chapter of this book, for the neurological theory of the brain has been interpreted as evidence that the mind is dual. The findings of neurological research demonstrate that given the usual definition of mind, a normal person has two minds. Here, however, it is argued that these "minds" are contained in the mental order, which includes distinguishable component parts, including the functions of the left and right cerebral hemispheres, but is itself essentially unitary. The mental order constitutes a dialectical synthesis transcending the functions carried out by each particular layer of mind. It is this dialectical organization of the mind that provides the basis for all inquiries.

● ● ● ● ●

This book is difficult on many counts, for unavoidable reasons. The topic, the structure of inquiry, has led us to a consideration of materials that may, at first glance, seem unrelated or, at best, not crucially related to each other or to inquiry itself. Some of these materials, beginning with the structure of the human brain in Chapter 2, may be foreign to most readers. An effort is made to express these neurological data in a way that presupposes little or no knowledge on the reader's part of neurology and physiology. Similarly, the inquiries we are calling synthetic, those presented in Chapter 3, may seem disturbingly alien at first. Again we must ask the reader's indulgence. It is our belief that if one is ever to understand the nature of nonscientific inquiries—their operations and how they illuminate the process of discovery—one must first experience its methods directly. To talk about these methods in the abstract would not be likely to provide the perspective we want for the reader. Given problems of space, we have settled on the idea of a brief excursion into the aforementioned systems—the **I Ching**, the **Tarot**, and the vision quest of an Indian American. Chapter 4, entitled **Concepts**, explores the crucial concepts of order and mind, form and structure, culture and nature, as we understand them to relate to the problem of inquiry. Chapter 5 attempts a linguistic comparison of English and Hopi in order to illustrate the dramatically different ways in which language is employed to encourage and reinforce ways of perceiving reality, and also attempts to describe language as a tool for inquiry.

By now it is probably clear that with each succeeding chapter the reader is abruptly brought into some new, probably unfamiliar, terrain. He must take it—generally on good faith—that the experience of these terrains is a viable preparation for the analyses in Chapters 6 through 9. At the least, it is the authors' preparation, so that we enter into an analysis of inquiry having shared the same materials. These first chapters, 2 through 5, present the key materials for an analysis that must come to terms with such questions as: Why is it important to understand nonscientific thought? What is the relation of scientific thought to nonscientific thought? What difficulties can be seen in the current reliance on scientific thinking as the way to develop knowledge?

In a sense, the organization of this book, with all its disjunctions, is in itself an exercise in alternative approaches to inquiry. In the book's first part the reader is provided with the raw ingredients of the theory.

NOTES

1. This idealism dominates numerous Eastern philosophical and religious systems; in the West, it is derived from a tradition of philosophical idealism that preceded Hegel.

2. Dean E. Wooldridge, **The Machinery of the Brain**, New York: McGraw-Hill, 1963, p. 234; statement after colon emphasized in text.

3. Ibid., p. 239. Cf. C. U. M. Smith, **The Brain: Toward an Understanding** New York: Capricorn, 1970, pp. 25–36, 348–366. While Smith does not reject the mind–body dualism, he does advocate a position of "psychoneural unity," such that the mind and the brain are the same thing looked at from different positions. This position embraces Schopenhauer's philosophy, which asserted that every immediate act of will is also directly a manifestation of body. See Arthur Schopenhauer, **The World as Will and Idea**, vol. I, trans. R. B. Haldane and J. Kemp, London: Routledge & Kegan Paul, 1957.

4. Michael Polanyi, **Personal Knowledge: Toward a Post-Critical Philosophy**, Chicago: University of Chicago Press, 1958, pp. 262–263.

5. Wooldridge, op. cit., p. 240.

6. Karl R. Popper, **The Poverty of Historicism**, New York: Harper & Row, 1961.

7. Joseph E. Bogen, "The Other Side of the Brain II: An Appositional Mind," **Bulletin of the Los Angeles Neurological Societies**, vol. 34, 1969, pp. 145–147.

8. Such an assumption is made in the metascientific school of thought known as logical empiricism (also called logical positivism) in which logic, including mathematics, is seen as the only respectable inquiry besides empirical science. See Morton White, **The Age of Analysis: 20th Century Philosophers**, Boston: Houghton Mifflin, 1955, p. 205, and Gerard Radnitzky, **Anglo-Saxon Schools of Metascience**, vol. 1, Göteborg, Sweden: Berlingska Boktrgckeriet Land, 1968.

Part One

The Materials

A Scientific Theory of the Brain

THE LEFT AND RIGHT SIDES OF THE BRAIN

Our point of departure for a comparative analysis of scientific and synthetic inquiries is provided by recent advances in scientific knowledge of brain functioning. The higher brain functions are carried out in the cerebrum, which in man has exploded upward and outward from the brain stem. The cerebrum contains a variety of structures connected by systems of nerve fibers. One of its fundamental features is its division into left and right hemispheres that are gross mirror images of each other.[1] Similarities in weight and metabolic rate suggest that each performs the same amount of work. Bogen writes that "the informational capacity of the one is just as great as the other; or, put differently, the other . . . is not only working just as hard, but also just as intricately."[2] Despite such overall structural similarities, impressive evidence indicates that the two hemispheres differ in cognitive functioning. The left dominates the verbal functions of speech, writing, and reading.[3] Neurologist John Hughlings Jackson wrote, in 1864, that the distinguishing feature of the left hemisphere is not possession of words, but rather its use of words in propositions, that is, in sequences in which the meanings of the words are interdependent.[4] He concluded that in cases of damage to the left hemisphere "the words removed are those employed in the formation of propositions; those which remain to the speechless patient are the same words used non-propositionally."[5] Bogen follows Jackson's term "propositionizing" and names the totality of functions of the left hemisphere **propositional**.

Jackson stated further that "if . . . the faculty of expression resides in one hemisphere, there is no absurdity in raising the question as to whether perception—its corresponding opposite—may not be seated in the other."[6] Recent neurological studies have borne out the pertinence of Jackson's question. There is diverse evidence indicating that while the left hemisphere dominates propositional thought, the right hemisphere dominates certain visual and constructive tasks, such as drawing, copying, and assembling block designs, and constructive activity in the arts, such as poetry, literature, and painting. More generally, the right hemisphere dominates thought based on the simultaneous grasping or enclosing of fragments or particulars as a whole, or **gestalt**. Bogen has given the name **appositional** to the totality of functions of the right hemisphere, which suggests an analogy with the role of man's appositional thumb in grasping an object. He writes that the term "implies a capacity for apposing or comparing of perception, schemas, . . . , etc., but has in addition the virtue that it implies very little else."[7] J. Levy-Agresti and Roger W. Sperry's terminology is also useful, as they contrast the left hemisphere's "logical—analytic" thought to the right hemisphere's "gestalt-synthetic" thought.[8]

The idea of two modes of thought has been presented in a number of scientific theories. Ivan P. Pavlov regarded human thought as divided into two signaling systems. The first is concerned with concrete perceptions immediately connected with responses to the natural world, the second with language and abstraction.[9] Aleksandr R. Luriia wrote that the cerebrum has two basic types of integrative activities, which he classified as "temporally organized successive series" and "simultaneous primary spatial groups."[10] Bogen writes that although this distinction suggests no lateralization of brain function, "it implies what well may be the most important distinction between the left and the right hemisphere modes; that is, the extent to which a linear concept of time participates in the ordering of thought."[11]

Sigmund Freud also hypothesized two modes of cognition, although his theories differed radically from Pavlov's. According to Freud's view, "secondary process" thought develops with the attainment of language, while "primary process" thought is concrete rather than verbal, employs pictorial images, and can be described as "primitive."[12] Otto Fenichel wrote that the type of thought described by Freud "is remote from any logic. But it is thinking nevertheless because it consists of imaginations according to which later actions are performed."[13]

I. Macfarlane Smith has been a primary exponent of the view that spatial ability is an independent factor in mental performance. In his research on the role of spatial thought in education, he argues that tests that are most closely associated with spatial ability involve the capacity to perceive or recognize the structure of a figure as a whole, rather than the ability to recognize details.[14] When C. Spearman read Smith's 1937 thesis, he was reluctant to accept the existence of such a spatial factor in human thought.[15] Yet by 1950 Spearman's research led him to a similar conclusion: "The senior writer happened to notice that such tests can readily be performed in two distinct manners. One may be

 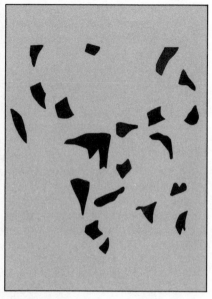

(handwritten in left margin: Fig) upside down — w J)

Figure 1.
Source: Roy F. Street, **A Gestalt Completion Test: A Study of a Cross Section of Intellect,**
New York: Teachers College Press, copyright 1931 by Teachers College, Columbia University, Items 8, 9. Reprinted by permission of the publisher.

called **analytic** in the sense that attention wanders from one element of the figure to another. The other mode of operation is comparatively **synthetic** in that the figures (or their constituents) are mentally grasped in much larger units (sometimes called 'wholes')."[16]

That grasping a whole constitutes appositional thought can be shown by visual example. Consider the two items in Figure 1, taken from the Roy F. Street Gestalt Completion Test. The fragments can be seen as a horse and rider and a rabbit only by a simultaneous grasping of all the particular fragments. Recognition does not come about through any sequence of logical operations constituting an analysis of these fragments; words and propositions about the fragments are of no value. Recognition comes about instantaneously; the animals are seen all at once or not at all. The problem is solved not through analysis but through synthesis; such appositional thought consists of silent and nonverbal perception. Now consider an isomorphic situation in nature (Figure 2). The copperhead snake hides the edges of its form through disruptive coloration. An engineer might not notice it, seeing only a pile of leaves; but a "primitive" would be more apt to grasp the form of the snake, seeing the patches of color as a whole.[17]

An extensive program of factor analytic research by Spearman and Wynn Jones has produced a typology of three factors in human intelligence—verbal, spatial, and general.[18] The general intelligence factor in all probability involves participation by both cerebral hemispheres and may reflect integration of the two modes.

In the 1930s psychologists began to employ mental tests standardized on

Figure 2.
Source: Reproduced from **Aspects of Form,** edited by Lancelot Law Whyte, London: Lund Humphries, 1968, Figure 2.2.

"normal" persons in the study of neurological patients. Theodore Weisenburg and Katharine E. McBride administered an extensive battery of mental tests to over 200 persons either suffering or not suffering from aphasia (an inability to speak or to understand words). They report that "the pathological materials afford ample evidence that language plays a tremendous part in thinking and in intelligent behavior but at the same time it is evident that purposeful and effective thinking may be carried through when language is extremely inadequate or confused, and must therefore depend largely on non-linguistic symbols such as visual or kinaesthetic images."[19] David Wechsler reduced these tests (which had taken about 18 hours per patient to administer) to a more convenient battery of six verbal and five nonverbal or performance subtests that have been widely used in clinical psychology.[20] A. Lloyd Anderson first used the subtests to examine patients with one-sided brain lesions; he found that patients with left-sided lesions experienced greater loss in the verbal subtests, whereas those patients with right-sided lesions experienced greater loss in the nonverbal subtests.[21] These findings, though qualified by numerous methodological problems, do provide suggestive evidence in support of the theory and have been confirmed by a number of other studies.[22]

Disorders of spatial thought are often associated with diffuse or two-sided brain damage, but may also occur when a lesion is restricted to one hemisphere.[23] Macdonald Critchley found that for 12 patients with disorders of spatial thought, unilateral damage was thought to be present in the left hemisphere of one patient (not verified), and on the right side for the other 11 patients (9 verified). He concludes that "the clinical occurrence of marked disorders of spatial thought should . . . lead to the strong suspicion of a lesion of the hinder part of the brain. . . . Other things being equal, it is the right . . . side of the brain which comes under greatest suspicion."[24] Henri Hécaen summarized findings in 415 patients with a variety of lesions in the back of the brain and found disorders of spatial thought to be associated with right-sided lesions. Of 59 cases of one-sided spatial agnosia (Freud defined **agnosia** as "disturbances in the recognition of objects"[25]), 15 had right hemisphere lesions, and 3 of the 4 patients with left hemisphere lesions were left-handed.[26] (Roughly one-half of left-handers have the propositional functions in the right hemisphere.) Inability to identify known faces occurred in 22 patients, of whom 16 had predominantly right-sided lesions (one was a left-hander). Hécaen and R. Angelergues conclude from these data that "the right hemisphere appears to play a special role in the appreciation of space and the recognition of faces. . . ."[27]

Studies of patients with brain tumors often are confounded by the presence of secondary symptoms. Operational removal of brain tissue for the purpose of relieving epileptic seizures, however, yields lesions with well-defined boundaries. Research on such patients is consequently of particular value in the study of hemispheric specialization. A program of research on such patients conducted by Brenda Milner and her co-workers contributes an imposing body of evidence in support of the notion of hemispheric specialization.[28] While their findings are qualified by changes in brain functioning as a result of long-term epilepsy and earlier head injuries, they consistently find that patients with left temporal lobe removal experience verbal deficits and that patients with right temporal lobe removal are impaired in perceiving pictures and in related visual performances.

L. D. Costa and H. G. Vaughn observed 54 patients in a carefully designed study. In their sample, 18 subjects had lesions in the left hemisphere, 18 had lesions in the right hemisphere, and a control group of 18 subjects had no lesions.[29] The sampling design controlled factors such as age, sex, severity of brain damage, and brain wave data. Verbal and performance tests—the Mill–Hill Vocabulary Test and the Wechsler Block Design Test—were administered. Results showed that patients with right hemisphere lesions performed significantly better on the vocabulary test, and patients with left hemisphere lesions achieved higher scores on the Block Design Test.

The term **constructional apraxia** is defined as "a disturbance in formative activities (arranging, building, drawing) in which the overall spatial part of the task is missing, although there is no apraxia of single movements."[30] The phenomenon of construction apraxia, as one might expect, has also been linked to the functioning of the right hemisphere. Malcolm Piercy writes that "it is now clear that failure on constructional tasks under visual control occurs more commonly and takes more severe form with right than with left hemisphere lesions. . . ."[31]

The Split Brain

The cerebral commissures (the largest of which is called the **corpus callosum**) are a mass of an estimated two million nerve fibers that connect the left and right hemispheres and provide the primary means of interhemispheric communication. Michael C. Corballis and Ivan L. Beale write that "such connections would create a kind of neural mirror that serves to 'reflect' neural activity across the midline. We believe the process might apply particularly to the transfer of memory traces between hemispheres: If a trace is established in one hemisphere, its mirror-image will be traced to the other."[32] A lesion in one hemisphere frequently results in abnormal functioning in the mirror-image position of the other.

A. L. Wigan was the first neurologist to advance a theory of the duality of the mind. He observed that autopsies occasionally reveal the absence of an entire cerebral hemisphere in persons who appeared to be normal and to possess a mind up to the time of their death. From this startling discovery he inferred that since most persons have two functioning hemispheres, most persons have two minds.[33]

Wigan's findings are supported by studies of patients who have undergone removal of an entire hemisphere (hemispherectomy). These patients typically experience only limited impairment of intellectual capability.[34] Even more direct evidence in support of Wigan's observation is provided by "split brain" surgery, in which the separation of the two hemispheres is effected by severing the nerve fibers of the corpus callosum and all other fibers directly connecting the hemispheres. This procedure has been carried out on humans in order to relieve generalized epileptic-seizure activity and on cats and monkeys in order to study brain functioning. Both eyes of higher animals are connected by fibers to both cerebral hemispheres. The optic nerves that go from the left eye to the right hemisphere and from the right eye to the left hemisphere meet in what is called the **optic chiasm**. It is possible to cut the optic chiasm to eliminate the crossed paths so that inputs from the right eye go **only** to the right hemisphere and inputs from the left eye go **only** to the left hemisphere. Ronald E. Myers trained monkeys that had undergone such surgery to choose between two symbols presented to just one eye and found these animals able to make a later correct choice with the other eye.[35] This finding suggests that the corpus callosum can transfer learned visual discrimination from one hemisphere to the other. In a second preparation, both the optic chiasm **and** the corpus callosum were severed. After this surgery, learning did **not** transfer from one hemisphere to the other as it did when the optic chiasm alone was severed. The other eye, in fact, can be trained to choose the **opposite** number of the two stimuli, so that the "correct" symbol depends on which eye is covered. In this way, the two hemispheres are shown to solve a problem in different ways and (as Wigan imagined they could) to function **independently**. More recently, M. S. Gazzaniga and E. D. Young have demonstrated that monkeys whose optic chiasms and cerebral commissures are cut can learn to solve a problem with one hand while simultaneously solving an independent problem with the other hand, a feat that monkeys that have not been operated on are barely able to perform.[36]

John Noble carried out essentially the same experiment, except that the two stimuli used were left-right mirror images of each other (see Figure 3). He severed the optic chiasm and covered one of the monkeys' eyes; then he taught them to select one of two stimuli (Figure 3a). After training, the monkeys were presented the same stimuli with the sight of the trained eye blocked off (Figure 3b), and they eventually showed a preference for the cue that had not been rewarded, the mirror image of the "correct" answer. He concluded that the information was reversed during its transfer across the corpus callosum. To test this conclusion, he repeated the one-eyed training (Figure 3c), except after learning had taken place, he split the corpus callosum before presenting the pair of stimuli to the untrained eye (Figure 3d). Here, the trained hemisphere was rendered unable to transfer the mirror image of what it had learned, and the mon-

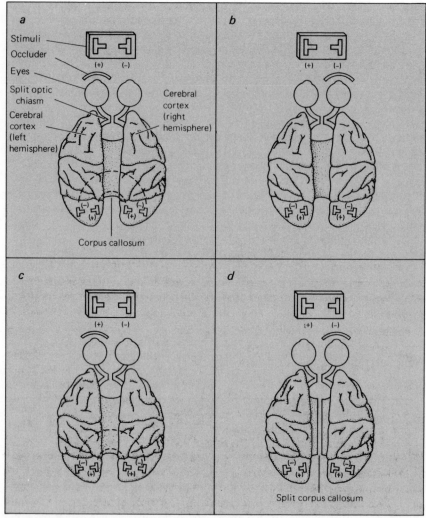

Figure 3. Information transfer in mirror image form in Noble's experiment with monkey subjects.

Source: From Michael C. Corballis and Ivan L. Beale, "On Telling Left from Right," copyright © 1971 by **Scientific American, Inc.** All rights reserved.

keys were able to select, by other ways, the cue they had originally learned.[37] Observations that persons who write with the right hand are often able to learn mirror writing (from right to left) with their left hand more effectively than nonmirrored writing also supports the notion of mirror-image reversal in interhemispheric transfer.

At least 50 humans have undergone the split-brain operation (cerebral commissurotomy). Performed primarily to diminish the spread and severity of epileptic seizures, the procedure provides an opportunity to study the independent functioning of the two hemispheres. Following the operation, the right side

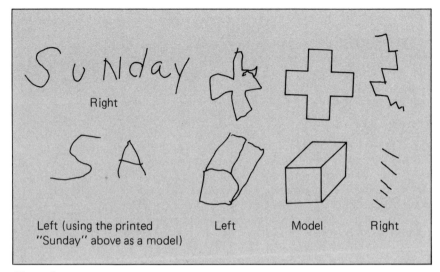

Figure 4.
Source: Joseph E. Bogen, "The Other Side of the Brain I: Dysgraphia and Dyscopia Following Cerebral Commissurotomy," **Bulletin of the Los Angeles Neurological Society,** vol. 34, 1969, Figure 5b, p. 83.

of the body is controlled by the left hemisphere, and vice versa. Therefore performances carried out by the right hand result from left hemisphere activity, and performances carried out by the left are related to the activity of the right hemisphere.

In a study of the first eight patients undergoing this surgery, Bogen found that all patients experienced a reduced capability to write (dysgraphia) with the left hand but not with the right hand.[38] This suggests that writing is controlled by the left hemisphere. These patients also experienced a reduced capacity to copy figures (dyscopia) with the right hand, but not with the left, suggesting that this ability is controlled by the right hemisphere.

The dysgraphia–dyscopia (D–D) phenomenon is illustrated in Figure 4 by responses of one of the split-brain patients. To measure dysgraphia, a written model of the word "Sunday" was used. The patient copied the word with his right hand, but could manage only a crude "S A" with his left. His dyscopia is illustrated by his effort to copy a Greek cross and a solid cube. He copied the figures quite well with his left hand but not with his right hand.

These eight patients varied considerably in their degree of incapacity, and also in the length of time D-D persisted. Factors such as low ability to develop ipsilateral control (for example, of the right hand by the right hemisphere), early brain damage, and low measured intelligence contributed to long periods of D–D.[39]

Music and the Right Hemisphere
S. E. Henschen reports that "in many cases of motor aphasia the faculty of singing is conserved in spite of the inability to speak a single word. In such cases the patient probably sings by means of the right hemisphere."[40] Aaron Smith describes a patient who had his entire left hemisphere removed in surgery and

could not speak at all, but who could sing a number of songs he had learned at an earlier age.[41] There is ample evidence that while much musical ability does not suffer from left hemisphere lesions (excluding capacity for understanding written music), it does suffer as a result of right hemisphere lesions, which do not damage speech. Milner, for example, reports that scores on the timbre and tonal subtests of the Seashore Measure of Musical Ability Test are depressed by right temporal lobectomy, but not by left temporal lobectomy.[42]

Doreen Kimura used listening experiments to further validate the specialization of music in the right hemisphere. She hypothesized that if two different melodies were presented simultaneously one in each ear (a procedure called "dichotic listening"), the subjects should best remember the melody played into the left ear,[43] which disproportionately informs the right hemisphere. This result has been consistently obtained; samples of normal subjects give more accurate identifications for the left ear than for the right ear.

The participation of appositional thought in music is also illustrated by the gestalt psychologist Max Wertheimer. Wertheimer makes no reference to brain functioning, but his analysis pertains to the concepts of propositional and appositional thought. He posed a problem of classifying four lines of written music:[44] A **propositional** classification might put lines A and B together as one class and C and D as a second class on the ground that each class begins with the same two notes (Figure 5), assuming that the structures can be understood through a reduction of the melodies to sequences of notes. Such an analysis is exact, but misses the point. For it is the melodies, characterized by simultaneous understanding of all of the notes, that reflect the "inner structure." C is a transposition of the melody in A, and D is a transposition of the melody in B. Hence the (AB/CD) classifications are "not the same for somebody who **grasps** the melodies. For him the two notes which the classification, with its atomistic procedure, regards as identical, are actually very different as to the roles they play in the melody."[45] Thus the inner structure of the melodies involves the synthetic capacities of appositional thought, a grasping of the whole.

The tonal aspects of music also belong to the appositional domain. Wertheimer notes that "the second note in A is the tonic, the 'identical' second note in B is far from being a tonic; it is the leading tone which asks for, drives toward the tonic which here is the third note."[46] Wertheimer's remarks on the problem of classifying these four lines of music merits direct quotation.

> In regard to the question of classification the main point boils down to the old proverb,
>
> si duo faciunt idem, non est idem,
>
> if two do the same, it is not the same. In exact terms: Two items or two groups of items which are identical from an atomistic point of view (cf. above AB/CD), may mean very different things structurally, and may in fact be different in nature. A necessary addition is the opposite sentence: If, from an atomistic point of view, two do very different things (cf. above AC/BD), their actions may nevertheless be structurally the same. In order to do the same in a changed situation one has to do it differently. In exact terms: Different items may be structurally the same.[47]

Figure 5.
Source: Max Wertheimer, **Productive Thinking,** enlarged edition, ed. Michael Wertheimer,
New York: Harper & Row, 1959, Figure 163, p. 253.

EXPERIMENTS IN SIGN SUBCEPTION

The propositional-appositional distinction receives indirect support from psychological experiments designed to demonstrate relations between two events, only
one of which is known at the verbal level. R. S. Lazarus and R. A. Cleary presented subjects with a large number of nonsense syllables. After the display of
certain of these syllables, an electric shock was administered. The subjects sub-
sequently became apprehensive when the "shock syllables" were presented, but
were unable to identify these syllables verbally.[48] In a related experiment, C. W.
Eriksen and J. L. Kuethe presented words to subjects, and administered shocks
to associations uttered to certain "shock words." The subjects learned to avoid
shocks by not uttering these words, but could not explain this learning.[49] In
both experiments, subceptions (perceptions without verbal correlates) were
induced by electric shocks, where the shock-producing particulars (syllables,
words) remained tacit.

In analyzing these experiments, Polanyi describes such subcepts as tacit
knowing, which consists of two elements (the shock syllables or shock words
and the shocks). The first term is known only by attending to the second. Thus
the electric shock is seen by Polanyi as "**specifiably** known. But we know the
shock-producing particulars only by relying on our awareness of them for attending to . . . the electric shock, and hence our knowledge of them remains
tacit."[50]

Polanyi also argues that face recognition is a type of tacit knowing, according to which "we are attending **from** the features **to** the face, and thus may be
unable to specify the features."[51] That is, the features or particulars that pre-
cede the total event (a shock, or a recognized face) are known only in that they
signify the whole. In such subceptive thought the particulars exist only as signs.

We shall call these elements of configurations **sign-particulars,** a notion that is pursued in Chapter 8.

Face recognition, and recognition of wholes or gestalts, are known to be right hemisphere functions.[52] Thus we can regard responses to sign-particulars as appositional thought. These experiments, and research in gestalt psychology, demonstrate that an object can be known through simultaneous consideration of members of a set of particulars in which the particulars are not known at the verbal level.

CULTURE, NATURE, AND BRAIN ASYMMETRY

The neurological theory indicates the mirror-image quality of the two hemispheres. In the socialization process they come to be specialized, the left hemisphere becoming increasingly involved in speech and the right hemisphere in perceptual and visual tasks. More generally, the left hemisphere deals with culture, and with language and propositional logic, which do not exist in nature but are essential to the development and transmission of culture. It is a widely held view among social scientists that capacity for language is **the** basis for culture and that man's development and retention of culture derives from this capacity. The right hemisphere's orientation is toward perception and observation. Included in this domain are perceptions of one's body and perceptions of phenomena external to it. The distinction between a person's body and the rest of nature is culturally learned. In sum, it can be said that the basic activities of the left and right cerebral hemispheres pertain to the comprehensions of culture and nature, respectively. Note the correspondence to Pavlov's first and second signaling systems.[53]

Given man's bilateral symmetry, it is difficult for children to tell left from right. Corballis and Beale contend, however, that unilateral asymmetric responses, such as the predominant use of one hand, a consistently directed eye movement, or a tilt of the head to one side, are sufficient for learning even the most complex mirror-image discriminations. For example, children can learn left from right by writing or throwing with a single hand. While recognition of asymmetry has obvious survival value, the preservation of symmetry also is functional. Corballis and Beale generalize: "In the natural environment there is more to be gained from mirror-image equivalence than from mirror-image discrimination."[54] For example, an attack from the left provides later recognition of an attack from the right, and vice versa.

Nature is generally symmetrical, with respect to both living and inanimate structures. Plants characteristically have radial symmetry, and animals bilateral symmetry. A picture of a landscape contains essentially the same information when seen in a mirror. Martin Gardner notes that "if you take a photograph of a lake and reverse the negative to obtain a print in which right is left and left is right, it still looks like a perfectly ordinary lake."[55] He adds that "it is difficult to tell if a photograph of **any** natural scene is reversed unless the picture happens to contain some bilaterally **asymmetrical** man-made object, such as a sign with printing on it or streets with cars driving on one side of the road."[56] Many cultural objects, such as writing, look much different when seen in a mirror, and can be interpreted only with difficulty.

Bilateral symmetry is a recurring theme in primitive art, especially in split representation of animals and men portrayed in drawings and in masks. This symmetry is found also in Medieval art, but is not present in later painting. A painting loses some aesthetic appeal if transformed into its mirror image. It has been observed that a photograph of a painting has more aesthetic value than a mirror-image photograph of the painting. For music, in which sound tones flow along a time dimension, a mirror image of a melody is obtained by playing it backward (for example, with a tape recorder). Gardner points out that when this is done, "in most cases the backward music is a meaningless jumble of sounds, not pleasant to hear."[57] Speech also may be thought of as a series of sounds ordered along a single dimension of time. And speech, a fundamental component of culture, is also rendered unintelligible when heard as its mirror image. On the importance of asymmetrical entities to the cultural order, Corballis and Beale conclude:

> In general, it appears that the left-right asymmetries are particularly associated with the kinds of behavior that are no longer restricted to the natural environment. This conclusion re-emphasizes our point that the large majority of left-right asymmetries exist only in the man-made environment. In tool use, in communication and in other kinds of symbolic behavior man is essentially freed from the symmetrical constraints imposed by the natural world. It is primarily with respect to these types of behavior that the human brain and nervous system have become lateralized.[58]

It is probable that nearly all cultures attribute left and right to the natural and cultural domains, with the natural regarded as profane and the cultural as sacred. The left hand is invidiously stereotyped from the standpoint of culture. For example, in describing Maori culture Robert Hertz wrote:

> Among the Maori the right is the sacred side, the seat of good and creative powers; the left is the profane side, possessing no virtue other than . . . certain disturbing and suspect powers. The same contrast reappears in the course of the evolution of religion, in more precise and less impersonal forms: the right is the side of the gods, where hovers the white figure of a good guardian angel; the left side is dedicated to demons, the devil; a black and wicked angel holds it in dominion. Even today . . . the right hand is still called good and beautiful and the left bad and ugly.[59]

Hertz reported that the Maori also name the right side by a term designating man's masculine nature, and the left side by a term designating man's feminine nature.[60]

While the right side is considered sacred among the Maori and numerous other cultures, the left hand and the female element—while profane from the perspective of the cultural order—are not viewed as lacking in resources. On this Hertz writes: "If a woman is powerless and passive in the religious order, she has her revenge in the domain of magic: She is particularly fitted for works of sorcery. 'All evils, misery, and death,' says a Maori proverb, 'come from the female element.' "[61] Inquiries such as sorcery, and related investigations of the "dark forces" are called "left-handed practices."

In some contexts the left hand is apt to be repressed in addition to being negatively stereotyped. Devaluation of the left hand has been demonstrated in the cultures of Hindus, American Mohave Indians, American Chippewa Indians, and Arabs. G. William Domhoff, in a study of stereotyping of left and right, reports that samples of American white children, adolescents, and adults make similar distinctions.[62]

PSYCHOLOGICAL MANIFESTATIONS OF COGNITIVE MODES

While the evidence is clear that there are propositional and appositional modes of thought lateralized in the two sides of the brain, it does not necessarily follow logically that there are propositional and appositional thinkers—persons specialized in one mode or the other. However, evidence exists that such may be the case.

Pavlov, as mentioned, conceived of thought as divided into two signaling systems, the first involving perception and the second language. He is quoted by Y. P. Frolov as saying: "The mass of human beings can be divided into artistic, thinking, and intermediate types. The last named combines the work of both systems in the requisite degree."[63]

Psychologist Merle E. Day's research shows that most persons, when asked questions such as "What is 12 times 13?" or "Who is your favorite composer?" immediately look to the left or to the right.[64] While the physiological mechanism of the conjugate lateral eye movements (CLEMs) is not entirely clear, it appears that left-movers are primarily utilizers of the right hemisphere, and right-movers primarily use the left hemisphere. When the left hemisphere's oculomotor areas are stimulated, the eyes move right; when the right hemisphere's oculomotor areas are stimulated, the eyes move left. Apart from the actual physical explanation for the process involved, a reasonable interpretation for the CLEM phenomenon is that the hemisphere that first goes to work in response to a question diverts the eyes to the side of the visual field most apt to contain the needed kind of information. (The left eye disproportionately informs the right hemisphere, and vice versa.)

Day finds that most persons consistently look either right or left in response to a question. On the average, about three-fourths of a person's CLEMs go in one direction. Further, he finds differences in personality organization between right-movers and left-movers. Right-movers (propositional thinkers) score high on reading ability tests, display analytic activity, and are generally abstract thinkers; left-movers are more responsive to music, more sensitive to sounds around them, and quicker to respond to a person's tone of voice or manner of speaking. In addition, they have a tendency to focus their attention on internal subjective experiences, to be sensitive to impulses from within. These are all known properties of appositional thought. Differences in language use are also reported: Right-movers use language in a consistent, assertive, matter-of-fact style; left-movers are more given to flowery adjectives and poetic expression.[65]

Psychologist Paul Bakan's research on right-movers and left-movers suggests that right-movers are more apt to choose "hard" majors in college—mathematics, biology, engineering, economics, and physics; left-movers select "soft" subjects as their majors—psychology, political science, English, and history. Nine of 17 right-movers were in hard sciences, and 15 of 18 left-movers were in soft subjects. Furthermore, the left-movers were found to be more hypnotizable and to report clearer visual images.[66]

The research of Day and Bakan also suggest that right-movers are active and left-movers passive. The left hemisphere functions at a higher level of arousal than does the right: For example, the production of 8- to 13-cycle-per-second alpha waves in the brain's electrical activity are more apparent in a relaxed subject with closed eyes. Bakan reports that the right hemisphere is most productive of these alpha waves, indicating it is passively receptive to inner structural processes.

Research by I. M. Smith indicates there may be basic personality differences between men of science and men of letters, and that these differences are manifested in facial expressions. A sample of 81 students were asked to distinguish between portraits of eminent men of science and men of letters. The students were able to make these distinctions. Men of science were stereotyped as thin-faced, tight-lipped, with keen penetrating eyes, hard and severe expressions, and cold temperaments. Literary men were characterized as fat, full-lipped, possibly feminine, with soft expressions and warm temperaments.[67]

While acceptance of such distinctions between men in what C. P. Snow has called the "two cultures"[68] cannot be made on the basis of I. M. Smith's study, and while the hypothesized relation of body type to cognitive mode must await adequate research, there may be some reason to suspect that cerebral organization influences physical appearance as well as intellectual interests and personality organization. Bakan's finding that right-movers are active and left-movers passive corresponds to the above description. In addition, "left-brained" thinkers are undoubtedly more selective in the information admitted than are "right-brained" thinkers. The former are concerned with materials that are verbal and conceptual, whereas men of letters deal with perceptions and with materials of lower verbal identifiability. In fact, it is characteristic of the right hemisphere that it admits stimuli with minimal "editing," hence its capacity for simultaneous consideration of stimuli and the construction of gestalts.

The distinction between men of science and men of letters as possessing cold and warm temperaments may refer to the association of emotion with right hemisphere thinkers. The activities of both cerebral hemispheres are involved with cognition. There is physiological evidence that emotions are the property of neither hemisphere, but are lower-brain functions. Since appositional thought is inclusive in the stimuli it entertains, the right hemisphere may be predisposed to admit emotions as well as sensory inputs and information pertaining to internal states as data. The stereotyping of appositional as emotional may occur for this reason.

Before turning to the next chapter, we would like to cite Jerome S. Bruner's thoughts on the involvement of nonpropositional activities in a scientific inquiry:

> The right is order and lawfulness, le droit. . . . Reaching for knowledge with the right hand is science. Yet to say only that much of science is to overlook one of its excitements, for the great hypotheses of science are gifts carried in the left hand. . . . One thing has become increasingly clear in pursuing the nature of knowing. It is that the conventional apparatus of the psychologist—both his instruments of investigation and the conceptual tools he uses in the investigation and the conceptual tools he uses in the interpretation of his data—leaves one approach unexplored. It is an approach whose medium of exchange seems to be the metaphor paid out by

the left hand. It is a way that grows happy hunches and "lucky" guesses, that is stirred into connective activity by the poet and the necromancer looking sideways rather than directly. Their hunches and intuitions generate a grammar of their own—searching out connections, suggesting similarities, weaving ideas loosely in a trial web. . . . If he is lucky or if he has subtle psychological intuition, he will from time to time come up with hunches, combinatorial products of his own subjectivity, he will go so far as to tame the metaphors that have produced the hunches, tame them in the sense of shifting them from the left hand to the right by rendering them into notions that can be tested.[69]

While the formulation of formalized scientific theories may be primarily the work of propositional thought, the act of constructing a theory may, as implied by Bruner, involve appositional thought integrated with propositional thought. In science, the most creative endeavors may be related to levels of thought that transcend the functions of either cortex. And although we will argue that the products of science are founded on rationalities that are primarily propositional, science as a **practice** is not confined to these rationalities. While we contend that the scientific and synthetic inquiries are based on rationalities that are mirror images of one another, these sets of rationalities are capable of integration and are fundamentally complementary. The involvement of both propositional and appositional thought in nonscientific inquiry, the obverse of Bruner's statement, is well described by Steven Spender when he writes about the creation of a poem:

> Obviously these lines are attempts to sketch out an idea which exists clearly enough on some level of the mind where it yet eludes the attempt to state it. At this stage, a poem is like a face which one seems to be able to visualize clearly in the eye of memory, but when one examines it mentally or tries to think it out, feature by feature, it seems to fade. . . .[70]

NOTES

1. Joseph E. Bogen, "The Other Side of the Brain I: Dysgraphia and Dyscopia Following Cerebral Commissurotomy," **Bulletin of the Los Angeles Neurological Societies,** vol. 1, 1969, p. 165.
2. Ibid.
3. Bogen, "Other Side of the Brain II," pp. 146–150.
4. **Selected Writings of John Hughlings Jackson,** ed. James Taylor, New York: Basic Books, vol. 2, 1958, pp. 129–132.
5. Henry Head, **Aphasia and Kindred Disorders of Speech,** London: Cambridge University Press, vol. 1, 1926, p. 206.
6. Jackson, op. cit., p. 220.
7. Bogen, "Other Side of the Brain II," p. 150.
8. J. Levy-Agresti and R. W. Sperry, "Differential Perceptual Capacities in Major and Minor Hemispheres," **Proceedings of the National Academy of Sciences,** vol. 61, 1969, p. 1151.
9. Y. P. Frolov, **Pavlov and His School,** trans. C. P. Dutt, New York: Oxford University Press, 1937, pp. 78–82.
10. Aleksandr Romanovich Luriia, **Human Brain and Psychological Processes,** trans. Basil Haigh, New York: Harper & Row, 1966, p. 74.
11. Bogen, "Other Side of the Brain II," p. 160.

12. The Standard Edition of the Complete Psychological Works of Sigmund Freud, trans. James Strachey, London: Hogarth, 1953, vol. 5, p. 601. Freud saw the "primary process" as lacking its own rationality, as dominated by affect and pleasure, and as confusing to perception. This he refers not to appositional thought, but to thought that is unconscious and irrational.

13. Otto Fenichel, The Psychoanalytic Theory of Neurosis, New York: Norton, 1945, p. 47.

14. I. Macfarlane Smith, Spatial Ability: Its Educational and Social Significance, San Diego: Robert K. Knapp, 1964, pp. 202–203.

15. C. Spearman, Psychology Down The Ages, London: Macmillan, 1937, vol. 1, as quoted in Smith, op. cit., p. 204.

16. C. Spearman and L. Wynn Jones, Human Abilities, London: Macmillan, 1950, as quoted in Smith, op. cit., p. 203.

17. Roy F. Street, A Gestalt Completion Test: A Study of a Cross Section of Intellect, New York: Teachers College, 1931. In this test the only verbal content is an instruction, "What is that?" and a one-word answer. E. DeRenzi and H. Spinnler, in "Visual Recognition in Patients with Unilateral Cerebral Disease," Journal of Nervous and Mental Disorders, vol. 142, 1966, pp. 515–525, report that right hemisphere damage impairs performance on the Street Test more than damage to the left hemisphere. Since the split-brain operation most seriously impairs performance peculiar to the right hemisphere (see R. W. Sperry, M. S. Gazzaniga, and J. E. Bogen, "The Neocortical Commissures: Syndrome of Hemisphere Disconnection," Handbook of Clinical Neurology, vol. 4, chap. 14, Amsterdam: North Holland Publishing Company, 1969), it can be expected that these patients would score low on the test relative to a test of propositional performance. Bogen administered the Street Test and a well-known measure of propositional performance, the Wechsler Similarities Test, and found the performances on the Street Test relative to the Similarities to be low, further supporting the contention that this test is solved by the right hemisphere. See Joseph E. Bogen, R. DeZure, W. D. TenHouten, and J. F. Marsh, "The Other Side of the Brain IV: The A/P Ratio," Bulletin of the Los Angeles Neurological Societies, vol. 37, 1972, pp. 49–61. That members of "primitive" culture can see the snake is indirectly supported by the finding that Hopi Indians outperform U.S. urban whites, urban blacks, and rural whites on the Street Test. See ibid., and Warren D. TenHouten, Cognitive Styles and the Social Order, Final Report, Part II, O.E.O. Study BOO-5135, "Thought, Race, and Opportunity," Los Angeles, California, 1971. For 12 of 13 items the Hopi mean is 9.3 (N = 49), compared with 6.7 (N = 681) for urban whites, 6.9 (N = 532) for urban blacks, and 7.2 (N = 81) for rural whites.

18. Theodore Weisenburg and Katherine E. McBride, Aphasia: A Clinical and Psychological Study, New York: Commonwealth Fund, 1936, pp. 425–426.

19. David Wechsler, The Measurement of Adult Intelligence, 2nd ed., Baltimore: Williams & Wilkins, 1952.

20. A. Lloyd Anderson, "The Effect of Laterality Localization of Focal Brain Lesions on the Wechsler-Bellevue Subtests," Journal of Clinical Psychology, vol. 7, 1951, pp. 149–153.

21. E. E. Balthazar et al., "Visuo-Constructive and Verbal Responses in Chronic Brain Damaged Patients and Familial Retardates," Journal of Clinical Psychology, vol. 17, 1961, pp. 293–296; A. L. Benton, "Differential Behavioral Effects in Frontal Lobe Disease," Neuropsychologia, vol. 6, 1968, pp. 53–60. For additional references, see Joseph E. Bogen and Glenda M. Bogen, "The Other Side of the Brain III: The Corpus Callosum and Creativity," Bulletin of the Los Angeles Neurological Society, vol. 34, 1969, references 98a–107, pp. 206–207.

22. J. M. Neilson, "Unilateral Cerebral Dominance as Related to Mind Blindness: Minimal Lesion Capable of Causing Visual Agnosia for Objects," Archives of Neurology and Psychiatry, vol. 38, 1937, pp. 108–135; J. M. Neilson, "Dominance of the Right Occipital Lobe," Bulletin of the Los Angeles Neurological Societies, vol. 5, 1940, pp. 135–145.

23. Macdonald Critchley, The Parietal Lobes, New York: Hafner, 1966, p. 172.

24. Sigmund Freud, On Aphasia, trans. E. Stengel, New York: International Universities, 1953.

25. Henri Hécaen, "Clinical Symptomatology in Right and Left Hemisphere Lesions," in Interhemispheric Relations and Cerebral Dominance, ed. V. B. Mountcastle, Baltimore: Johns Hopkins Press, 1962, pp. 215–243.

26. Henri Hyacinthe Octave Hécaen and R. Angelergues, La Cecito Psychique: Etude Critique de la Notion d'Agnosie, Paris: Masson, 1963, p. 132.

27. E. DeRenzi, P. Faglioni, and H. Spinnler, "The Performance of Patients with Unilateral Brain Damage on Face Recognition Tasks," **Cortex,** vol. 4, 1968, pp. 17–34; H. Lansdell, "Effect of Extent of Temporal Lobe Ablations on Two Lateralized Deficits," **Physiology and Behavior,** vol. 3, 1968, pp. 271–273; B. Milner, "Visual Recognition and Recall after Right Temporal-Lobe Excision in Man," **Neuropsychologia,** vol. 6, 1968, pp. 191–209; E. K. Warrington and M. James, "An Experimental Investigation of Facial Recognition in Patients with Unilateral Cerebral Lesions," **Cortex,** vol. 3, 1967, pp. 317–326.

28. Brenda Milner, "Interhemispheric Differences in the Localization of Psychological Processes in Man," **British Medical Bulletin,** vol. 27, 1971, pp. 272–277.

29. L. D. Costa and H. G. Vaughn, "Performance of Patients with Lateralized Cerebral Lesions: I. Verbal and Perceptual Tests," **Journal of Nervous and Mental Disorders,** vol. 134, 1962, pp. 162–168.

30. Critchley, op. cit., p. 172.

31. Malcolm Piercy, "The Effects of Cerebral Lesions on Intellectual Functions: A Review of Current Research Trends," **British Journal of Psychiatry,** vol. 110, 1964, p. 310.

32. Michael C. Corballis and Ivan L. Beale, "On Telling Left from Right," **Scientific American,** vol. 224, 1971, p. 100.

33. A. L. Wigan, **The Duality of the Mind,** London: Longman, 1844.

34. P. Glees, **Experimental Neurology,** London: Oxford University Press, 1961, p. 486; Harry Houston White, "Cerebral Hemispherectomy in the Treatment of Infantile Hemiplegia," **Confinia Neurologica,** vol. 21, pp. 1–50; L. S. Basser, "Hemiplegia of Early Onset and the Faculty of Speech with Special Reference to the Effects of Hemispherectomy," **Brain,** vol. 85, 1962, pp. 427–460.

35. Ronald E. Myers, "Discussion," Mountcastle op. cit., pp. 117-129.

36. M. S. Gazzaniga and E. D. Young, "Effects of Commissurotomy on the Processing of Increasing Visual Information," **Experimental Brain Research,** vol. 3, 1967, pp. 368–371.

37. John Noble, "Paradoxical Interocular Transfer of Mirror-Image Discriminations in the Optic Chiasm Sectioned Monkey," **Brain Research,** vol. 10, 1968, pp. 127–151.

38. Bogen, "Other Side of the Brain I."

39. Ibid.

40. S. E. Henschen, "On the Function of the Right Hemisphere of the Brain in Relation to the Left in Speech, Music, and Calculation," **Brain,** vol. 49, 1926, p. 118.

41. Aaron Smith, "Speech and Other Functions After Left (Dominant) Hemispherectomy," Journal of Neurology, Neurosurgery and Psychiatry, vol. 29, 1966, pp. 467–471.

42. Milner, "Visual Recognition," **op. cit.**

43. Doreen Kimura, "Left-Right Differences in the Perception of Melodies," **Quarterly Journal of Experimental Psychology,** vol. 16, 1964, pp. 355–358.

44. Max Wertheimer, **Productive Thinking** enlarged edition, ed. Michael Wertheimer, New York: Harper & Row, 1959, p. 253.

45. Ibid., p. 253.

46. Ibid., pp. 253–254.

47. Ibid., p. 255.

48. R. S. Lazarus and R. A. McCleary, "Autonomic Discrimination without Awareness: An Interim Report," Journal of Personality, vol. 18, 1949, pp. 171–179; R. S. Lazarus and R. A. McCleary, "Autonomic Discrimination without Awareness: A Study of Subception," **Psychological Review,** vol. 58, 1951, pp. 113–122.

49. C. W. Eriksen and J. L. Kuethe, "Avoidance Conditioning of Verbal Behavior Without Awareness: A Paradigm of Repression," Journal of Abnormal and Social Psychology, vol. 53, 1956, pp. 203–209; C. W. Eriksen, "Discrimination and Learning Without Awareness: A Methodological Survey and Evaluation," **Psychological Review,** vol. 67, 1960, pp. 279–300.

50. Michael Polanyi, **The Tacit Dimension,** Garden City, N.Y.: Anchor Books, 1967, pp. 9–10.

51. Ibid., p. 10.

52. Bogen, "Other Side of the Brain II," p. 140.

53. Frolov, op. cit., p. 74.

54. Corballis and Beale, op. cit., p. 104.

55. Martin Gardner, **The Ambidextrous Universe,** New York: Basic Books, 1964, p. 35.

56. Ibid., p. 35.

57. Ibid., p. 38.

58. Corballis and Beale, **op. cit.,** p. 104.
59. Robert Hertz, **Death and the Right Hand,** trans. Rodney and Claudia Needham, New York: Free Press, 1960, p. 100.
60. Ibid., p. 97.
61. Ibid.
62. G. William Domhoff, "But Why Did They Sit on the King's Right Hand in the First Place?" **Psychoanalytic Review,** vol. 56, 1970, pp. 586–596.
63. Frolov, **op. cit.,** p. 74.
64. Merle E. Day, "An Eye-Movement Indicator of Individual Differences in the Physiological Organization of Attentional Processes and Anxiety," **Journal of Psychology,** vol. 66, 1967, pp. 51–62.
65. Ibid.
66. Paul Bakan, "The Eyes Have It," **Psychology Today,** vol. 4, 1971, pp. 64-67 and p. 97.
67. I. M. Smith, **op. cit.,** pp. 302–308.
68. Sir Charles Percy Snow, **The Two Cultures and the Scientific Revolution,** New York: Cambridge University Press, 1960.
69. Jerome S. Bruner, **On Knowing: Essays for the Left Hand,** Cambridge: Harvard University Press, 1963, pp. 2–4, cited in Bogen and Bogen, **op. cit.,** p. 200.
70. Stephen Spender, "The Making of a Poem," **The Creative Process: A Symposium,** ed. B. Ghiselin, New York: New American Library, 1952, cited in Bogen and Bogen, **op. cit.,** p. 149.

Synthetic Inquiries: Three Case Studies

With
RONALD DeZURE

This chapter presents a description of the three synthetic inquiries to be used as case studies: the **Tarot**, the **I Ching**, and the vision quest of don Juan. These inquiries occur in different cultures. The **Tarot** is grounded in systems of Western occult thought; the **I Ching** is of Chinese origin; don Juan's practices are an instance of an ancient traditional inquiry in Indian American cultures. It is hypothesized that each one constitutes a **discipline** within the general class of inquiries that we call synthetic. While there are differences between them, they are hypothesized to be as closely related as are disciplines within the general class of inquiries that are scientific. For instance, there is as close a relation between the **Tarot** and **I Ching** as there is between sociology and neurology. While there is virtually no overlap between sociology and neurology, they are both scientific disciplines, governed by the criteria for rationality peculiar to science. Sociology and neurology study phenomena that must be understood on their own level, so that one is not reducible to the other. Yet interpenetration is possible. A neurologist can contribute to sociology, and a sociologist can contribute to neurology; in collaboration, practitioners of the two disciplines can contribute to theories not contained by either discipline's topic.

In the synthetic inquiries there is also a high level of interpenetration.

Persons who are practitioners of one synthetic inquiry are apt to be, or have been, practitioners of others as well. In our work among **I Ching** and **Tarot** practitioners and sorcerers, it was rare to find practitioners of one of these disciplines that had not been involved in others of the same kind. Competent practitioners of any synthetic inquiry must have adequate knowledge of the units of meaning in the system such that knowledge about a situation or topic can be generated within these units. While the units of meaning vary from discipline to discipline, the rationalities governing the use of these units of meaning are invariant. The general rationalities peculiar to synthetic inquiries enable practitioners of one system to become involved in others.

THE TAROT

The **Tarot** is an ancient philosophical system that has been preserved as a strange and beautiful deck of 78 cards, each symbolizing an idea called an **arcanum**. The deck is divided into two parts: 22 picture cards called the Major Arcana; and 56 other cards called the Minor Arcana.

The origins of the **Tarot** are lost in antiquity. One legend has it that the Major Arcana evolved from pictures in what may be the world's oldest book, originated by Hermes Trismegistus, a councillor to King Osiris of Egypt. Osiris, with the aid of his wife Isis, was a wise and beneficent ruler in his life, who became the immortal god of the underworld and judge of the dead.

Another version ties the **Tarot** to Arabic culture. A great university of the occult sciences was located in Fez, Morocco, about A.D. 1200. The scholars, magicians, and sages who gathered at this intellectual center, not sharing a common language, invented the **Tarot** as a book of pictures containing occult symbols from many traditions. In describing this gathering, Eden Gray notes: "A key to the interpretation of these universal symbols and their infinite combinations, it is said, enabled the sages to understand one another and to create a common store of wisdom."[1]

While **Tarot** practitioners have taken issue with one another regarding the origins of the **Tarot** and the systems of interpretations that are attached to the numbers, hieroglyphs, letters, and symbols on the cards,[2] these issues are largely extrinsic to the practice itself, which consists of reflecting and meditating on the meanings of the cards, and using the cards in divination.

The Deck

The 56 Minor Arcana cards are divided into four suits of 14 cards each. The suits are wands, cups, swords, and pentacles, which correspond to clubs, hearts, spades, and diamonds, respectively, in ordinary playing cards. Within each suit there are 10 cards numbered 1 through 10 and 4 court cards—the King, Queen, Knight, and Page—which symbolize the spirit, the soul, the ego, and the body, respectively.[3]

One Major Arcanum, the Fool, is numbered either 0 or 21, and the other Major Arcana are numbered 1 to 21 or 22 depending on the number assigned to the Fool. The names of the arcana vary from version to version. The description here is confined to selected cards from a widely used deck, the Albano–Waite Tarot,[4] which is supplemented by illustrations of three arcana prepared for Mouni Sadhu's encyclopedic study on the **Tarot**.[5]

A listing of the titles of the Major Arcana in the Albano–Waite deck illustrates the range of the ideas contained in the system:

1. The Magician	10. Wheel of Fortune	19. The Sun
2. The High Priestess	11. Justice	20. The Last Judgment
3. The Empress	12. The Hanged Man	21. The World
4. The Emperor	13. Death	0. The Fool
5. The Hierophant	14. Temperance	
6. The Lovers	15. The Devil	
7. The Chariot	16. The Tower	
8. Fortitude	17. The Star	
9. The Hermit	18. The Moon	

According to Sadhu, whose views are not universally held, the **Tarot** includes four subdivisions of occult thought—alchemy, astrology, Kabbalah (Jewish mysticism), and ceremonial magic. He argues that the Great Law that organizes the **Tarot** is derived from the Biblical name of God, Jehovah, originally constructed from four Hebrew letters:

Yod (ﬡ), Hé (ﬣ), Vau (ﬡ), Hé (ﬣ).

According to the Great Law, any manifestation of a phenomenon requires a first, acting element or power, which initiates the process. This principle is symbolized by the number 1 and the letter **Yod**. It is positive, active, and masculine. Manifestation also requires a second element, which is receptive to the active. It is symbolized by the number 2 and the letter **Hé**. This principle is the opposite of the first in that it is negative, passive, and feminine.

When the first element acts with the second, a third element appears, having the number 3 and the letter **Vau**. The two opposites constitute a "binary," which is "neutralized" by the third element.[6] This third element is neutral, reflecting in itself the quality of the two independent principles. A binary so neutralized is called a "ternary" and is symbolized by a triangle.

The primary three—the ternary—in turn brings into being a new element. This principle is symbolized by the number 4 and the second **Hé** in **Yod-Hé-Vau-Hé**. This letter is not passive like the first **Hé**, but is an active principle and is the **Yod** of the next triangle. This fourth element is placed in the center of the first triangle, and is the top of the second triangle. Sadhu associates the 22 letters of the Hebrew alphabet to form an overlapping set of 7 triangles, with the Fool numbered 21 and the World 22. The scheme is shown in Figure 6. Each of the 7 triangles pertains to a topic consisting of an active, a passive, and a neutral idea.

The first triangle has **mind** as its topic, which is a concept of interest here; therefore these cards will be shown and discussed in some detail. The analysis of particular cards shows the **ideal viewpoint** in the system, consisting of practitioners' developing views of the meanings of tools and manipulations.

Arcanum 1: The Magician
The letter symbolizing the first arcanum is **aleph** (א). Its idea is unity, and its hieroglyph is a man standing with right hand raised grasping a scepter, a symbol

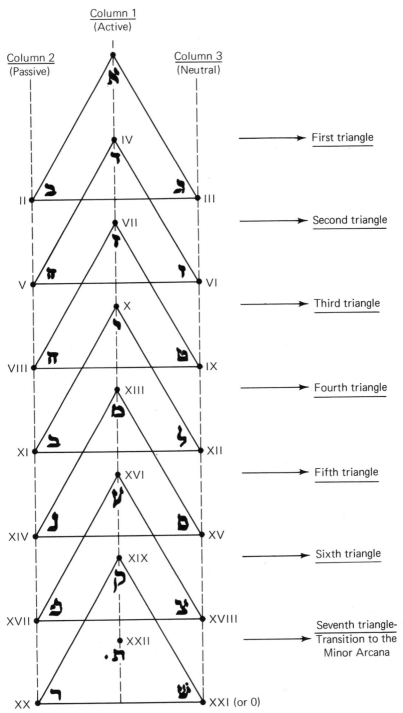

Figure 6. General Scheme of the Tarot (Major Arcana—1 to 22).
Source: Mouni Sadhu, **The Tarot: A Contemporary Course of the Quintessence of Hermetic Occultism,** North Hollywood, Ca.: Wilshire Book Company, 1970, Figure 1.

Figure 7. The First Arcanum: Left, the Albano-Waite Magician; Right, the Sadhu Magician.

Source: Left, P. C. Smith and A. E. Waite, **The Deck of Tarot Cards Called the "Albano-Waite** Tarot Deck," Los Angeles, Ca.: Tarot Productions, Inc.; Right, Mouni Sadhu, **The Tarot: A Contemporary Course of the Quintessence of Hermetic Occultism,** North Hollywood, Ca.: Wilshire Book Company, 1970, p. 32.

of order and authority (Figure 7). The left hand is lowered, with the index finger pointed toward the earth. Papus observes that the hand points to "the symbol of Nature."[7] Papus adds that the position of the Magician's hands "represents the two principles, active and passive."[8]

The Magician's standing position stresses his active nature. In some versions of the **Tarot**, the first arcanum is called the Juggler, or a "male inquirer."[9] His outer red garment represents "desire, passion, and activity. Its color is that of the planet Mars, which astrology associates with action and initiative."[10]

The infinity sign above the Magician's head symbolizes eternal life. It also signifies his propensity for abstraction and analytic thought, which he directs, through his will, into manifestation.

The word "magician" had a different meaning in ancient times, when "magic" (as distinguished from sorcery) was a name for science.[11] Thus the idea represented by this arcanum includes scientific inquiry, which begins at the level of abstraction in language and culture and endeavors to establish laws of nature. In describing this arcanum Paul F. Case writes: "Every true magician knows that all his practice has a mathematical, geometrical basis. By the aid of occult geometry he has traced nature to her concealed recesses. He uses geometric formulae and diagrams in his practical work."[12]

Figure 8. The Second Arcanum: Left, the Albano-Waite High Priestess; Right, the Sadhu Gnosis.

Source: Left, P. C. Smith and A. E. Waite, **The Deck of Tarot Cards Called the "Albano-Waite Tarot Deck,"** Los Angeles, Ca.: Tarot Productions, Inc.; Right, Mouni Sadhu, **The Tarot: A Contemporary Course of the Quintessence of Hermetic Occultism,** North Hollywood, Ca.: Wilshire Book Company, 1970, p. 42.

The four implements on the table before the Magician, according to Waite, signify "the elements of natural life, which lie like counters before the adept, and he adopts them as he wills."[13] Case adds: "As elements of natural life, they are water (cup), fire (wand), air (sword), and earth (pentacle)."[14] It appears that the problem to which the Magician's will and desire are directed is nature.

Arcanum 2: The High Priestess (Gnosis)
The second arcanum is Gnosis, or knowledge. Its letter is **beth (ב)**, its number, two (Figure 8). Occultists refer to this card as the Door of the Sanctuary, as its general meanings refer to hidden or veiled influences, silence, and mystery; when reversed, the idea means direct sensory knowing.

Gnosis holds the **Torah**, the book of knowledge of the world. Eden Gray notes that "it is only slightly unrolled, for the instruction contained therein is hidden, save for a partial glimpse, from the ordinary human eye. A veil also covers half of the scroll, thus intimating that only one-half of the mystery of being can be comprehended."[15]

The column to her left is white and labeled **J**, and the column to her right is black and labeled **B**. The white column, **Jakin**, represents a positive life principle; the black column, **Boaz**, represents a negative life principle.[16] Case argues

Figure 9. The Third Arcanum: Left, the Albano-Waite Empress; Right, the Sadhu Venus.

Source: Left, P. C. Smith and A. E. Waite, **The Deck of** Tarot **Cards Called the "Albano-Waite** Tarot **Deck,"** Los Angeles, Ca.: Tarot Productions, Inc.; Right, Mouni Sadhu, **The** Tarot: **A Contemporary Course of the Quintessence of Hermetic Occultism,** North Hollywood, Ca.: Wilshire Book Company, 1970, p. 54.

that the two pillars are those of Solomon and Hermes: "Opposite in color, but alike in form, they represent affirmation . . . and negation."[17] In innumerable synthetic systems white is associated with the abstract, as it has the property of reflection, of image; black is associated with the concrete and with perception, as it absorbs all colors. In Sadhu's version, the column to Gnosis's left is blue and that to her right is red. This alternative color coding has the same interpretation, as blue is associated with what is abstract and unavailable for manipulation (heaven), and red is associated with the concrete (earth).[18]

Sadhu does not connect the two columns, but refers to the space between them as the " 'middle' space"; the woman in this space is intended to "neutralize this binary."[19] Gray notes that "the veil between the pillars is decorated with pomegranates (female) and palms (male) symbols, indicating that the subconscious is only potentially reproductive. Only when this veil is penetrated by conscious thought desires, can creativity be actualized."[20]

Sadhu also writes that the "binary of the male and female" exists in the relation between this card and the Magician. Over the head of the Magician there are signs for unity and infinity; here, we have the horns of Isis, with a full moon between them.[21] This symbolizes a distinction between the two arcana—the Magician being regarded as spiritual and abstract, and the High Priestess as material and concrete. The standing Magician is active and willful; the sitting High

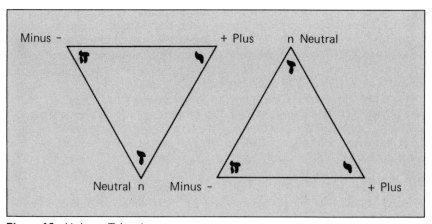

Figure 10. Unitary Triangles.
Source: Mouni Sadhu, The Tarot: A Contemporary Course of the Quintessence of Hermetic
Occultism, North Hollywood, Ca.: Wilshire Book Company, 1970, Figure 4.

Priestess, in contrast, is passive and accepting. Her astrological sign is the moon,
which reflects the light of the sun, the sign for the Magician.

The High Priestess is the eternal virgin, the second marriage of a prince
whose first marriage was sexual. Waite explains that she is a higher Garden of
Eden, a paradise where the tree of knowledge grows. To marry the High Priestess
thus means to know the bright reflection of inner glory obtained by knowing the
laws of nature. Her veil can be penetrated only by conscious thought, by the will
and power directing the Magician's activities.[22]

Arcanum 3: The Empress (Venus)

The letter for the third arcanum is **ghimel** (**ℷ**), its number is three, and "the
hieroglyph is a hand with the fist folded so that it forms a **narrow tunnel**, which
can contain something."[23] The tunnel represents the process of birth (the
womb), which is connected with the idea of love and its creative potential. The
creation is not an independent process, for it is a basic principle in the Tarot that
"nothing is created, but everything is born."[24] The pregnant woman illustrates
the basic law, "there is always **℩** (**Yod**) which fecundates **ה** (**Hé**) and therefore
brings about the birth of the third element **℩** (**Vau**)."[25] The role played by
Venus in linking the two independent principles is illustrated by a triangle, in
which the neutral third element brings about a dialectical synthesis of the dualism created by the two. Sadhu writes: "A neutralizing of the binaries . . . simply
means the birth of a third or intermediary element which offers us a passage
from one extreme to the other. In such a way is created the idea of the threefold
manifestation, the TWO merging together, with the help of the THIRD to form a
UNIT."[26] He explains that in the triangles (Figure 10) the "+" symbolizes "that
beginning of the binary which we consider as the active . . . (male) pole, while
the '−' is the passive (female) one which attracts the former."[27] Sadhu adds: "In
many cases it is possible to begin with the neutral element and separate it in
order to determine both of the poles."[28]

The picture of the Empress (Figure 9) shows a woman crowned with the
twelve stars of the zodiac, symbolizing the relation between phases of solar ener-

gy and physical birth, which Sadhu considers a basis of creativity. In her left hand she holds a scepter with the sign of Venus (♀), thereby reigning over all life. "The sign ♀ itself is a synthesis of two symbols: ☉ belongs to the Sun (creative emanations) and + being . . . the world of elements, or the complex of all the influences of the surroundings. Therefore love brings a victory for creative emanations over all obstacles, arising from those surroundings."[29]

In her right hand is a shield inscribed with an eagle, indicating that "the idea of creation extends itself over the highest regions."[30] The cross affixed to the eagle's neck indicates that "birth is a natural consequence of the union between the active and passive principles."[31] The moon beneath Venus's foot symbolizes the sublunar world, regarded as the lowest realm of creativity.

• • • • •

The analogy between the brain theory and the idea of mind embodied in the first three arcana of the **Tarot** is striking. The Magician is a principle of mind that is abstract, active, and generally coordinate with the activities of a scientist. This principle bears a resemblance to propositional thought. The High Priestess is a principle of mind that is concrete, passive, associated with hidden or veiled influences, and generally coordinate with the direct perception of nature. This principle resembles appositional thought. The Empress is a principle of mind connecting the two independent principles, like a tunnel which can contain something, leading to creative emanation. This principle of mind suggests the working of the corpus callosum, which Joseph and Glenda Bogen have related to creativity, since creative thinking involves integrated thought and cooperation of the two hemispheres.[32] While the direct reference in the **Tarot** interpretations is to the womb, a tunnel that creates life by transferring the fetus from one world to another, the corpus callosum may work in an analogous way: as a tunnel that creates integrated thought by transferring sensory-motor information and ideas from one hemisphere to the other. In this connection Sadhu's statement that "it is possible to begin with the neutral element and separate it in order to determine both of the poles" is of interest, because it is suggestive of the split-brain surgery, in which separation of the neutral element in the brain, the corpus callosum, provided evidence regarding the functions of the two hemispheres.

Manipulatory Techniques

In any synthetic inquiry there are manipulatory techniques for using the basic tools involved in the production of knowledge. These techniques function as constraints that lend discipline to a practice. In the **Tarot** the cards constitute the basic tools and it is through manipulation of cards that inquiry into a particular question proceeds. It is in the shuffling and laying out of cards that a practitioner consults an "oracle"—a reading of the cards that provides an opportunity for fortune-telling and divination. A competent practitioner must have carried through protracted study of the ideas contained in the 78 cards in preparation for interpreting an array of cards. The above discussion of the first three cards in the Major Arcana provides only a preliminary to the comprehension of the ideas contained therein. An adequate understanding of these cards cannot be rendered in words, and written descriptions are intended only to initiate the process of becoming a practitioner. A practitioner knows that the real meaning of the cards is in the **seeing**.

Just as there are a wide variety of **Tarot** decks, so there are numerous techniques for reading the cards. Many practitioners keep their cards wrapped in silk and in a special box to protect their "vibrations." Often a practitioner will let no one else touch or use his or her deck of cards, although it is a common practice when doing a reading for another to have that person touch or shuffle the deck while framing the question. The essence of the practice is so highly visual and nonverbal that the question is often kept in silence.

In a typical statement to beginning practitioners, Gray offers this advice:

While the subject is shuffling the cards, with his mind concentrated on the question he wants answered, the reader must quietly ask that only the highest spiritual forces surround the procedure, and that the answer given by the cards will be of a constructive and helpful nature. The reader asks that he will be guided to interpret them correctly and so illumined as to give positive help to the seeker.[33]

There are innumerable techniques for shuffling the cards, some using the entire deck and others only the Major Arcana.[34] While most advanced practitioners use the entire deck, we present here a simple method described by Ralph Metzner that requires only the Major Arcana.[35] The cards are shuffled and five cards laid out in the following order which, according to Metzner, constitutes a model of "the astrological map of the 24-hour cycle and uses the basic form of the cross."[36]

```
            3

      1     5     2

            4
```

The card in position 1 represents **what is coming** into the situation. The astrological correspondent to this card is the ascendent: the sign or planet rising over the horizon. It is the dawning, the morning time, the beginning. In the Celtic method of laying out cards described by Waite it is called "what will come."[37]

Position 2 represents **what is passing**, what is leaving the scene. In astrology it is the descendent: the sign or planet setting below the horizon. It is the time of sunset, the evening. In the Celtic technique it is called "what is behind him."

Position 3 is **what is manifesting** in the present situation. In astrology it is the zenith, the sign or planet that is overhead. The Celtic technique refers to this card as "what crowns him."

Position 4 represents **what is hidden** from the inquirer. It is the unmanifest, the unconscious, the latent factor. Astrologically, it corresponds to the nadir, the midnight time. In the Celtic technique it is called "what is beneath him."

Metzner calls position 5 the **key card**, as it is "the integrating factor, that which is needed or indicated to bring these four tendencies or influences into balance."[38]

Figure 11. A Tarot reading with the Major Arcanum.
Source: P. C. Smith and A. E. Waite, **The Deck of** Tarot **Cards Called the** "Albano-Waite Tarot **Deck,"** Los Angeles, Ca.: Tarot Productions, Inc.

Figure 11 shows the results of an actual reading carried out by a male practitioner regarding a woman he loves. Note that cards 1 and 2 were dealt upside down, which has significance in the interpretation of the cards. A person with no knowledge of **Tarot** would encounter these condensed hints regarding the divinatory meaning of these five cards in the Albano–Waite deck:

1. The Sun: "Material happiness, fortunate marriage, contentment. **Reversed:** The same in a lesser sense."
2. Strength, reversed: "Despotism, abuse of power, weakness, discord, sometimes even disgrace."
3. The Hierophant: "Marriage, alliance, captivity, servitude; by another account, mercy and goodness; inspiration. . . ."
4. The Lovers: "Attraction, love, beauty, trials overcome."
5. Wheel of Fortune: "Destiny, fortune, success, elevation, luck, felicity."[39]

In this particular reading, the cards indicate that the relationship has been beset with the abuse of power, but that this or it is passing, and that some alliance or marriage has happiness and some degree of contentment in the future. The attraction and beauty of the relationship is hidden, and the fortune or success in projects and personal development holds the key to the outcome. At any rate, this is essentially what the practitioner said about the reading, which he did for himself rather than for another person. Beyond these superficial observations, the meaning of the situation presented by the cards is to be seen rather than talked about. While each of these cards in itself constitutes a complex idea, the array as a whole provides an even more complex and veiled meaning that cannot be understood through any sequence of propositions, but must be seen as a gestalt. A method of reading cards that employs the entire deck and uses 10 or 15 cards provides an even more complex situation for a practitioner.

THE I CHING

The **I Ching**, or **Book of Changes**, is an ancient Chinese book of wisdom. It is believed that it first consisted of a collection of linear signs used as an oracle. As with the **Tarot**, chance is seen as a mechanism by which persons possessing mediumistic powers can perceive a communication from some suprahuman source and thereby receive an answer to a question. Originally, the oracle was designed to provide only a yes or no answer, indicated by a firm line (———) or a broken line (— —), respectively. The firm and yielding lines were combined to form two-lined figures, and again combined to form three-lined figures called **trigrams.** The eight possible trigrams were then combined to form a collection of 64 six-lined figures called **hexagrams.**

The originators of the **I Ching** in preliterate China have been referred to as the Holy Sages. The system was first codified by King Wên, the progenitor of the Chou dynasty, circa 1100 B.C. King Wên was imprisoned by the scrofulous tyrant Chou Hsin, and during this time he added brief judgments to the hexagrams, which reflect political stress and social upheaval.

Additional material was added by the Duke of Chou, the son of King Wên. His contribution was to the text pertaining to the individual lines in the hexagrams.

Confucius edited and annotated the **Book of Changes,** and his whole philosophy is permeated with its influence. He is reported to have said at an old age: "If some years were added to my life, I would give fifty to the study of the [**I Ching**], and might then escape falling into great error."[40] The portion of the text called the **Commentary on the Decision** is attributed to Confucius or his school.

The philosopher Lao Tzu, who may or may not have been an historical person,[41] was said to have been inspired by the book, and his Taoist philosophy is closely related to it. Metzner is one scholar who sees the **I Ching** as a Taoist system.

> The eighty-one verses of the **Tao Tê Ching**[42] are excursions on the physical, biological, social, and psychological implications of **Tao** variously called "process," "energy," "way," "design," "spirit," or "that which cannot be named," or "the great." The **I Ching** takes this a step further and builds the Taoist philosophy into a structured system of practical divination of psychic programming.[43]

The Lines

A line, by itself, represents oneness; distinctions are said to come into the world as a result of this unity, for the perception of a line posits an above and a below, a left and a right, a front and a back, a world of dimensions and a world of opposites.[44] The meanings of the firm and yielding lines were elaborated in the doctrine of **yang** and **yin,** which developed in China about 300 B.C. Originally yang meant "banner waving in the sun," or "something shone upon," or "bright," while yin referred to "the cloudy" or "the overcast."[45] Firm yang lines are light, and yielding yin lines are dark. The properties of activity, abstraction, and the male are consistently attributed to the yang principle, whereas the yin principle has the properties of receptivity, concreteness, and the female. Although yang and yin are not in the **I Ching,** they are so close in meaning to the firm and the yielding that practitioners refer to "yang lines" and "yin lines." Yang lines are solid, ————; yin lines are divided, —— ——. Yang and yin lines represent two opposite principles, and transformations (yang to yin) and changes (yin to yang) are the basis of a dialectical unity of opposites.

The Trigrams

Trigrams are figures composed of three horizontal lines arranged in a vertical hierarchy. Each of the eight trigrams represents a basic archetype or idea of the system. The trigrams are given a number of interpretations: They are assigned attributes, positions in a metaphorical family, and processes in nature (Images). They are classified as follows:

Symbol	Name	Attribute	Family Relationship	Image
≡	**Ch'ien,** the Creative	strong	father	heaven
≡≡	**K'un,** the Receptive	yielding	mother	earth

Symbol	Name	Attribute	Family Relationship	Image
☳	Chên, the Arousing	inciting movement	first son	thunder
☵	K'an, the Abysmal	dangerous	second son	water
☶	Kên, Keeping Still	resting	third son	mountain
☴	Sun, the Gentle	penetrating	first daughter	wind, wood
☲	Li, the Clinging	light-giving	second daughter	fire
☱	Tui, the Joyous	joyful	third daughter	lake

The Hexagrams

The hexagrams are formed by combining trigrams; each of the hexagrams has an upper trigram and a lower trigram. The sixty-four hexagrams are arranged in a definite order that is called the **sequence.**

As with the **Tarot,** there are a number of versions of the I Ching available in English. The trigrams and hexagrams, however, are invariant across the versions. We shall confine our attention to an excellent version widely used by English-speaking practitioners. This is the I **Ching** that was translated into German by Richard Wilhelm and then rendered into English by Cary F. Baynes.[46]

Hexagram 1: Ch'ien, the Creative

The first hexagram consists of six firm lines, having Ch'ien as both the upper and lower trigrams:

☰ **Ch'ien, the Creative**   above: the trigram **Ch'ien**
below: the trigram **Ch'ien**

The attribute of the hexagram is strength or power, its image is heaven, and its gender is male (the father). It embodies four Chinese virtues—sublimity, success, furthering, and perseverance. The unbroken lines are "light giving, active, strong, and of the spirit."[47]

The energy of **Ch'ien** is described as "unrestricted by any fixed condition in space and is therefore conceived of as motion. Time is regarded as the basis of this motion. Thus the hexagram includes . . . the power of time and the power of persistence in time, that is, duration."[48] The generation of time by the idea **Ch'ien** is described as follows:

> Since there is only one heaven, the doubling of the trigram Ch'ien, of which heaven is the image, indicates the movement of heaven. One com-

plete revolution of heaven makes a day, and the repetition of the trigram means that each day is followed by another. This creates the idea of time. Since it is the same heaven moving with untiring power, there is also created the idea of duration both in and beyond time. . . . This duration in time is the image of the power inherent in the Creative.[49]

The idea of power also is embodied in **Ch'ien**. Wilhelm comments that in the human world the attribute of this hexagram denotes "the creative action of the holy man or sage, of the ruler or leader of men, who through his power awakens and develops their higher nature."[50] The concept of power implies an ordering of persons, according to which some are more powerful than others. Thus social order and political change exist in the idea of **Ch'ien** and with the original meaning of yang—"banner waving in the sun." In explaining **Ch'ien,** Wilhelm wrote: "The great man brings peace and security to the world through his activity in creating order."[51]

Associated with each hexagram are two poetic statements, the Judgment and the Image. The Judgment describes behavior in culture appropriate to the situation represented by the hexagram, and the Image describes the situation in nature. These words, along with statements pertaining to the six lines, constitute the text of the **I Ching**. The Judgment for **Ch'ien** pertains to the concept of achievement, or furthering:[52]

> The Creative works sublime success,
> Furthering through perseverance.[53]

The Image reads:

> The movement of heaven is full of power.
> Thus the superior man makes himself strong and untiring.[54]

Wilhelm explained: "The urge to life—that which furthers and is right for each being—lays the foundation of its nature, and this nature acts according to fixed laws."[55] Moreover, the Creative "furthers by virtue of what eternally belongs to it, by virtue of its very nature. . . . In the phenomenal world, each thing has its specific nature: This is the principle of individuation. At the same time this specific nature fixes a boundary that separates each individual from every other."[56]

Hexagram 2: K'un, the Receptive
The hexagram occupying the second place in the sequence is the complement of **Ch'ien**, consisting of six divided yin lines:

☷	K'un, the Receptive	above: the trigram **K'un**
		below: the trigram **K'un**

K'un portrays the dark, yielding, and receptive character of yin. Wilhelm wrote: "It is the perfect complement of the Creative. . . . It represents nature in contrast to spirit, earth in contrast to heaven, space as against time, the female-maternal as against the male-paternal."[57]

The spatial nature of **K'un** is elaborated in Wilhelm's commentary: "In the hexagram of heaven the doubling of the trigram implies duration in time, but in the hexagram of earth the doubling connotes the solidity and extension in space by virtue of which the earth is able to carry and preserve all things that live and move upon it."[58] Wilhelm also wrote of **K'un**:

> Here, in contrast to the relationships in the hexagram of the Creative, the single lines do not have a developmental relation to one another, but stand side by side without interrelation. Each line represents a separate situation. This is in accord with the nature of the two hexagrams. The Creative represents time, producing sequence; the Receptive represents space, which indicates juxtaposition.[59]

Ch'ien and **K'un** are contrasted as abstract and concrete, respectively. Wilhelm wrote that the Creative "produces invisible seeds of all development. At first these seeds are purely abstract. . . . While the Creative acts in the world of the invisible, with spirit and time for its field, the Receptive acts upon matter in space and brings material things to completion."[60]

The Judgment for **K'un** reads:

> The Receptive brings about sublime success,
> Furthering through the perseverance of a mare.
> If the superior man undertakes something and tries to lead,
> He goes astray;
> But if he follows, he finds guidance.
> It is favorable to find friends in the west and south,
> To forego friends in the east and north.
> Quiet perseverance brings good fortune.[61]

Wilhelm explained:

> Applied to human affairs, therefore, what the hexagram indicates is action in conformity with the situation. . . .
> Since there is something to be accomplished, we need friends and helpers in the hours of toil and effort, once the ideas to be realized are firmly set. The time of toil and effort is indicated by the west and south, for west and south symbolize the place where the Receptive works for the Creative, as nature does in summer and autumn. . . . Hence to find friends there means to find guidance.[62]

That toil and effort are associated with the yielding principle is explained in the text's statement:

> The Creative knows through the easy.
> The Receptive can do things through the simple.[63]

The Creative, through movement, unites with ease what is divided. Further, "since the direction of movements is determined in the germinal stage of being, everything else develops quite effortlessly of itself."[64] The Receptive, in contrast, has repose as its nature. "Through repose the absolutely simple becomes possible in the spatial world. This simplicity, which arises out of pure receptivity, becomes the germ of all spatial diversity."[65] Thus **K'un** works through simple division, but this work requires effort; **Ch'ien** works with ease but not simplicity. An abstract theory, for example, if clearly expressed, is easy to read, but it is not simple. Perceiving a hexagram is a simple act, but to grasp its meaning is not easy.

The Image for **K'un** is:

The earth's condition is receptive devotion.
Thus the superior man who has breadth of character
Carries the outer world.[66]

Wilhelm explained: "The earth in its devotion carries all things, good and evil, without exception. In the same way the superior man gives to his character breadth, purity, and sustaining power, so that he is able both to support and to bear with people and things."[67]

● ● ● ● ●

The **I Ching** stresses that the firm and yielding principles are complementary. There are conditions of equilibrium and disequilibrium, harmony and struggle, and integration and disintegration. There exists an asymmetry between the firm and yielding lines which provides an interpretation of integration and disintegration. Firm lines have a tendency to rise; yielding lines tend to descend.
Thus situations in which all firm lines are below the yielding lines should portray integration, and situations in which all firm lines are above should portray disintegration. To explore these relations it is sufficient to describe two additional hexagrams, **T'ai** and **P'i**.

Hexagram 11: T'ai, Peace
The hexagram with three firm lines below and three yielding lines above is called Peace, and its Image is that of heaven below the earth:

≡ ≡   **T'ai**, Peace   above: **K'un**: the Receptive, earth
≡   below: **Ch'ien**: the Creative, heaven

Wilhelm commented:

The Receptive, which moves downward, stands above; the Creative, which moves upward, is below. Hence their influences meet and are in harmony, so that all living things bloom and prosper. . . . This hexagram denotes a time when heaven seems to be on earth. Heaven has placed itself beneath the earth, and so their powers unite in deep harmony. Then peace and blessings descend upon all living things.[68]

Hexagram 12: P'i, Stagnation
In the sequence, **T'ai** is followed by its "mirror image"[69] hexagram **P'i**:

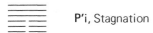 **P'i**, Stagnation   above: **Ch'ien**: the Creative, heaven
below: **K'un**: the Receptive, earth

Wilhelm wrote:

> Heaven is above, drawing farther and farther away, while the earth below
> sinks farther into the depths. The creative powers are not in relation. It is a
> time of standstill and decline. . . . Heaven and earth are out of communica-
> tion, and all things are benumbed. What is above has no relation to what is
> below, and on earth confusion and disorder prevail. The dark place is with-
> in, the light power without.[70]

As might be expected, the hexagram **T'ai** is favorable and the hexagram **P'i** is
unfavorable.

Since Bogen and Bogen relate the integration of propositional and appositional thought to creativity, and since creativity is the major idea in the third
arcanum of the **Tarot**, the hexagram **T'ai**, which portrays the coming together of
the firm and the yielding, should pertain to creativity. The Image for this hexagram reads:

> Heaven and earth unite: the Image of Peace.
> Thus the ruler
> Divides and completes the course of heaven and
> earth . . .
> And so aids the people.[71]

Wilhelm added this commentary:

> **Heaven and earth are in contact and combine their influences, producing a
> time of universal flowering and prosperity. This stream of energy must be
> regulated by the ruler of men. It is done by a process of division.** Thus men
> divide the uniform flow of time into the seasons, according to the succes-
> sion of natural phenomena, and mark off infinite space by the points of
> the compass. In this way nature in its overwhelming profusion of phenom-
> ena is bounded and controlled. On the other hand, nature must be fur-
> thered in her productiveness. This is done by adjusting the products to the
> right time and the right place, which increases the natural yield. This con-
> trolling and furthering activity of man in his relation to nature is the work
> of nature that rewards him.[72]

Thus **T'ai** describes the creation of culture through understanding, codifying,
and controlling nature. Nature is described both temporally and spatially, in
accordance with the properties of **Ch'ien** and **K'un**. Although **Ch'ien** is called the
Creative, the creation of culture is more closely linked to **T'ai**.

The remarks on creativity in the **Tarot** discussion suggest that the active
and passive principles can be understood through a separation of the neutral
element. Since the **I Ching** is based on principles that are analogous to propositional and appositional thought, the same sort of statement might be expected in
the context of the hexagram **T'ai**. The emphasized sentences in the above com-

mentary on the Image for **T'ai** can be given such an interpretation. First of all, the physical vehicle for the "contact" between heaven and earth is represented in the metaphor of a stream. The principles, heaven and earth, bear analogy to propositional and appositional thought, and the phrase "are in contact" is analogous to the functioning of the corpus callosum in connecting the two cerebral hemispheres. The stream of energy between heaven and earth is regulated "by a process of division."

Manipulatory Techniques

In ancient China there existed a variety of oracles used for divinatory purposes. The **I Ching** derived from the yarrow stalk oracle. The yarrow plant had a mystical significance in China, for yarrow was planted by the graves of the dead. Folklore has it that the yarrow derived from this location a connection with the "other world," such that advice on problems in "this world" could be obtained from one's dead ancestors, whose spirits were believed to be able to intervene in an otherwise random process. Such a belief is not essential to the practice, and many users of the **I Ching** make no such contention.

An oracle is obtained in the practice of the **I Ching** by the construction of a hexagram. There are two widely used methods called the yarrow stalk oracle and the coin oracle. The method of manipulating yarrow stalks to obtain a hexagram is a complex procedure that takes about twenty minutes. It is preferred by many practitioners because it provides an opportunity to concentrate on the question while obtaining the answer. A detailed account of this method is provided by Wilhelm.[73]

It is sufficient for this discussion to describe the coin oracle. The inscribed side of a coin (tails) is given the value 2 and the noninscribed side (heads) the value 3. Three coins are thrown simultaneously to construct each line; the line is determined by the sum of the three values—6, 7, 8, or 9. Firm lines that are transforming are 9; yielding nonchanging lines are 8; firm nontransforming lines, 7; and yielding changing lines, 6. Firm transforming lines are denoted ——O—— and yielding changing lines are denoted ——X——. When lines change, they change into their opposites: yielding lines into firm lines, and vice versa. The bottom line is constructed first, then the second line from the bottom, and so forth. Thus the phrase "nine at the beginning" means that a changing firm line occupies the lowest position in a hexagram.

For example, the practitioner who provided the example of a **Tarot** reading, also being an **I Ching** practitioner, consulted the coin oracle regarding the same situation. He obtained the values 7, 7, 6, 8, 8, 9, which results in the hexagram **Sun** (Decrease) with change lines in the third and sixth positions:

 Sun, Decrease   above: **Kên**: Keeping Still, mountain
below: **Tui**: the Joyous, lake

The Image for Decrease is:

At the foot of the mountain, the lake:
The Image of Decrease.
Thus the superior man controls his anger
And restrains his instincts.[74]

Wilhelm wrote: "The lake at the foot of the mountain evaporates. In this way it decreases to the benefit of the mountain, which is enriched by its moisture. The mountain stands as the symbol of a stubborn strength that can harden into anger."[75] Also: "What is below is decreased to the benefit of what is above."[76] Wilhelm further explained that "this hexagram represents a decrease of the lower trigram in favor of the upper, because the third line, originally strong, has moved up to the top, and the top line, originally weak, has replaced it. What is below is decreased to the benefit of what is above. This is out-and-out decrease."[77]

Thus the situation is seen as one in which there is movement of a line from the third place to the top. But this situation is the hexagram **T'ai**, which is closely related to **Sun**. In this particular throwing, the relation is even more striking, because in this situation the yielding line in the third place is growing together, and the firm line in the sixth place is dividing. The result of these two changes is the hexagram **T'ai**.

The text associated with each hexagram provides commentary on each line. In a throwing, only the lines that are changing (6s and 9s) are consulted. The following passages are found in the hexagram **Sun**:

Six in the third place means:
When three people journey together,
Their number decreases by one.
When one man journeys alone,
He finds a companion.[78]

Nine at the top means:
If one is increased without depriving others,
There is no blame.
Preseverance brings good fortune.
It furthers one to undertake something.
One obtains servants
But no longer has a separate home.[79]

Both of these passages are favorable, as might be expected, for together they change the situation from Decrease to Peace. Note that both the **Tarot** reading and the **I Ching** throwing imply that misuse of power in the relation in question is passing from the scene, and that fate—the outcome of effort—holds the key to the situation. Here this is expressed in the advice, "It furthers one to undertake something."

The occurrence of a hexagram can have a profound influence on a practitioner, for it brings into a focus a situation that can be dwelled in. In this case, the practitioner, after obtaining the hexagram Decrease four times in a row in response to the same question, sold or gave away the bulk of his material possessions and was last seen living in a state of Decrease, cheered by the passage: "When decrease has reached its goal, flowering is sure to begin."[80]

THE VISION QUEST OF DON JUAN

Anthropologist Carlos Castaneda has spent a decade studying a Mexican Indian sorcerer named Juan Matus. Castaneda's methodology for studying the practices of this man, whom he calls don Juan, consists of becoming don Juan's apprentice and then making the practice, including the teaching, the topic of his ethnographic research. Castaneda's three books on his study of don Juan, **The Teachings of Don Juan, A Separate Reality,** and **Journey to Ixtlan,** constitute a highly personal account of the practice of sorcery and the kind of knowledge, called **seeing,** that it produces.

The opportunity to have access to the profound thoughts of don Juan provided through these books does not imply that this kind of inquiry is idiosyncratic to one man. Castaneda notes: "For the American Indian, perhaps for thousands of years, the vague phenomenon we call sorcery has been a serious, bona fide practice, comparable to that of our science."[81]

It may be that don Juan's practices are an instance of the Indian American **vision quest.** For don Juan sees the central concern of his practice, and of his teaching of Castaneda, as an effort in learning how to **see.** This involves use of psychotropic plants, a basic but not essential tool for the inquiry. These plants, which contain hallucinatory or mind-altering drugs, are pictured in Figure 12. They are peyote, **Lophophora williamasii,** which don Juan calls "Mescalito"; jimson weed, **Datura inoxia;** and a mushroom identified as **Psylocybe Mexicana,** which don Juan inhales in dust form in conjunction with a mixture of five plants—called Humito, or his "little smoke." Through the systematic use of these plants, Castaneda was able to experience a "nonordinary reality." Not all such vision quests involve the use of psychotropic plants. But frequently there exists some method of producing stress, such as fatigue, hunger, exposure to the elements, which alters one's ordinary reality. Another account of a vision quest is presented in Black Elk's description of the Oglala Sioux rite called **Hanblecheyapi** (Crying for a Vision):

> Every man can cry for a vision, or "lament"; and in the old days we all—men and women—"lamented" all the time. What is received through the "lamenting" is determined in part by the character of the person who does this, for it is only those people who are very qualified who receive the great visions, which are interpreted by our holy man, and which give strength and health to our nation. It is very important for a person who wishes to "lament" to receive aid and advice from a **wichasha wakan** (holy man), so that everything is done correctly, for if things are not done in the right way, something very bad can happen, and even a serpent could come and wrap itself around the "lamenter." . . . But perhaps the most important reason for "lamenting" is that it helps us to realize our oneness with all things, to know that all things are our relatives; and then in behalf of all things we pray **Wakan-Tanka** that He may give to us knowledge of Him who is the source of all things, yet greater than all things.[82]

And poet Gary Snyder writes:

> In many American Indian tribes it is obligatory for every member to get out of the society, out of the human nexus, and 'out of his head,' at least once in his life. He returns from his solitary vision quest with a secret name, a protective animal spirit, a secret song. It is his 'power.' The culture honors the man who has visited other realms.
>
> Peyote, the mushroom, morning-glory seeds, and Jimson-weed are some

 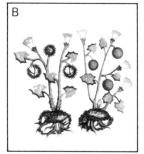 

"Mescalito"	Jimson weed	Mushroom for the
Lophophora	Datura inoxia	"Little Smoke"
williamasii		Psylocybe mexicana

Figure 12. Hallucinogenic plants used in don Juan's vision quest.
Source: Left and right, **Psylocybe mexicana** and **Lophophora williamsii** from Frank Barron,
Murray E. Jarvik, and Sterling Bunnell, Jr., "The Hallucinogenic Drugs," copyright © 1964
by Scientific American, Inc., all rights reserved; Center, **Datura inoxia** from an Aztec herbal,
The Badianus Manuscript, ed. E. W. Emmart, Baltimore: Johns Hopkins Press, 1940, plate
49.

of the best-known herbal aids used by Indian cultures to assist in the
quest. Most tribes apparently achieve these results simply through yogic-
type discipline: including sweat-baths, hours of dancing, fasting and total
isolation.[83]

The Practice: Sorcery and Seeing
The first two books describe separate phases of Castaneda's apprenticeship.
According to the first book (**The Teachings**), when confronted by alien concepts
Castaneda senses that "don Juan's teachings possessed an internal cohesion."[84]
By the end of the first phase Castaneda concludes:

> Nearly six years after I had begun the apprenticeship, don Juan's knowl-
> edge became a coherent whole for the first time. . . . And the strenuous
> experiences I had undergone, which were so overwhelming to me, were but
> a very small fragment of a system of logical thought from which don Juan
> drew meaningful inferences for his day-to-day life, a vastly complex sys-
> tem of beliefs in which inquiry was an experience leading to exultation.[85]

It is important to distinguish between don Juan as sorcerer and don Juan as
teacher. His sorcery dazzles Castaneda's imagination and challenges his sensibilities; nevertheless, the first book is entitled **The Teachings of Don Juan**. Note the
following conversation:

> "To be a sorcerer is a terrible burden," [don Juan] said in a reassuring tone.
> "I've told you that it is much better to learn to **see**. A man who **sees** is every-
> thing; in comparison, the sorcerer is a sad fellow."
> "What is sorcery, don Juan?"
> He looked at me for a long time and he shook his head almost imper-
> ceptibly.

"Sorcery is to apply one's will to a key joint," he said. "Sorcery is inter-
ference. A sorcerer searches and finds the key joint of anything he wants to
affect and then he applies his will to it. A sorcerer doesn't have to **see** to be a
sorcerer, all he has to know is how to use his will."[86]

Later on don Juan said:

"The world is indeed full of frightening things and we are helpless creatures surrounded by forces that are inexplicable and unbending. The average
man, in ignorance, believes that those forces can be explained or changed; he
doesn't really know how to do that, but he expects that the actions of mankind
will explain them or change them sooner or later. The sorcerer, on the other
hand, does not think of explaining or changing them; instead, he learns to use
such forces by redirecting himself and adapting to their direction. That's his
trick. A sorcerer is only slightly better off than the average man. Sorcery does
not help him to live a better life; in fact I should say that sorcery hinders him; it
makes his life cumbersome, precarious. By opening himself to knowledge a sorcerer becomes more vulnerable than the average man."[87]

At this point—the point of knowing—man as sorcerer and man as seeker of
knowledge converge. Both must develop the character of a warrior because
"only as a warrior can one survive the path of knowledge."[88]

"It is my commitment to teach you to **see**. Not because I personally want
to do so but because you were chosen; you were pointed out to me by Mescalito. I am compelled by my personal desire, however, to teach you to feel and
act like a warrior. I personally believe that to be a warrior is more suitable than
anything else. Therefore I have endeavored to show you those forces as a sorcerer perceives them, because only under their terrifying impact can one become
a warrior. To **see** without first becoming a warrior would make you weak; it
would give you a false meekness, a desire to retreat; your body would decay
because you would become indifferent. It is my personal commitment to make
you a warrior so you won't crumble. . . ."
     "The spirit of a warrior is not geared to indulging and complaining, nor is
it geared to winning or losing. The spirit of a warrior is geared only to struggle,
and every struggle is a warrior's last battle on earth. Thus the outcome matters
very little to him. In his last battle on earth a warrior lets his spirit flow free and
clear. And as he wages his battle, knowing that his will is impeccable, a warrior
laughs and laughs."
     I finished writing and looked up. Don Juan was staring at me. He shook his
head from side to side and smiled.
     "You really write everything?" he asked in an incredulous tone. "Genaro
says that he can never be serious with you because you're always writing. He's
right; how can anyone be serious if you're always writing?"
     He chuckled and I tried to defend my position.
     "It doesn't matter," he said. "If you ever learn to **see**, I suppose you must
do it in your own weird way."[89]

A person who would attain knowledge must have an ally. Don Juan says: "An
ally is a power capable of carrying a man beyond the boundaries of himself. This

is how an ally can reveal matters no human being could."[90] The allies are contained in various drugs. They are vehicles to be used for special purposes such as divination, bodily flight, movement by adopting an alternative form—or seeing. To achieve these purposes one enters into an apprenticeship, a commitment to learning manipulatory techniques aimed at contacting and ultimately mastering the ally. There are inflexible rules for handling each ally, for preparing the drug and then inhaling it, ingesting it, rubbing it on, and so forth. In his growing obsession with seeing, Castaneda turns again and again to an ally, an hallucinogenic smoking mixture used in conjunction with inhaling the mushroom. But don Juan has told him this is not enough, that without his first becoming a warrior, seeing would only lead him to ruin. Together they continuously examine Castaneda's character, in an ongoing critique. Knowledge in depth might involve the patient cultivation of extraordinary abilities facilitated by the catalytic action of allies. But, if one is to survive, it always requires the development of extraordinary character. Mescalito, for example—which don Juan indicates is the "spirit" in peyote—is not an ally because there are no rules for its manipulation. It is available to any man and without long apprenticeship. Its value rests in teaching us the right way to live. Don Juan advises Castaneda: "You must come to him without fear and, little by little, he will teach you how to live a better life."[91] In comparing Mescalito to the "little smoke," don Juan says: "Mescalito takes you out of yourself to teach you. An ally takes you out to give you power."[92]

Don Juan speaks out against self-indulgence and against attachment to anything, including his personal history. He calls for the emergence of "impeccable will." These terms and others already mentioned have special and fascinating meanings within the system of his wisdom, and it is not possible to amplify every meaning here. But it is important to understand that perhaps the crucial variable in becoming a "man of knowledge" is character. Thus, don Juan draws Castaneda beyond the technology of manipulating allies (correct behavior) and into the problem of correct being.

Castaneda writes that "becoming a man of knowledge was not a permanent accomplishment, but rather a process."[93] And don Juan says, "To be a man of knowledge has no permanence. One is never a man of knowledge, not really. Rather, one becomes a man of knowledge for a very brief instant, after defeating the four natural enemies."[94] The first enemy one must defeat is **Fear:** "He must be fully afraid, and yet he must not stop. . . . And a moment will come when . . . [h] is intention becomes stronger. Learning is no longer a terrifying task."[95] The second enemy is **Clarity:** "That clarity of mind, which is so hard to obtain, dispels fear, but also blinds. . . . [H] e must defy his clarity and use it only to see. . . . And a moment will come when he will understand that his clarity was only a point before his eyes."[96] At the moment clarity is overcome the third enemy is encountered. It is **Power:** "Power is the strongest of all enemies. And naturally the easiest thing to do is to give in; after all, the man is truly invincible. He commands; he begins by taking calculated risks, and ends in making rules, because he is a master."[97] However, "he has to defy it, deliberately. He has to come to realize the power he has seemingly conquered is in reality never his. . . . If he can see that clarity and power, without his control over himself, are worse than mistakes, he will reach a point where everything is held in check. He will know then when and how to use his power."[98] A man who has mastered these three enemies finally encounters the fourth, and cruelest of all,

Old Age: "[H] e has an unyielding desire to rest. . . . But if the man sloughs off his tiredness, and lives his fate through, he can then be called a man of knowledge, if only for the brief moment when he succeeds in fighting off his last, invincible enemy. That moment of clarity, power, and knowledge is enough."[99]

There is poetry in this conception. Knowledge, unalloyed, is the precious metal; it takes its highest forms through the purification of the alchemist's own structure. One becomes one's own instructor, in time, inquiring in depth into the structure of nature and one's own nature with quite the intensity that science reserves for developing formal linguistic clarity and theoretical formulation. To be a warrior is to struggle with the crucial imperfection of character. Impeccable character, enlightened and unfolding, is the only nature prepared for the highest inquiries into structure.

At the conclusion of the first phase of his apprenticeship Castaneda decides to abandon his quest because, he says, "I do believe that I have succumbed to the first enemy of a man of knowledge."[100] He does return, however, but soon insists that once again he finds himself afraid to continue. This time don Juan tells him, "You're not afraid, . . . but now you hate to lose your clarity, and since you're a fool, you call that fear."[101] Then Castaneda continues on, driven by the desire to see.

In Chapter 6 it will be noted that scientific knowledge is rooted in its attendance to language and linguistic clarification and that therein lies a discipline and a rationality. According to don Juan there is a problem, too, with our everyday language—both spoken and in our internalized thought. Language, he insists, serves to confound our sensibilities and seriously limit the possibilities of our seeing. He tells Castaneda: "You get confused only when you talk."[102] The following conversation explains this:

"You talk to yourself too much. You're not unique at that. Every one of us does that. We carry on an internal talk. Think about it. Whenever you are alone, what do you do?"

"I talk to myself."

"What do you talk to yourself about?"

"I don't know; anything, I suppose."

"I'll tell you what we talk to ourselves about. We talk about our world. In fact we maintain our world with our internal talk."

"How do we do that?"

"Whenever we finish talking to ourselves the world is always as it should be. We renew it, we kindle it with life, we uphold it with our internal talk. Not only that, but we also choose our paths as we talk to ourselves. Thus we repeat the same choice over and over until the day we die, because we keep on repeating the same internal talk over and over until the day we die."

"A warrior is aware of this and strives to stop his talking. This is the last point you have to know if you want to live like a warrior."

"How can I stop talking to myself?"

"First of all you must use your ears to take some of the burden from your eyes. We have been using our eyes to judge the world since the time we were born. We talk to others and to ourselves mainly about what we see. A warrior is aware of this and listens to the world. . . ."

"A warrior is aware that the world will change as soon as he stops talking to himself," he said, "and he must be prepared for that monumental jolt."

"What do you mean, don Juan?"

"The world is such-and-such or so-and-so only because we tell ourselves that that is the way it is. If we stop telling ourselves that the world is so-and-so, the world will stop being so-and-so. . . ."

"Your problem is that you confuse the world with what people do. Again you're not unique at that. . . . The things people do are the shields against the forces that surround us; what we do as people gives us comfort and makes us feel safe; what people do is rightfully very important, but only as a shield. We never learn that the things we do as people are only shields and we let them dominate and topple our lives. . . ."

"A warrior is aware of this confusion and learns to treat things properly. The things that people do cannot under any conditions be more important than the world. And thus a warrior treats the world as an endless mystery and what people do as an endless folly."[103]

Don Juan says: "An average man who is equally surrounded by those inexplicable forces is oblivious to them because he has other kinds of special shields to protect himself."[104] Those shields are what people do. But Castaneda, at the edge of becoming a warrior, is told that he can no longer count on those commonplace shields: "Act like a warrior and select the items of your world. . . . Now for the first time you are not safe in your old way of life."[105] This sobering revelation lends deep drama to Castaneda's attempts to see and to discipline his character.

Don Juan has been quoted to the effect that everyday language, both spoken and internal, and ordinary commonsense action determine our perceptual field and serve to shield us from extraordinary realities. We have learned, he says, to think about everything, and we have trained our eyes to look as we think. **Seeing** stands in sharp contrast to **looking** at things this way. It involves experiencing a multilayered, deep, and vibratory world. But for don Juan it is not inherently better than looking. However, to train the eyes only for looking is, in his opinion, an unnecessary loss. He says: "For instance, we need to look with our eyes to laugh, . . . because only when we look at things can we catch the funny edge of the world. On the other hand, when our eyes **see**, everything is so equal that nothing is funny."[106]

Nor is anything sad, for that matter. Don Juan tells Castaneda of the time when his son, working on the construction of the Pan-American Highway, was crushed by rocks. At the scene, witnessing his son's mangled, almost dead body, don Juan reports:

"I shifted my eyes so I would **see** his personal life disintegrating, expanding uncontrollably beyond its limits, like a fog of crystals, because that is the way life and death mix and expand. That is what I did at the time of my son's death. That's all one could ever do, and that is controlled folly. Had I looked at him I would have watched him becoming immobile and I would have felt a cry inside of me, because never again would I look at his fine figure pacing the earth. I **saw** his death instead, and there was no sadness, no feeling. His death was equal to everything else."[107]

"In order to become a man of knowledge one must be a warrior, not a whimpering child. One must strive without giving up, without complaint, without flinching, until one **sees**, only to realize then that nothing matters."[108] And yet: "Everything is filled to the brim and everything is equal and my struggle was worth my while."[109]

That a warrior has the capacity to become a man of knowledge is further explicated in **Journey to Ixtlan**. It is a warrior's responsibility to wield power, and don Juan remarks "Knowledge is power."[110] He explains that "Every warrior has a specific form, a specific posture, which he develops under the influence of his personal power."[111] The movements of the dance are learned in struggling with worthy opponents. Don Juan concludes: "The posture, the form of a warrior, is the story of his life, a dance that grows as he grows in personal power."[112] Then he claims that persons possess "rings of power" that are "hooked to the **doing** of the world in order to make the world."[113] When pressed for an example, he tells Castaneda:

> "For instance, our rings of power, yours and mine, are hooked right now to the **doing** in this room. We are making this room. Our rings of power are spinning this room into being at this very moment. . . . You see," he continued, "every one of us knows the doing of rooms because, in one way or another, we have spent much of our lives in rooms. A man of knowledge, on the other hand, develops another ring of power. I would call it the ring of **not-doing**, because it is hooked to **not-doing**. With that ring, therefore, he can spin another world."[114]

Then Castaneda attains "stopping the world," that is, experiencing another world, and reports he has had a "conversation" with a coyote. In this experience, Castaneda has stopped the world in that in communicating with a magical being, the world of sorcery comes into being. Don Juan explains:

> "In that world coyotes talk and so do deer, as I once told you, and so do rattlesnakes and trees and all other living beings. . . . Perhaps you know now that **seeing** happens only when one sneaks between the worlds, the world of ordinary people and the world of sorcerers."[115]

Don Juan has spoken for himself about these difficult matters of inquiry—about sorcery and the struggle to see—and he always leads us back to the paradoxes of character and the structure of an appositional inquiry in which nothing truly matters. Action and inaction alike represent "controlled folly,"[116] and "a man of knowledge has no honor, no dignity, no family, no name, no country, but only life to be lived."[117]

Castaneda struggles to understand, but don Juan says to him:

> "You think about your acts. . . . Therefore you have to believe your acts are as important as you think they are, when in reality nothing of what one does is important. . . . It would be more simple to die; that's what you say and believe, because you're thinking about life, just as you're thinking now what **seeing** would be like. You wanted me to describe it to you so you could begin to think about it, the way you do with everything

else. . . . I cannot tell you what it is like to **see**. Now you want me to describe the reasons for my controlled folly and I can only tell you that
controlled folly is very much like **seeing**; it is something you cannot think
about."[118]

At last, after months of listening to the sounds of the world, of listening without
looking, and of shutting off internal dialogue, Castaneda again smokes the hallucinogenic mixture and hunts for "the holes between the sounds."[119] By listening carefully to sounds, distinguishing them, he finds that together they create
what he calls an "order, . . . an order of sounds that had a pattern; that is, every
sound happened in a sequence." The spaces or pauses between sounds became
"holes in a structure."[120] When the sounds ceased, Castaneda perceived the
cessation as a hole, and at that moment he shifted "attention from hearing to
looking."

The silhouette of the hills was arranged in such a way that . . . there
seemed to be a hole on the side of one of the hills. . . . For a moment . . .
[it] was as if the hole I was looking at was the "hole" in the sound. . . . At
a given moment the pauses became crystallized in my mind and formed a
sort of solid grid, a structure. I was not seeing or hearing it. I was feeling it
with some unknown part of myself.[121]

These descriptions by Castaneda call to mind some statements of Maurice Merleau-Ponty concerning mescaline. In his **Phenomenology of Perception** he wrote:

The influence of mescaline, by weakening the attitude of impartiality and
surrendering the subject to his vitality, should . . . favor forms of synaesthetic experience. And indeed, under mescaline the sound of a flute gives a
bluish-green colour, the tick of a metronome, in darkness, is translated as
grey patches, the spatial interval between them corresponding to the intervals of time between the ticks, the size of the patch to the loudness of the
tick, and its height to the pitch of the sound. A subject under mescaline
finds a piece of iron, strikes the windowsill with it and exclaims: "This is
magic"; the trees are growing greener. The barking of a dog is found to
attract light in an indescribable way, and is re-echoed in the right foot. It is
as if one could sometimes see the occasional collapse of the barriers established, in the course of evolution, between the senses. Seen in the
perspective of the objective world, with its opaque qualities, and the objective body with its separate organs, the phenomenon of synaesthetic experience is paradoxical. The attempt is therefore made to explain it independently of the concept of sensation: It is thought necessary, for example, to
suppose that the excitations ordinarily restricted to one region of the
brain—the optical or auditory zone—become capable of playing a part
outside these limits, and that in this way a specific quality is associated
with a non-specific one. Whether or not his explanation is supported by
arguments drawn from brain physiology, this explanation does not account for synaesthetic experience, which thus becomes one more occasion
for questioning the concept of sensation and objective thought. **For the
subject does not say only that he has had the sensation both of a sound**

and a color: it is the sound itself that he sees where colors are formed. This formulation is literally meaningless if vision is defined by the visual **quale,*** and the sound by the acoustic **quale.** . . . Synaesthetic perception is the rule, and we are unaware of it only because scientific knowledge shifts the centre of gravity of experience, so that we have unlearned how to see, hear, and generally speaking, feel, in order to deduce, from our bodily organization and the world as the physicist conceives it, what we are to see, hear, and feel.[122]

Continuing the phenomenological analysis of the interdependence of the senses, Merleau-Ponty added:

Sight, it is said, can bring us only colours or lights, and with them forms which are the outlines of colours, and movements which are the patches of colour changing position. But how shall we place transparency or "muddy" colours in the scale? In reality, each colour, in its inmost depths, is nothing but the **inner structure** of the thing overtly revealed. . . . The senses intercommunicate by opening on to the structure of the thing. . . . The form of objects is not their geometrical shape: it stands in a certain relation to their specific nature, and appeals to all our other senses as well as sight. The form of a fold in linen or cotton shows us the resilience or dryness of the fibre, the coldness or warmth of the material. Furthermore, the movement of visible objects is not the mere transference from place to place of coloured patches. . . . Gradually we should come to find that there was no longer any difference between the perceptual and the intellectual syntheses. The unity of the senses would then be of the same order as the unity of the objects of science.[123]

It should be pointed out that experience with psychedelic drugs may constitute hallucinations, in which perceptions are not only "nonordinary," but may also indicate disorder and confusion. Insofar as this is so, these drugs are experienced at a level that does not constitute **seeing.** The visual experiences possible—with or without such drugs—do not imply seeing a world that is clear and distinct, and as the practice progresses, visual hallucinations disappear, and vision becomes a vision.

We conclude that the teachings of don Juan are intended to convey the unity of the senses, and that the entire enterprise is directed toward an inquiry into structure, into the inner layers of order. It is for this reason that such an inquiry can properly be called **synthetic.** In logic, a synthetic judgment is one that attributes to a subject a predicate that is not contained in the essence or connotation of that subject. It would appear, as Merleau-Ponty suggested, that **perceptual** synthesis corresponds to this logical operation whereby the senses— acting simultaneously upon the world as perceived—are able to bring into being a level of reality, a perception of the whole, that transcends the categories of the individual senses. With our eyes, we can **look at** an object, but to the extent that we **grasp** the inner structure of the object and are able to **see** in a way that transcends merely looking, our perceptions act in concert and it can be said that we gain insight into order.

---

* **Quale** means with respect to its own particular quality, independent of other senses—Ed.

NOTES

1. Eden Gray, **The Tarot Revealed**, New York: Bell, 1970, p. 1.

2. The view that the Tarot is of Egyptian origin was advanced by French occultist Eliphus Levy and elaborated by Papus (M. Gerard Encausse), Mouni Sadhu, and many others. However, an outstanding student of the Tarot, Arthur E. Waite, took strong exception to such speculations, attacking both Levy and his ideas. In his preface to the English translation of Papus, **The Tarot of the Bohemians** (trans. A. P. Morton, North Hollywood, Cal.: Wilshire, 1971, p. xi), Waite wrote: "In respect to Eliphus Levy, it is a matter of common familiarity that his opinion on any question of fact was sometimes more than worthless and occasionally a little bit less than intellectually honest." Waite added: "I conclude generally that the cards are prior to the end of the fourteenth century, and that we know nothing further concerning them." **Ibid.**, p. xii.

3. Gray, **op. cit.**, p. 5.

4. For this widely used Tarot deck the artist was Pamela Coleman Smith, in collaboration with Waite. Published by Tarot Productions, Inc., Los Angeles, California, 1968.

5. Mouni Sadhu, **The Tarot: A Contemporary Course of the Quintessence of Hermetic Occultism**, North Hollywood, Ca.: Wilshire Book Company, 1970, p. 29.

6. Ibid., p. 25.

7. Papus, **op. cit.**, p. 106.

8. Ibid.

9. Paul Foster Case, **The Tarot: A Key to the Wisdom of the Ages**, Richmond, Virginia: Macoy Publishing Company, 1947, p. 40.

10. Ibid., p. 43.

11. Ibid., p. 41.

12. Ibid.

13. Ibid., pp. 43–44.

14. Ibid., p. 49.

15. Gray, **op. cit.**, p. 19.

16. Ibid., p. 79.

17. Case, **op. cit.**, p. 51.

18. Sadhu, **op. cit.**, p. 43.

19. Ibid., pp. 43, 45.

20. Gray, **op. cit.**, p. 79.

21. Sadhu, **op. cit.**, p. 45.

22. Arthur Edward Waite, **The Pictorial Key to the Tarot**, New Hyde Park, N.Y.: University Books, 1959, p. 79.

23. Sadhu, **op. cit.**, p. 55.

24. Ibid., p. 56, capitalized in text.

25. Ibid., emphasis added.

26. Ibid., p. 35.

27. Ibid., p. 36.

28. Ibid., emphasis added.

29. Ibid. p. 56.

30. Ibid.

31. Ibid.

32. Bogen and Bogen, **op. cit.** This thought can also be called **dialectical**.

33. Gray, **op. cit.**, p. 99.

34. Ralph Metzner, **Maps of Consciousness: I Ching, Tantra, Alchemy, Astrology, Actualism**, New York: Collier, 1971, p. 80; Waite, **op. cit.**, p. 306.

35. Metzner, **op. cit.**, p. 80.

36. Ibid.

37. Waite, **op. cit.**, p. 305.

38. Metzner, **op. cit.**

39. Waite, **op. cit.**, pp. 283–287.

40. James Legge, trans. **I Ching: Book of Changes**, New York: Dover, 1963, p. 1.

41. Archie J. Bahm writes: "When, where and how the author of the **Tao Teh King** lived have been questions of long and ardent, but largely futile, speculation." He adds: "The name Lao means old, ancient, venerable, and . . . Tzu is a common term of respect, like Sir, Master, or Worthy One. The Chinese early and late, have venerated the wisdom of their elders. Since Tao Teh King expounds ideals which are exceedingly primitive, and which it attributes to the men of old, one may easily infer that the name of the author means simply 'Ancient Thinker.' " Bahm translates Tao as Nature and Teh as Intelligence. Archie J. Bahm, trans., Lao Tze, Tao Teh King, New York: Ungar, 1958, p. 71.

42. Bahm, ibid.

43. Metzner, op. cit., p. 18.

44. Richard Wilhelm and Cary F. Baynes, trans., The I Ching, or Book of Changes, Princeton, N. J.: Princeton University Press, Bollingen Series, 1967, p. lv.

45. Ibid., p. xlvii.

46. Ibid. Another widely used version is John Blofeld, trans. and ed., I Ching: The Book of Change, New York: Dutton, 1965.

47. Ibid., p. 3.

48. Ibid.

49. Ibid., pp. 6–7.

50. Ibid., p. 3.

51. Ibid., p. 5.

52. Ibid., p. 4.

53. Ibid.

54. Ibid., p. 6.

55. Ibid., p. 377.

56. Ibid. p. 378.

57. Ibid., p. 10.

58. Ibid., p. 396.

59. Ibid., p. 11.

60. Ibid., pp. 285–286.

61. Ibid., p. 11.

62. Ibid., p. 12.

63. Ibid., p. 286.

64. Ibid.

65. Ibid.

66. Ibid., p. 12.

67. Ibid., p. 13.

68. Ibid., p. 48.

69. A mirror image hexagram will be defined as the image of a hexagram reflected from above or below; an opposite hexagram, by replacement of all six lines by their opposites, yang into yin, and yin into yang. T'ai and P'i are both mirror images and opposites.

70. Wilhelm and Baynes, op. cit., pp. 52–53.

71. Ibid., p. 49.

72. Ibid., emphasis added.

73. Ibid. pp. 721–723. See also Blofeld, op. cit., pp. 59–71.

74. Ibid. p. 159.

75. Ibid.

76. Ibid.

77. Ibid., p. 158.

78. Ibid., p. 160.

79. Ibid., p. 161.

80. Ibid. p. 590.

81. Carlos Castaneda, A Separate Reality: Further Conversations With Don Juan, New York: Simon & Schuster, 1971, p. 19.

82. Black Elk, recorded and edited by Jose Epes Brown, The Sacred Pipe: Black Elk's Account of the Seven Rites of the Oglala Sioux, Norman, Okla.: University of Oklahoma Press, 1953, pp. 44–46.

83. Gary Snyder, Earth House Hold, New York: New Directions, 1957, p. 107.

84. Carlos Castaneda, The Teachings of Don Juan: A Yaqui Way of Knowledge, New York: Ballantine, 1968, p. 8.

85. Ibid., pp. 254–255.

86. Castaneda, Separate Reality, p. 240, emphasis in text.

87. Ibid., p. 258.

88. Ibid.

89. Ibid., pp. 258–260.
90. Castaneda, Teachings, p. 45.
91. Castaneda, Separate Reality, p. 85.
92. Castaneda, Teachings, p. 45. Don Juan describes jimson weed as a "female" ally, being possessive, violent, and unpredictable. Psylocybe is a "male" ally with the opposite characteristics, being dispassionate, gentle, and predictable. Ibid., pp. 214–219.
93. Ibid., p. 253.
94. Ibid., p. 78.
95. Ibid., pp. 79–80.
96. Ibid., pp. 80–81.
97. Ibid., p. 81.
98. Ibid., p. 82.
99. Ibid., p. 83.
100. Ibid., p. 198.
101. Castaneda, Separate Reality, p. 142.
102. Ibid., p. 205.
103. Ibid. pp. 263–265.
104. Ibid., p. 260.
105. Ibid., p. 261.
106. Ibid., p. 104.
107. Ibid., p. 113.
108. Ibid., p. 110.
109. Ibid.
110. Carlos Castaneda, Journey to Ixtlan: The Lessons of Don Juan, New York: Simon and Schuster, 1972, p. 186.
111. Ibid., p. 188.
112. Ibid.
113. Ibid., p. 252.
114. Ibid.
115. Ibid., p. 300.
116. Castaneda, Separate Reality, p. 107.
117. Ibid.
118. Ibid., pp. 107–108.
119. Ibid., p. 267.
120. Ibid., pp. 269–270.
121. Ibid., p. 270.
122. Maurice Merleau-Ponty, trans. Colin Smith, Phenomenology of Perception, New York: Humanities, 1962, pp. 228–229, emphasis in text.
123. Ibid., pp. 229–230, emphasis added. It is known that stimulation in one sense, for example, in vision, produces responses in others, including auditory and somatosensory areas.

Concepts: Order and Mind; Form and Structure

This chapter explicates a number of concepts necessary for the comparative analysis of inquiry. The first concept to be taken up is **order**. Sociologist Louis Guttman's theory for measuring objects so that they can be ordered from left to right consistent with the extent to which they possess some variable provides a vehicle for explicating the notion of order itself. His analysis shows that the rank ordering of objects on a directed continuum of numbers running from left to right—the **direction** of order—does not exhaust the topic of order. This analysis suggests that order prevails in both propositional and appositional kinds of thought; that these kinds of thinking involve the concepts of form and structure, respectively; and that the relation between form and structure has to do with the outside and the inside, such that it is meaningful to refer to outer form and inner structure, but not to inner form and outer structure.

ORDER
Before analyzing order, it is useful to distinguish between an **order** and a **system**. An **order** constitutes a whole, or ensemble, containing constant factors (the "environment") and factors that change (the "system"); it has the characteristic that what happens at every point is determined by what happens at every other

point. **Order** thus describes the workings of a whole rather than a system.[1] Scientists and engineers deal with systems rather than orders to the extent that they disregard the environment. The orientation to systems rather than orders pervades Western science and engineering and often results in misfits between environments and systems. The costs of such misfits can be seen in the observed performances of traffic systems, educational systems, economic systems, political systems, and so on.

In general, social scientists also focus on systems rather than orders. For example, American sociology was dominated for a period of time by the work of Talcott Parsons and his collaborators.[2] One could, for example, read Parsons's **The Social System** without being reminded that social systems are not self-contained, but are productions of one species of animals that share an environment with other species of animals and plants. Current interest in ecology and the environment is in large measure a result of recognized misfits between environments and systems. It can be expected that a new sociology will eventually emerge with its topic not the social system but the social order.

An order containing a system and its environment can be thought of as a form in its structural context. Examples are a soap bubble, a game of chess, or a musical composition. Here the form is, as Merleau-Ponty wrote, "a visible or sonorous configuration (or even a configuration which is prior to the distinction of the senses) in which the sensory value of every element is determined by its function in the whole and varies with it."[3] In the moment form is grasped, "consciousness is nothing other than the dialectic of milieu and action."[4] And forms must be defined as perceptible wholes. Merleau-Ponty credited the gestalt psychologist Wolfgang Köhler with this concept, "when he wrote that the order in a form 'rests . . . on the fact that each local event, one could almost say, "dynamically knows" the other.' "[5] Gestalt psychology has shown that perceptual space, like physical space, is non-Euclidean, so that perceived objects change in their properties according to their movements and locations. Merleau-Ponty wrote:

> The thresholds of perception in an organism . . . are among the individual constants which express its essence. This signifies that the organism itself **measures** the action of things upon it and itself delimits its milieu by a circular process which is without analogy in the physical world. The relations of the organic individual and its milieu are truly **dialectical** relations, therefore, and this dialectic brings about the appearance of new relations which cannot be compared to those of a physical system and its entourage or even understood when the organism is reduced to the mirage which anatomy and the physical sciences give of it.[6]

ORDER AND MEASUREMENT

To pursue the notion of order, we can now make use of Guttman's theory of ordinal measurement, which—by means of its very abstractness—contributes to an understanding of order itself. The relationship between order and measure is fundamental, inasmuch as objects can be arranged in an order from left to right only by the measurement of some variable characterizing every object in a domain.

In the most general sense, measurement is the assignment of numbers to objects according to clearly defined rules. Scientific investigations usually include observation of empirical phenomena, which in general concern some unit of analysis consisting of objects or measurable properties. The properties of interest can, of course, include relations between these objects or elements.

Category Measurement

At the simplest level, the elements being studied by a scientist can be grouped into distinct categories. A rule can be constructed for assigning each element to exactly one category, and giving each category a unique number. For example, every person in a work group could be identified by giving him or her a different number. These same persons could also be categorized by sex, such that males are numbered 1 and females 2. In the first example, there are as many categories as persons, but in the second, there are just two measurement categories.

In such category measurement, two persons, i and j, can be given different measurement numbers, m_i and m_j, respectively, **only** if they are members of different categories—so that the true category for person i, t_i, differs from the true category for person j, t_j. This measurement rule can be stated formally:[7]

Rule 1: $m_i = m_j$ only if $t_i = t_j$.

For example, group members named Ben and Amy, could be identified by the numbers 5 and 8, respectively, and then categorized by their sex, $m_5 = 1$ and $m_8 = 2$.

Ordinal Measurement

Each element being studied can vary in the magnitudes of certain properties. For example, the group of persons, in addition to being identified and categorized by sex, can be measured for their age, their income last year, their level of opposition to war, and so on. Suppose the property to be measured is "work alienation," and that there is some number t representing the true level of work alienation for each member of the work group. Also suppose there is some measuring procedure—such as asking each person a number of questions—by which a measurement number m can be assigned to each member of the group. There are two rules here for assigning measurement numbers. First, persons i and j should be given **different** measurement numbers only if they differ in their true levels of work alienation; in other words, Rule 1 applies to both category and ordinal measurement. Second, person i should be assigned a **larger** measurement number than j only if he or she is more alienated from the work group. This rule can be stated formally:[8]

Rule 2: $m_i \neq m_j$ only if $t_i \neq t_j$.

If Rules 1 and 2 both hold, it becomes possible to rank order the persons by their level of work alienation.

Interval Measurement

There are also properties or variables for which the rank orderings of measurement numbers have meaning, and in addition these numbers can be given interpretation—such that the difference between two measurement numbers, the width of the interval, has a direct interpretation. Temperature in degrees Fahrenheit is such a variable. If Ben's temperature is 98.6, Amy's 98.8, and David's 99.2, then the difference in temperature between Ben and Amy is half that of the difference between Amy and David. If the measurement numbers contain this level of information, it is said that interval-level measurement is attained, and the measurement numbers constitute a **metric**. Technically, this means that there is a straight-line (linear) relation between the measurement numbers and the true magnitudes for the variable being measured:[9]

Rule 3: $m_i = a \, (t_i) + b$, where a and b are constants and $a \neq 0$

For a variable such as work alienation, which exists only as an attitude of mind, there is no known way to achieve direct physical measurement. An attitude weighs nothing and is invisible, so there is no physical scale on which it can be placed. In spite of this limitation, there is methodology for measuring such attitudes and for ordering persons along a continuum of numbers.

Ordinal Scaling

Social scientists are concerned with many variables that do not lend themselves to measurement by instruments or devices that can be assigned metric scores. There is no scale or yardstick by which concepts such as "work alienation," "authoritarianism," and "self-esteem" can be measured. It is difficult to attain interval-level measurement for such variables. Moreover, it is unclear whether such concepts exist in the minds of persons as unitary variables or as multivariate complexes.

   In an effort to deal with such problems, Louis Guttman developed a methodology called **scale analysis**.[10] A **scale** is defined as a set of items (questions put to respondents), each of which is hypothesized to provide an independent empirical measure of some single universe of content—that is, some single variable. As an example, consider weight. It is clear that weight constitutes a single variable, and that there is an interval metric for this variable. Imagine that each person to be measured possesses a scale, but that the researcher does not. Further, imagine that the researcher's method is restricted to questioning these persons. The persons could be asked to agree or disagree with three questions, each of which provides a crude measure of weight:

   A. I weigh at least 100 pounds.
   B. I do not weigh less than 150 pounds.
   C. I weigh at least 172 pounds.

To construct a numerical measure of weight, the researcher could assign the following numerical scores to responses, where 1 is a response showing more weight than 0:

   A. Agree = 1; disagree = 0.
   B. Agree = 0; disagree = 1.
   C. Agree = 1; disagree = 0.

   A measure of weight can be constructed for each person by adding these numbers, so that the heaviest persons are given a "scale score" of 3 and the lightest persons a "scale score" of zero. The following relation between the scale scores provide a measure of weight in pounds:

Weight in pounds	Scale score
Less than 100	0
$100 \leqslant$ weight < 150	1
$150 \leqslant$ weight < 172	2
172 or more	3

Because there is a monotonic relation between weight in pounds and the scale scores, the scale scores are sufficient to order the persons on a left–right continuum.[11] It is clear that the criterion for ordinal measurement is satisfied: One person can be assigned a higher score than another only if his true weight in pounds is greater.

Before pursuing the analysis, a few obvious points should be made. This procedure would not actually be used for measuring weight, because accurate measurement scales exist and are available to any researcher. Social scientists, however, have legitimate interests in concepts such as "work alienation" and "self-esteem" for which external physical scales are unavailable. When questioned about such concepts, persons answer from an "internal scale" existing only in mind. Although there may be an underlying metric, such concepts cannot be measured in the same way that weight can be measured.

Let us now pursue the example considering the problem of the underlying metric. The hypothesis that weight constitutes a single variable—a universe of content—and that each question provides an independent measure of that variable makes it possible to predict the **pattern of responses** for each person, from this person's score. For example, if a person scores one on two of the three statements, his scale score is 2, and we can expect that the answers are one for items A and B and zero for C. For any person's answers to the items, ordered (A,B,C), all one scores should be to the left of all zero scores. This provides a definition of a **perfect scale:** For any set of items ordered from left to right, everyone scoring one on the jth item also scores one on the (j −1)th item. Suppose, for example, that 10 persons respond to the statements and the following response pattern is obtained:

Respondent	Item A	B	C	Scale Score
1	0	0	0	0
2	0	0	0	0
3	1	0	0	1
4	1	1	0	2
5	1	1	0	2
6	1	1	0	2
7	1	1	0	2
8	1	0	1	2
9	1	1	1	3
10	1	1	1	3

For a scale with r items, there are 2^r possible response patterns, only (r + 1) of which conform to the model of a perfect scale. In the above example the patterns (0, 0, 0), (1, 0, 0), (1, 1, 0) and (1, 1, 1) fit the model of a scale. But the responses of person 8 do not fit this model: This person claims to weigh less than 150 pounds, but also to weigh 172 pounds or more. Confronted with such answers the researcher has to decide either that weight does not constitute a single variable, or that there are "errors" in the answers of person 8. In this case the correct decision is that weight is a single variable and there are errors in the answers of person 8.

Such a decision is difficult to make when one is attempting to measure a variable such as work alienation. Suppose, for example, that a group of workers were asked to agree or disagree with each of the following five questions:

A. I really don't feel a sense of pride or accomplishment as a result of the type of work that I do.
B. My work gives me a feeling of pride in having done the job well.
C. I very much like the type of work that I am doing.
D. My job gives me a chance to do the things that I do best.
E. My work is my most rewarding experience.[12]

Persons highest on work alienation should agree with the first item and disagree with the rest. It would be appropriate to assign the score 1 to an "agree" answer to A, and the score 1 to the "disagree" answer to items B through E. The ordering of the items is determined by the proportion of persons scored 1 for each item. In such a situation, it is doubtful that all response patterns will be perfect. Thus the existence of a single variable becomes a statistical problem.[13]

The methodologies for the statistical analysis of ordinal measurement is not our present concern. Instead, the concept of a perfect scale is used to study the topic of order itself. To this end, we shall draw on an analysis of perfect scales developed by Guttman. Guttman's theory of "The Principal Components of Scale Analysis" involves a complex mathematical analysis. Here, some of the major features of the analysis are described in nonmathematical form.

In a perfect scale all respondents can be ranked from lowest to highest for the variable measured by the items, according to their scale scores. The assignment of **metric** scores to the ranks can be inferred through a formal argument. Guttman presents a theory relating scale scores in a perfect scale to the underlying metric, where the scale scores are of ordinal-level measurement and the metric is of interval-level measurement. For any particular problem there are a multiplicity of metric scores that can be thought of as a solution to the problem of metric. These solutions are called **principal components**.[14] We will refer to these components as the **layers of order**.

Guttman explains his theory as follows:

In quantifying a set of qualitative items, there are two different sets of numerical values that can be determined. One set is the **weight** to be assigned the categories of the items, and the other is the **scores** to be assigned the people. The principle we shall use for quantification, or obtaining a metric, for each of these sets is that of maximizing internal consistency in the sense of least squares. . . .

The most internally consistent scores to assign the people on the basis of their responses to the items are those that satisfy the following condition. All people who fall in one category of an item should have scores as similar as possible among themselves, and as different as possible from the scores of the people in the other categories of the item; this should be true to the best extent possible for all items simultaneously. The total variance of the persons' scores can be expressed as the sum of two parts: the variance of the scores **within** categories, and the variance **between** categories. Maximizing similarities within categories and differences between categories implies maximizing the ratio that the variance between categories has to the total variance. The square root of such a ratio is called technically a **correlation ratio**, so our problem resolves itself into finding the set of scores that has the largest possible correlation ratio with respect to all items.[15]

The solution of finding the scores for people is independent of the solution of weights for categories. Also, the maximum possible correlation ratio for scores equals the maximum possible correlation ratio for weights. "The score of a person is proportional to the arithmetic mean of the weights of the categories by which he is characterized, and the weight of a category is proportional to the arithmetic mean of the scores of the people who are in it."[16]

Guttman then states that the equations of internal consistency provide justification for assigning weights to items added up to provide scores for the people. He writes:

The solution to the equations of internal consistency can be put in the following terms. Find a set of scores for the people such that, if weights are derived from these weights by adding them up for each person, then the new scores will be exactly proportional to the original scores. That is, find a set of scores that "go in a circle": they yield weights that give back the same scores. Such a set of scores is called a principal component of the system.[17]

The "size" of such a "circle" is provided by the correlation ratio described above. An outstanding result of this analysis is that:

There are many principal components for a configuration of responses. It turns out that, for any configuration of responses to items, **whether it is the scale pattern or not**, there exist scores and weights that go in a circle, and hence are the most internally consistent for that configuration. Equally important is the fact that there is **more than one** set of scores and of weights which go in a circle, albeit the circles will vary in size. There are many such sets, in fact, usually at least as many as there are distinct types of items. Any such set is also called a principal component of the system. A set of scores that goes in a circle is a principal component of the score system, or the quantification of the persons' ranks; a set of weights that goes in a circle is a principal component of the weight system, or the quantification of categories of values.

TABLE 1. A PERFECT SCALE OF FIVE ITEMS FOR THE VARIABLE "WORK ALIENATION"

Scale				Response Category						
Score	(Ia)*	(2a)	(3a)	(4a)	(5a)	(Ib)	(2b)	(3b)	(4b)	(5b)
5	x	x	x	x	x					
4		x	x	x	x	x				
3			x	x	x	x	x			
2				x	x	x	x	x		
1					x	x	x	x	x	
0						x	x	x	x	x
Number	1	2	3	4	5	5	4	3	2	1

* Ia = "agree" to item A; 2a, 3a, 4a, 5a = "disagree to items B, C, D, and E.

Source: Louis Guttman, "The Principal Components of Scale Analysis," in Samuel A. Stouffer, et al., Studies in Social Psychology in World War II, vol. IV, Measurement and Prediction, New York: Wiley, 1950, p. 317, Table 1.

Each principal component is associated with a correlation ratio,[18] the square of which is the "size of the circle." Hence, of the many principal components, the one with the largest correlation ratio is the most consistent quantification. The one with the next largest correlation ratio is the most consistent **after** the first component is subtracted out, etc. It is the first component, or the one with the largest correlation ratio, that defines our desired metric; we shall call this the **metric** component.[19]

Consider a concrete example. Imagine that the five-item scale of work alienation is administered to 30 workers and that their answers fit the model of a perfect scale, such that there were 5 respondents of each of the "scale types" 0 through 5. These responses are arranged in order in Table 1. In the table x shows the response chosen by persons of each scale score. For example, the persons scored 5 for work alienation, the most alienated, are those whose responses are scored 1 for all five items, who agree with item A and disagree with the other four.

In this example it is seen that the scale scores "go in a circle" that is larger than any other circle and is said to constitute the first principal component. Actually, it is necessary that principal component scores have a mean of zero, so the scores 5, 4, 3, 2, 1, 0 on the m axis of Figure 13 are a linear function of the principal component scores on the t axis, which are 5, 3, 1, -1, -3, and -5. The rule for expressing the m scores as a linear function of the metric score t is m = ½(t) + 2½ as shown in Figure 13. Guttman explains:

To see that the scores "go in a circle," let us first ascertain the weights they yield for the categories. Category 1a has only one kind of person, whose new score is 5. Category 2a has two kinds of people, one with score 5 and the other with score 3. Since each type is equally frequent for this example, the mean is 4. Category 3a has the mean score of three kinds of people:

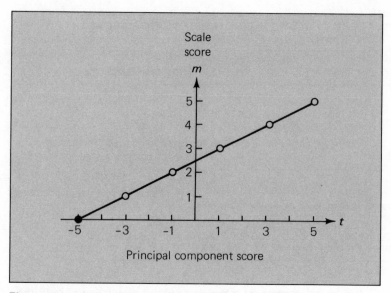

Figure 13.
Source: Derived from Table 2.

$$\frac{5 + 3 + 1}{3} = 3,$$

and so on.[20]

The category weights for the ten columns in Table 1—two categories for each item—are 5, 4, 3, 2, 1, −1, −2, −3, −4, and −5. These category weights give the metric scores back again, by finding the mean of the category weights for each type of person. For example, persons with scale scores of 5 have weights 5, 4, 3, 2, 1, the average of which is 3; persons with scale scores of 4 have weights 4, 3, 2, 1, −1, so the mean is 1.8. Continuing this procedure gives "circular scores" of .6, −.6, −1.8, and −3.0. Each circular score is exactly .6 times the original score, and this proportionality verifies that these scores go in a circle. Guttman shows also that his constant of proportionality is the square of the correlation ratio for the first component and that the constants for each higher-order principal component yields a smaller circle.

The derivation of these circular scores involves a complex mathematical argument that need not be taken up here. Instead, our attention will focus on the **substantive** interpretations of the distinct solutions to the problem of order.

For the example scale, the principal component scores for each "scale type" are shown in Table 2, and a graph showing these component scores (weighted by size of circle) is shown in Figure 14. For this example there are five principal components containing information; the sixth and higher-order solutions are constant.

The first solution—the largest or "outer" circle, is a measure of the true

TABLE 2. PRINCIPAL COMPONENT SCORES FOR THE
WORK ALIENATION SCALE

Scale Scores	Principal Component Scores					
	I	II	III	IV	V	VI
5	5	5	5	1	1	1
4	3	−1	−7	−3	−5	1
3	1	−4	−4	2	10	1
2	−1	−4	4	2	−10	1
1	−3	−1	7	−3	5	1
0	−5	5	−5	1	−1	1
Size of Circle	.60	.20	.10	.06	.04	1

Source: Louis Guttman, "The Principal Components of Scale Analysis," in Samuel A. Stouffer, et al., **Studies in Social Psychology in World War II**, vol. IV, **Measurement and Prediction**, New York: Wiley, 1950, p. 322, Table 4.

magnitude of the level of work alienation; these scores can thus be ranked from left to right on a numerical continuum.

The second best solution has a U-shaped relation to the scale scores, and the third best solution has a curve with two bends in it. Mathematically, there are at least as many solutions as items, and the **k**th best solution will, when plotted against the scale scores, provide a curve with **k** − 1 bends in it. For example, the third solution yields a curve with two bends in it, and the fourth solution yields a curve with three bends in it.

The first four principal components of scalable variables have been given interpretation in terms of attitude measurement.

The **first principal component,** scores that vary directly with the metric scores, is interpreted as the **direction** of the variable. That is, scale scores to the left, given small numbers, show low alienation, and scores to the right show high alienation.

The interpretation for the **second principal component** is **intensity.** Guttman writes:

If [a] scalable attitude has a meaningful zero point, . . . a **point of indifference** . . . , then as people have ranks farther and farther to the right of it, they should become more and more positive, and hence more and more intense. Similarly, as ranks get farther and farther to the left of the zero point, they should become more and more negative, and hence also indicate more intensity.[21]

The **third component, closure,** means the extent to which the mind is closed about the attitude in question. In the example variable, high closure might be

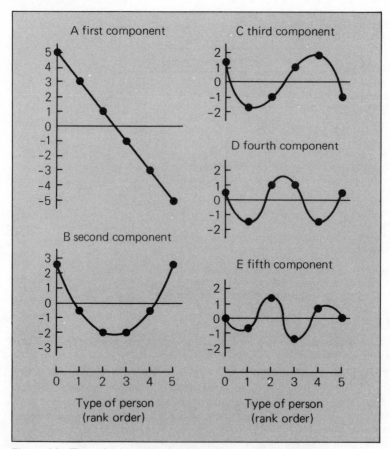

Figure 14. The principal components of the scale of Table 2.
Source: Louis Guttman, "The Principal Components of Scale Analysis," in Samuel A. Stouffer, et al., **Studies in Social Psychology in World War II**, vol. IV, **Measurement and Prediction**, New York: Wiley, 1950, p. 324.

elicited through answers to questions such as "How sure are you that your job does not provide meaningful work for you?"[22]

The **fourth component, involution,** is interpreted to mean that the person is turning the attitude over and over in his mind and is highly **involved** with the attitude. Low involution, in contrast, would mean that the person has ceased to reason through the attitude—that his or her mind is at rest with respect to it. Level of involution for a work alienation scale could be measured by a question such as "Do you spend much time in wondering whether your job provides rewarding work?"[23]

Although the theory implies the existence of additional components of scalable attitude, substantive interpretations have not been established for these components.

MIND AND THE MENTAL ORDER

When Wigan discovered that a person could function up to the time of death with an entire side of the brain withered away and yet clearly possess a mind, he reasoned that a person with two hemispheres must have two minds.[24] Neurologists have argued that the split-brain operation lends support to Wigan's conclusion. Cats with surgically divided brain hemispheres and optic chiasms can be trained to choose one of two symbols when one eye is covered and the opposite symbol when the other is covered. The two sides of the brain develop different solutions to the problem of choosing the rewarded symbol. Similar results have been attained on humans who have been subjected to the split-brain operation. M. S. Gazzaniga and Roger Sperry report that these patients can solve one problem with the left hand while solving a separate problem with the right.[25] Sperry writes: "Everything we have seen so far indicates that the surgery has left each of these people with two separate minds, that is, with two separate spheres of consciousness."[26] Bakan writes of "the inherent duality in man's behavior and experience."[27] The hypothesis of two independent spheres of consciousness is forcibly argued by Joseph Bogen. His statement merits quotation:

> Using special tests following a special operation, cerebral commissurotomy, we can regularly elicit a behavioral dissociation from which are inferred two separate, parallel streams of thought. The crucial question is whether these two minds exist with the commissures intact. It may be that an essential function of the corpus callosum is to keep the two hemispheres in exact synchrony, so that only one Mind can exist, that is, until the commissures are cut. This may be stated differently as a question: Does cerebral commissurotomy produce a splitting or doubling of the Mind, or is it more correctly considered a maneuver making possible the demonstration of a duality previously present?
>
> Every experiment involves the introduction of artifice or alteration, so that every experimental result can be explained as attributable more to the technique than to the process under investigation. Ultimately, this question is settled by production of the same result with a different technique. In this particular case, we can choose with certainty between the alternatives only if some other approach illustrates the same duality of mind.
>
> Pending further evidence, I believe (with Wigan) that each of us has two minds in one person. There is a host of detail to be marshalled in this case. But we must eventually confront directly the principal resistance to the Wigan view: that is, the subjective feeling possessed by each of us that we are One. This inner conviction of Oneness is a most cherished opinion of Western Man.[28] It is not only the common sense of the layman but also the usual assumption of the most prominent neurobiologists. Ramon y Cajal wrote: "It is impossible to understand the architectural plan of the brain if one does not admit as one of the guiding principles of this plan the unity of perception. . . ."[29] The issue was drawn with surpassing clarity by Sir Charles Sherrington:

> "This self is a unity . . . it regards itself as one, others treat it as one. It is addressed as one, by a name to which it answers. The Law and the State schedule it as one. It and they identify it with a body which is

considered by it and them to belong to it integrally. In short, unchallenged and unguarded conviction assumes it to be one. The logic of grammar endorses this by a pronoun in the singular. All its diversity is merged in oneness."[30]

The strength of this conviction is no assurance of its truth. . . .

The hypothesis which is the main burden of this paper may be summarized as follows:

One of the most obvious and fundamental features of the cerebrum is that it is double. Various kinds of evidence, especially from hemispherectomy, have made it clear that one hemisphere is sufficient to sustain a personality or mind. We may then conclude that the individual with two intact hemispheres has the capacity for two distinct minds. This conclusion finds its experimental proof in the split-brain animal whose two hemispheres can be trained to perceive, consider, and act independently.[31]

● ● ● ● ●

The scientists who maintain there are two minds have not provided an explicit definition of mind, but their usage seems to follow the Cartesian dictum by defining mind as a sphere of consciousness that solves problems for the body. Given a definition of this sort, the evidence supports the new contention that there are two minds.

At this point, it is useful to introduce the concept of the **mental order.** Like any order, the mental order contains distinguishable layers. The outer layer, concerned with form and direction, is propositional. The second layer of the mental order pertains to intensity, to inner structural processes, the visceral rhythms, and the emotions. Closure, the third layer of the mental order, refers to grasping or enclosing a whole or a gestalt, or grasping the meaning of a situation through perception of subtle changes in the perceptual field. To the extent that the layers of the mental order—which contain differing "proportions" of propositionality and appositionality—are not closed but open to each other, the mind as a whole is dynamically involved in the world.

Nevertheless, this description of the mental order does not suggest a dualistic view according to which the existence of two kinds of consciousness is considered evidence that there are two "minds" in a normal person. Instead, the mental order can be considered to be the dialectical mind, so that a normal person has just one.

As an individual, a person has no more than three layers of the mental order, but the theory of order suggests there may be additional layers of shared mental experience. For example, the fourth layer of the mental order includes our involvement in social structure. This layer of mental experience, in which we become involved in networks of social relations, transcends individual, unitary experience as an integrated thinking being. While social structure is not, per se, perceived by the senses—being invisible, untouchable, and without voice—its presence can nonetheless be perceived.

In the Eastern concept of Mind, involution would have a radically more inclusive meaning, meaning no less that involution into the Universal Mind in enlightenment or in death. By the definition given here, the mental order contains two minds. The Mind in the Eastern philosophical sense, if there is such a thing, would contain the mental order.

At this point it is possible to argue that the neurological data are not inconsistent with the concept of the mental order.

The split-brain operation destroys the direct connection between the first two layers of the mental order—thereby creating regions of consciousness that can know one another only indirectly. To some extent, these persons' "minds" are fragmented, and they are, to a limited degree, pathological instances of "dualistic man." But that layers of mental order can be partially fragmented by an operation that literally disconnects the two hemispheres does not prove that a normal person's two "minds" need be fragmented, or that one needs to dominate the other. For even after this operation the two hemispheres can communicate with one another, in such a way that the integration of personality survives.

First, Sperry notes that when both the optic chiasm and corpus callosum of a cat or monkey are divided along the midline, there is failure to transfer a learned pattern discrimination from a trained to an untrained eye.[32] Hence the corpus callosum appears to be necessary for the transfer of a pattern discrimination. However, a brightness discrimination might differ from a pattern discrimination. This distinction receives support in an experiment carried out by T. H. Meikle, et al., which shows that split-brain cats cannot transfer visual patterns from one hemisphere to the other, but can transfer brightness discriminations.[33] Furthermore, brightness discriminations are apparently unimpaired by the split-brain operation. This result, although not carried out on human subjects, implies that the corpus callosum is not essential in the transfer of a simple brightness discrimination and that such a discrimination is transferred subcortically. It thus appears that the cerebral hemispheres can communicate with each other through the lower brain stem. Messages can be sent across the corpus callosum, establishing a mediation of sensory-motor data, and they can be sent through subcortical structures, establishing a hypermediation of intensity discriminations. While this subcortical transfer in the human brain may be restricted to intensities and brightness discriminations, the communicative capacities of the lower brain structures are not yet known.

Second, propositional and appositional layers of the mental order can be kept in dynamic contact by means of the senses. For example, the human split-brain patients are able to transfer a verbal thought from the left hemisphere to the right by talking out loud to themselves. By doing this, words formed in the left hemisphere become available to the right hemisphere by being heard in the left ear. Similar contacts are maintained through vision. Bogen and Bogen note: "Every patient with a complete cerebral commissurotomy fails to name an unseen object [held] in the left hand, although recognition by the right hemisphere is obvious from the ability of the left hand to retrieve the test object when it is dropped into a bag containing a large number of similar objects."[34] While this controlled experiment dramatically shows that recognition of whole objects is a right hemisphere function and naming objects is a left hemisphere function, the experiment does not imply that these patients ordinarily are unable to define effectively the objects they see: When the artificial constraints of the experiment—specifying that the object is **unseen**—are removed, these patients can use both hands to retrieve an object and can bring the objects into view merely by emptying out the bag. In this case the dynamic connection is maintained in that an object grasped in the left hand and known by the right hemisphere can be associated with its name when both eyes look at it.

In summary, although the split-brain patients have lost an important **direct** link between the two hemispheres, the two kinds of thought maintain their dialectical connection by other means—through the brainstem and through the senses. It may be for this reason that their overall behavior demonstrates a fragmentation of consciousness only in the experimental setting in which indirect sensory linkages to the two hemispheres are denied. It would appear that the split-brain patients continue to function, on the whole, as normal persons. It may be the case that the mind is dual, so that the exchange between hemispheres is confined to the highest levels of creative thought, while in the day-to-day world the mind is double. This would explain why the operation makes such a small difference. At the same time, it may be that the mental order is unitary, its layers being dialectically connected so that exchange between the hemispheres comes about in so many ways that even surgical division of the direct connections fails to create, except in a controlled experiment denying indirect communications, anything that approaches a pathological fragmentation of the mental order into two isolated "minds."

FORM AND STRUCTURE

In claiming that the mind is unitary, the problem of dualism manifests itself on another level—that of the mind and body. There is an obvious difference between the mind and the body, in that the body has a spatiality in three dimensions and is visible; the mind has spatiality or a different order and is invisible. A surgeon can see the brain or the eye, but thought and sight are not seen. A sociologist can see persons in a group, but social structure itself is invisible. We need admit no dualism here; we simply note that there may be different levels to the world as perceived which are not reducible to each other. Moreover, the body itself can be studied at its cultural, social, biological, and physical levels simultaneously.

Because thought is invisible, it is necessary to resist the temptation to take any geometric model for the mental order too seriously. Guttman's analysis suggest that the components of an order can be thought of as concentric circles; the word **layer** is also visually evocative. But such interpretations may be inappropriate for a level of reality that is invisible.

We define the concepts of form and structure as the outer and inner layers of order, respectively. Consistent with this, it is appropriate to refer to outer form and inner structure. In Guttman's theory of order, each successive principal component explains **less** variance than the one before (which defines the sizes of the circles); that is to say, each successive component contains less information than the one before. The outer layer of order represents a maximal concentration of form, and each successive layer contains less form and more structure, until the layer is reached at which everything is constant in the sense that no additional information exists. This layer might be pure structure; or it might be without both form **and** structure—that is, it might be **disorder**.

CULTURE AND NATURE

The French anthropologist Claude Lévi-Strauss has written a book entitled **The Raw and the Cooked**[35] constituting an effort to introduce a scientific basis for

the study of myth. In dealing with his materials—myths gathered from Indian
tribes in the heart of tropical South America—Lévi-Strauss arrives at the position
that there exist parallels between myth and music. He contends that the arts of
myth-telling and music operate through the adjustment of two grids—one external and one internal. He writes that in music

> The external, or cultural, grid formed by the scale of intervals or the hier-
> archical relations among the notes, refers back to an inherent discontinu-
> ity: the discontinuity of musical sounds that are already wholly cultural
> objects in themselves, since they stand in contrast to noises, which are the
> only elements given **sub specie naturae**.[36]

Thus, while research has been cited showing that the tonal and melodic components of music may be specialized in the right hemisphere, the following statement by Lévi-Strauss implies that both propositional and appositional thought
participate in music:

> The inner, or natural, grid, which is a function of the brain, is reinforced
> by a second, and one might say, still more wholly natural grid: that con-
> stituted by the visceral rhythms. Consequently, in music the mediation
> between nature and culture that occurs in every language becomes a hyper-
> mediation; the connections are strengthened on either side. Since music is
> established at the point where two different spheres overlap, it runs well
> beyond boundaries that other arts are careful not to overstep. In the two
> opposite directions of nature and culture, it is able to go much further
> than they can.[37]

In the terminology developed here, it can be said that the second principal component, intensity, and the third, sensory grasp and closure, hypermediate culture
and nature. High intensity is associated with extremes of left and right, and
intensity in music (its visceral rhythms) sharpens distinctions between cultural
and natural components of music. Lévi-Strauss also writes:

> This explains the principle (though not the genesis and functioning, both
> of which . . . remain the great mysteries of the science of man) of music's
> extraordinary power to act simultaneously on the mind and the senses,
> stimulating both ideas and emotions and blending them in a common flow,
> so that they cease to exist side by side, except insofar as they correspond
> to, and bear witness to, each other.[38]

Lévi-Strauss's analysis of mythical inquiry is not chosen as a "case study" of
synthetic inquiry, but the system of mythology he describes certainly qualifies
as such an inquiry. The analysis provided by Lévi-Strauss contains a point requiring something akin to a modest critique. The structure of music is shown to
hypermediate the left-right and up-down "dualisms," but language, Lévi-Strauss
suggests, may be less dimensional than is music. For he writes "in music the
mediation between nature and culture that occurs within every language becomes a hypermediation."[39] What he is suggesting is that language involves the
domains of culture and nature—but does not connect this horizontal dimension

to the vertical, the intensity component. To deal with this limitation in the French language, Lévi-Strauss attempts to "musicalize" natural language: The format of **The Raw and the Cooked** parallels that of a musical symphony. This very act suggests that the music/language, hypermediation/mediation association may vary **within** a single language. If this is so, we might also expect that variations of this sort could occur **between** languages. That is, languages could exist that would hypermediate the first two components—that would be heavily involved in describing vibratory (intensity) phenomena. The existence of such a language certainly would have impact on inquiries carried out in that language. In particular, we should anticipate that "appositionally oriented" languages would lend themselves to synthetic inquiries, just as inquiry through music is synthetic inquiry and inquiry in "musicalized" natural language lends itself to the structural analysis of myth.

Up to this point we have related the left hemisphere to culture and language used propositionally and the right hemisphere to nature, myth, music, and the synthetic-perceptual in general. Bogen argues that a linear concept of time is characteristic of the left hemisphere's mode of thought; neurological and psychometric research shows spatial thought to be specialized in the right hemisphere. Lévi-Strauss argues that a musical composition and the myths constituting his ethnographic materials are isomorphic. He emphasizes that they must be perceived not sequentially but as totalities: "Every myth is an organized totality; the development of the narrative throws light on an underlying structure which is independent of the relation between what comes before and what comes after."[40] He explains that music and myth share the property of

> requiring a temporal dimension in which to unfold. But this relation to time is of a rather special nature: it is as if music and mythology needed time only in order to deny it. Both, indeed, are instruments for the obliteration of time. Below the level of sounds and rhythms, music acts upon a primitive terrain, which is the physiological time of the listener; this time is irreversible and therefore irredeemably diachronic, yet music transmutes the segment devoted to listening to it into a synchronic totality, enclosed within itself. Because of the internal organization of the musical work, the act of listening to it immobilizes passing time; it catches and enfolds it as one catches and enfolds a cloth flapping in the wind. It follows that by listening to music, and while we are listening to it, we enter into a kind of immortality.[41]

Thus it can be said that appositional cerebral structures such as gestalts, musical compositions, and myths enclose a time, immobilize time, and grasp a time. Hence inquiries through music, myth, and in general through the synthetic methods are fundamentally atemporal, if time is defined as linear.

Certainly arcana in the **Tarot** and hexagrams in the **I Ching** share the property Lévi-Strauss attributes to music. Arcana and hexagrams represent ideas that can be grasped and thereby enclosed, so that they hold time. A hexagram, for example, is explicitly defined in the **I Ching** as "the time," for it represents a situation that has accumulated. In this connection, Wilhelm writes that a hexagram constitutes "a contact transcending the limit of time. . . . True enough, speech and writing are imperfect transmitters of thought, but by means of the

Figure 15.
Source: Claude Lévi-Strauss, **The Savage Mind,** Chicago: University of Chicago Press, 1966,
Plate 4, Humanized Nature. Sketches by Grandville **(Bibl. Nationale).**

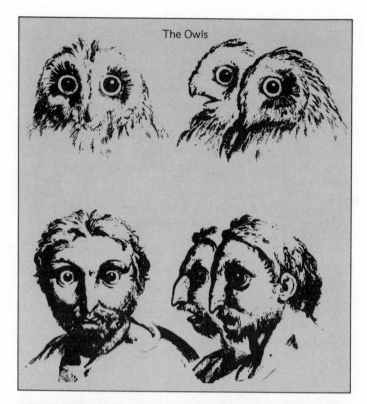

The Owls

The Foxes

Figure 16.
Source: Claude Lévi-Strauss, **The Savage Mind,** Chicago: University of Chicago Press, 1966, plate 3, Naturalized Man. Sketches by Le Brun.

images—we would say 'ideas'— . . . a spiritual force is set in motion whose action transcends the limits of time."[42] In this way, Wilhelm argued, it is possible for one epoch to understand another. The images of the arcana in the **Tarot**, so it is argued, have, at least in legend, been used in the same way: Scholars who did not share a common language were able to communicate and carry out collaborative inquiries through the time- and culture-transcending imagery of the arcana.

The relation between culture and nature, which parallels the disctinction between form and structure, such that culture is associated with·form and nature with structure, can be illustrated visually. Consider two sets of drawings (Figures 15 and 16) taken from Lévi-Strauss's **The Savage Mind**.[43] The first set shows culture superimposing on nature, such that culture contains nature, and structure contains form. The second set shows the opposite relation, nature superimposed on culture, such that culture is contained in nature. Here, form and structure have been defined so that form is most evident as the outer layer of order, and structure is more prevalent in the inner layers. Consistent with this, it can be said that culture is embedded in nature, rather than vice versa, and that nature contains culture. So the question becomes, Which set of pictures represents the situation as it is, and which represents the situation as it is not? The concepts defined here suggest that the first set of pictures portrays the world as it is not, and the second set portrays the world as it is. Birds are not included in human culture: They do not court one another as humans do; they do not live in families; they do not use tools; they do not live in houses; and they do not wear spats. The second set of pictures is startling in that humans are shown to resemble various animals; this strips away the cultural roles that we project onto faces. There is no fundamental distortion here, for man is a species of animal living in a community with other species and bearing resemblances to birds and other mammals.

It might be said that a problem in Western civilization is that the distinction between culture and nature is distorted by a tendency to project culture onto nature. It is for this reason that minerals, hydrocarbons, plants, and animals are so easily defined as "natural resources" existing for human consumption. To the extent that this is true, civilized man can be said to be confused about the relation between culture and nature. The "primitive," on the other hand, may be more apt to correctly see the first set of pictures as fantasy and the second set as a close approximation to reality. Because of this, "primitives" have attempted to impress upon the civilized world that they, and the entire ecological order, are not to be used as natural resources for modern technological societies.

NOTES

1. This distinction between system and environment is close to architect Christopher Alexander: "Every design problem begins with an effort to achieve fitness between two entities: the form in question and its context. The form is the solution to the problem; the context defines the problem. In other words, when we speak of design, the real object of discussion is not the form alone, but the ensemble comprising the form and its context. Good fit is a desired property of this ensemble which relates to some particular division of the ensemble into form and context. . . . [N]o one division of the ensemble is unique. . . . Fitness across any one such division is just one instance of the ensemble's internal coherence. . . . We ought always really to design with a number of nested, overlapped form—context boundaries in mind. Indeed, the form itself relies on its own inner organization and on the internal fitness between the pieces it's made of to control its fit as a whole to the context outside. . . . [T]he process of achieving good fit between two entities is a negative process of neutralizing the incongruities, or irritants, or forces, which cause misfit." Christopher Alexander, Notes on the Synthesis of Form, Cambridge: Harvard University Press, 1964, pp. 15–18, 24.

2. Talcott Parsons, The Structure of Social Action, New York: McGraw-Hill, 1937; Talcott Parsons, The Social System, New York: Free Press, 1951; Talcott Parsons, Robert F. Bales, and Edward A. Shils, Working Papers in the Theory of Action, New York: Free Press, 1953.

3. Maurice Merleau-Ponty, trans. Alden L. Fisher, The Structure of Behavior, Boston: Beacon, 1963, p. 168.

4. Ibid., p. 169.

5. Ibid., p. 143. Wolfgang Köhler Die Physischen Gestalten, in Ruhe und im Stationaren Zustand, Erlangen: Braunschweig, 1920, p. 180.

6. Merleau-Ponty, The Structure of Behavior, pp. 148–149, emphasis added.

7. S. S. Stevens, Handbook of Experimental Psychology, New York: Wiley, 1951. The particular form of these rules is used in William L. Hays, Statistics for Psychologists, New York: Holt, Rinehart & Winston, 1963, pp. 70–73.

8. Hays, op. cit., p. 70.

9. Ibid., p. 71.

10. Louis Guttman, "The Cornell Technique for Scale and Intensity Analysis," Education and Psychological Measurement, vol. 7, 1947, pp. 247–279. This method is currently called "cumulative scaling" or "Guttman scaling."

11. The scale scores must not decrease as weight increases, so that Rule 2 is satisfied.

12. This scale is used by George A. Miller, "Professionals in Bureaucracy: Alienation Among Industrial Scientists and Engineers," American Sociological Review, vol. 32, 1967, pp. 755–768.

13. Guttman, op. cit.; Leo A. Goodman, "Simple Statistical Methods for Scalogram Analysis," Psychometrika, vol. 24, 1959, pp. 29–43; Warren D. TenHouten, "Scale Gradient Analysis: A Statistical Method for Constructing and Evaluating Guttman Scales," Sociometry, vol. 32, 1969, pp. 80–98.

14. Guttman writes: "Principal components are an important concept in mathematics and in physics. It is interesting that they should also arise out of social-psychological considerations. Other names used for them include: principal axes, latent vectors, characteristic functions, characteristic vectors, eigenfunctions, and eigenvectors." In Louis Guttman, "The Principal Components of Scale Analysis," in Samuel A. Stouffer, et al., Studies in Social Psychology in World War II, vol. IV, Measurement and Prediction, New York: Wiley, 1950, p. 316 f.

15. Ibid., p. 314.

16. Ibid., p. 315.

17. Ibid., p. 316.

18. The correlation ratio is the ratio of the total sum of the variation within all categories to the total sum of squares of the deviations. See ibid., pp. 336–337.

19. Ibid., pp. 320–321, emphasis in text.

20. Ibid., p. 318.

21. Louis Guttman, "The Principal Components of Scalable Attitudes," in Paul F. Lazarsfeld, ed., Mathematical Thinking in the Social Sciences, New York: Free Press, 1954, pp. 224–226. The first component is the least squares metric, ibid., p. 229, emphasis in text.

22. Ibid., pp. 233–239.

23. Ibid., pp. 241–246.

24. Wigan wrote, "Each cerebrum is a distinct and perfect whole as an organ of thought," and "a separate and distinct process of thinking or ratiocination may be carried out in each cerebrum simultaneously." op. cit., p. 26, cited in Bogen, "Other Side of the Brain II," p. 151.

25. M. S. Gazzaniga and Roger W. Sperry, "Simultaneous Double Discrimination Response Following Brain Bisection," Psychoanalytic Science, vol. 4, 1966, pp. 261–262.

26. R. W. Sperry, "Problems Outstanding in the Evolution of Brain Function," James Arthur Lecture, American Museum of Natural History, New York, 1964.

27. Bakan, "The Eyes Have It."

28. And, of course, it is a dominant theme in Eastern religions and philosophical systems such as Hinduism, Buddhism, and Taoism.

29. S. Ramon y Cajal, "Anatomical and Physiological Considerations about the Brain," in G. Von Bonen, trans., **Some Papers on the Cerebral Cortex,** Springfield, Ill.: C. C. Thomas, 1960.

30. Charles Sherrington, **The Integrative Action of the Nervous System,** London: Cambridge University Press, 1947, p. xvii. A similar statement is set forth by philosopher Ludwig Wittgenstein, who wrote: "Why can't my right hand give my left hand money?—My right hand can put it into my left hand. My right hand can write a deed of gift and my left hand a receipt.—But the further practical consequences would not be those of a gift. When the left hand has taken the money from the right, etc., we shall ask: 'Well, and what of it?' And the same could be asked if a person had given himself a private definition of a word; I mean, if he has said the word to himself and at the same time has directed his attention to a sensation." Ludwig Wittgenstein, **Philosophical Investigations,** trans. G. E. M. Anscombe, Oxford: Blackwell, 1963, p. 94.

31. Bogen, "Other Side of the Brain II," pp. 155–157.

32. Roger W. Sperry, "Split-Brain Approaches to Learning Problems," in G. C. Quarton, T. Melnechuk, and F. O. Schmitt, eds., **The Neurosciences: A Study Program,** New York: Rockefeller University Press, 1967, pp. 714–722.

33. T. H. Meikle, J. A. Sechzer, and E. Stellar, "Interhemispheric Transfer of Tactile Conditioned Responses in Corpus Callosum—Sectioned Cats," **Journal of Neurophysiology,** vol. 25, 1962, pp. 530–543.

34. Bogen and Bogen, **op. cit.,** p. 195. They add: "Every such patient fails to replicate, with one hand, complicated postures imposed on the other. There is a wide variety of similar defects in interhemispheric transfer following commissural section," **ibid.** Also see R. W. Sperry, M. S. Gazzaniga, and J. E. Bogen, "Interhemispheric Relationships: The Neocortical Commissures; Syndromes of Hemispheric Disconnection," in P. J. Vinken and G. W. Bruyn, eds., **Handbook of Clinical Neurology,** vol. 4, Amsterdam: North Holland Publishers, 1969, pp. 273–290.

35. Claude Lévi-Strauss, **The Raw and the Cooked: Introduction to a Science of Mythology,** vol. 1, trans. John and Doreen Weightman, London: Jonathan Cape Ltd., and New York: Harper & Row, 1969.

36. Ibid., p. 27.

37. Ibid., pp. 29–30.

38. Ibid., p. 28.

39. Ibid., p. 27. Mediation can be defined as the connecting of two dimensions (e.g., culture and nature) along one axis; hypermediation is the simultaneous mediation of three or more dimensions.

40. Ibid., p. 111.

41. Ibid., pp. 15–16.

42. Wilhelm, **op. cit.,** p. 325 **f.**

43. Claude Lévi-Strauss, **The Savage Mind,** Chicago: University of Chicago Press, 1966, pp. 148–149.

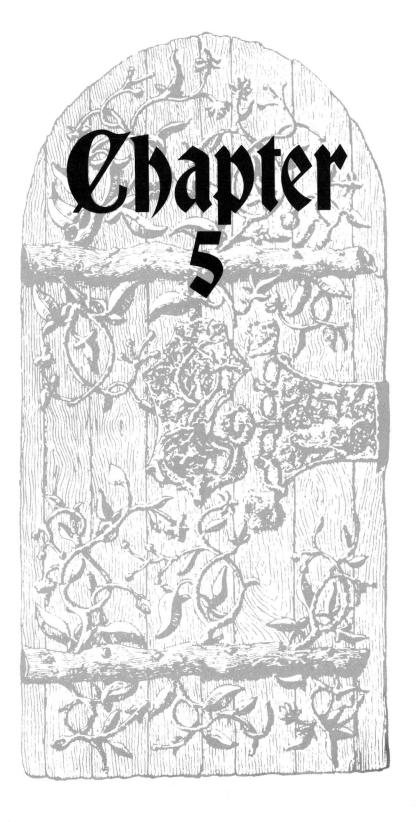

Chapter
5

Language in Inquiry

Language is used differently in propositional and appositional thinking. On this basis it is expected that different languages can differ in the emphasis given to the two modes of thought. This chapter presents a comparative description of two languages—English and Hopi—in order to demonstrate the extent to which languages can be specialized in a single cognitive mode. English, while it does lend itself to poetry, is in its predominant usage, primarily propositional and concerned with abstract form, the outer layer of the mental order; Hopi, in contrast, has its predominant usage more oriented to inner structural processes and sense experience, the second and third layers of the mental order.

ENGLISH AND HOPI COMPARISONS

This section undertakes a general comparison of two languages—English and Hopi. We contend that English is an instance of a primarily propositional language, and Hopi an instance of a primarily appositional language. A comparative analysis of scientific and synthetic inquiries—disproportionately involving propositional and appositional thought, respectively—suggests that such comparisons can be carried out. The following excerpt from Benjamin Lee Whorf's linguistic analysis is a good beginning:

When linguists became able to examine critically and scientifically a large number of languages of widely different patterns, their basis of reference was expanded; they experienced an interruption of phenomena hitherto held universal, and a whole new order of significances came into their ken. It was found that the background linguistic system (in other words, the grammar) of each language is not merely a reproducing instrument for voicing ideas but rather is itself the shaper of ideas, the program and guide for the individual's mental activity, for his analysis of impressions, for his synthesis of his mental stock in trade. Formulation of ideas is not an independent process, strictly rational in the old sense, but is part of a particular grammar, and differs, from slightly to greatly, as between different grammars. We dissect nature along lines laid down by our native languages. The categories and types that we isolate from the world of phenomena we do not find there because they stare every observer in the face: on the contrary, the world is presented in a kaleidoscopic flux of impressions which has to be organized by our minds—and this means largely by the linguistic system in our minds. We cut nature up, organize it into concepts, and ascribe significances as we do, largely because we are parties to an agreement to organize it in this way—an agreement that holds throughout our speech community and is codified in the patterns of our language. The agreement is, of course, an implicit and unstated one, but **its terms are absolutely obligatory;** we cannot talk at all except by subscribing to the organization and classification of data which the agreement decrees.

This fact is very significant for modern science, for it means that no individual is free to describe nature with absolute impartiality but is constrained to certain modes of interpretation even while he thinks himself most free.[1]

Whorf contends that language is not a passive and generalized medium of expression of mental reality; on the contrary, it is an active partner in the construction of this reality. Insofar as languages differ in relation to certain structural considerations, a uniformity of mental life cannot be assumed. Thus, one could expect the structure of a language to be directly related to the cognitive mode prevalent in a language community. It is possible that in various language communities different strategies might be used in solving similar problems and, conversely, that solutions appearing to be similar may be answers to fundamentally different questions. In this way, languages as well as perceptions of physical phenomena are governed by a principle of relativity.

The reality of the relativity of languages becomes salient in a comparison of English and Native American languages. In our field experience among the Hopi, relative reality became dramatically evident in the inability of bilingual Hopis to perform certain translations. Hopi words equivalent in meaning to English concepts contained in words like "love," "good," and "room" do not appear to exist.

A primary feature of the Hopi language seems to be that it compels a speaker to consider the **concrete** as fundamental. It involves the speaker with the perceptual and leads to the immediate **attendance** to nature. This feature can be contrasted directly with English, which seems to program the speaker to talk in a relatively **abstract** manner. The English language compels the speaker to attend to the "logical" or "analytic" level of reality and ultimately to a concern with culture. One is driven into the bounds of conversation itself. Participants in a conversation in English become enmeshed in culture as their talk comes to pertain to antecedent talk and becomes abstracted from the happenings of the immediately perceivable. In Hopi, on the other hand, the language structure ultimately leads away from the cultural dimension, compelling the speaker to go out alone in nature **to see for oneself** and in effect to discover the perceptual phenomena that compose the basis of the language.

In a general way, Hopi social gatherings are very quiet in comparison with those of English-speaking Americans, and conversations are short. It is as if the "what" to be discovered by talk is not fundamentally located in a talking situation itself. When one considers the richness of Hopi ceremony and ritual, when one observes an old Hopi carrying on a conversation with his corn plants, then one is led to hypothesize that this language is not fundamentally cultural, but leads the speaker to nature.

● ● ● ● ●

Such an hypothesis requires the careful examination of some specifics. Consider a simple case. When a Hopi speaks about a situation that in English would be expressed "my room," he must instead say "my ceiling," "my walls," or "my bed." A Hopi equivalent to "my room" does not exist. This usage seems to be derived from the concreteness that is basic to the Hopi language. In English, we are allowed to lump objects like ceiling, door, and wall together and call them some other thing. This illustrates our propensity to gloss over subtle concrete–perceptual distinctions and to group objects in abstract classes. In Hopi, on the other hand, these objects cannot be lumped together in one class. To the Hopi, doors and ceilings are very distinct things, immediately available to perception. A room, on the other hand, is not available to perception-as-thing, but comes to be known through **movement from one location to another.** A room is observable only through the recognition of the relation and not in the same way that nominative and objective things are observable. As Whorf contends, "It will be found that a **'pave'** belongs to a part of speech called LOCATORS, which include such words as 'here, there, above, below, in front, in back, north, south, east, west,' and a good many others, among them the Hopi geographical names such as Oraibi, Walpi, and Shipaulovi."[2] To understand the meaning of the Hopi **locators,** it is helpful to consider their usage. In Hopi, one would not say "the name of the village is Oraibi," but rather "standing house in the location of Oraibi." A Hopi does not say "the south," but must say "in the south," "to the south," or "from the south." These forms modify verbal actions and thus resemble English language adverbs. They do not stand alone as nominative or objective things of the same order as birds or walls.

In English, words can be classified as verbs or nouns. Each class carries varying local and definitive properties. In Hopi, verbs and nouns may be discerned, but these words do not have properties identical to those of their formal English equivalents. Instead, Hopi may be seen as consisting of **eventuations** and their respective modifiers. These eventuations can be classified and can then be translated into the English categories of nouns and verbs. The primary consideration in the classification of the eventuations is duration within the visual field of an observer. An eventuation that had a brief duration in the observational field is translated as an English verb; one of a longer duration, as an English noun. The Hopi words describing a flash, a gust of wind, or a sudden vibration are translated into English as "flashing," "gusting," and "vibrating," but not as the nouns "flash," "gust," and "vibration." But the Hopi words for eventuations such as crows and rocks, because of their enduring properties, would be translated into the English nouns "crow" and "rock." Thus the Hopi regard words as verbs or nouns on the basis of direct perception of the eventuations to which these words refer.

In English, the basic operation applied to verbs is that of tense: that is, verbs are conjugated in terms of their occurrence within a medium called time. They are classified according to whether they belong in the past, present, or future tense. The meaning of such an operation at the level of perception is not taken into account. Time is analogous to a hollow linear medium which objects and actions fill, stretching infinitely from the present "back" to the remote past or "forward" to the remote future.[3] Insofar as time can be calibrated, it can be named and can be considered to have the status of other named objects. Although this conception of time makes sense on the abstract level to which English fundamentally adheres, it seems fraught with difficulties on the perceptual level. For example, consider a phenomenon of very limited duration, like a flash of light in the sky. If we were to focus attention on a clock, we could not simultaneously attend to the light. If we shifted our attention to the sky, we could not also attend to the clock. A medium of time consisting of past, present, and future may be of central importance in conveying sense within a conversation, but may be superfluous with respect to the perceptual field.

Hopi, on the other hand, uses its verbs in such a way that the **operations** employed on them are indifferent toward time. An event expressed by a grammatical operation in English refers to a class of eventuations in Hopi. Whorf has isolated this class and called it **temporals.**

[Temporals] are a formal part of speech by themselves, distinct from nouns, verbs, and even other Hopi "adverbs." Such a word is not a case form or locative pattern, like "des Abends," or "in the morning." . . . It means "when it is morning" or "while morning-phase is occurring." These "temporals" are not used as subjects or objects, or at all like nouns. One does not say "it's a hot summer," or "summer is hot"; summer is not hot, summer is only **when** conditions are hot, **when** heat occurs. One does not say "THIS summer," but "summer now" or "summer recently." There is no objectification, as a region, an extent, a quantity, of subjective duration-feeling. Nothing is suggested about time except the perceptual "getting later" of it. And so there is no basis here for a formless item answering to our "time."[4]

Time as a linear medium does not seem to exist within the concrete Hopi language. Insofar as everything has its "time," this does not mean that everything is contained in a formless past, present, and future. To the Hopi, it is quite conceivable that certain things do not have a past, present, and future, but are at all times available for the looking. The stars and the mesas may be such "timeless" forms. As we shall see, the Hopi have a linguistic usage that gives expression to such timeless eventuations.

The argument that English is abstract and Hopi concrete involves the notion of **attendance,** the existential domain to which the speaker is oriented by virtue of his or her language. The hypothesis states that the Hopi language is concrete in that its attendance is to the domain of the immediately perceivable, that is, to the domain of nature. On the other hand, English seems to program the speaker to attend to the speaking itself, and to elaborations of verbalizations leading farther and farther away from the immediately perceivable domain of nature and toward the domain of culture. We will now endeavor to introduce some additional data in support of this contention.

Whorf has discussed in detail an aspect of Hopi "verbs" that he terms **punctual** and **segmentative.** His discussion is concluded:

[T] he Hopi language maps out a certain terrain of what might be termed primitive physics. We have observed how, with very thorough consistency and not a little true scientific precision, all sorts of vibratile phenomena in nature are classified by being referred to various elementary types of deformation process. The analysis of a certain field of nature which results is freely extensible, and all-in-all so harmonious with actual physics that such extension could be made with great appropriateness to a multiplicity of phenomena belonging entirely to the modern scientific and technical world—movements of machinery and mechanism, wave processes and vibrations, electrical and chemical phenomena—things that the Hopi have never known or imagined, and for which we ourselves lack definite names. The Hopi actually have a language better equipped to deal with such vibratile phenomena than is our latest scientific terminology. This is simply because their language establishes a general contrast between two types of experience, which corresponds to a contrast that, as our science has discovered, is all-pervading and fundamental in nature. According to the conceptions of modern physics, the contrast of particle and field of vibrations is more fundamental in the world of nature than such contrasts as space and time, or past, present, and future, which are the sort of contrasts that our own language imposes upon us. The Hopi aspect-contrast which we have observed, being obligatory upon their verb forms, practically forces the Hopi to notice and observe vibratory phenomena, and furthermore encourages them to find names for and to classify such phenomena. As a matter of fact the language is extraordinarily rich in terms for vibratory phenomena and for the punctual events to which they are related.[5]

As example, we will cite some instances of the Hopi usage adopted from Whorf which display the fundamental natural distinction between particle and field of vibration. The rule of conveying the distinction may be described as follows: From a base root of a verb[6] (the root having the properties of being in the third person singular, intransitive voice, punctual aspect, and present-past tense), the segmentative aspect is formed by duplicating the final syllable of this root and adding the suffix —ta (indicating duration). Whorf characterized the transformation in the meaning of the original root: "The phenomenon denoted by the root, shown in the punctual aspect as manifested about a point, becomes manifested as a series of repeated interconnected segments of one large phenomenon of a stretched out segmental character, its extension usually being predominantly in one dimension, indifferently of space or time, or both."[7]

Consider phenomena that are manifested in a solid or rigid substance, such as leather, cloth, earth, or wood. Hopi roots of such cases might include:

ho″ci	it forms a sharp acute angle
pa″ci	it is notched

To indicate the segmentative aspect with its engendered transformation of meaning we have only to apply the rule described by Whorf:

hoci′cita	it is zigzag
paci′cita	it is serrated

Consider now phenomena requiring a nonsolid medium as an observational field. The same rule applies, providing parallel examples:

wa′la	it . . . makes one wave
nö′ya	several come out (applied to objects or persons)

These are transformed into:

wala′lata	it is tossing in waves
nöya′yata	it is coming out in successive multitudes

The principle also applies to shocks and sudden disturbances:

ti′ri	he gives a sudden start
wi′wa	he trips over something

Transformed, these words are:

tiri′rita	he is quivering, trembling
wiwa′wata	he is stumbling or hobbling along[8]

The preeminence of the concrete observational field in Hopi also obtains in comparisons of equivalent English and Hopi verb meanings. Although it is possible to translate Hopi verbs into past, present, and future, our differences in time exist as a kind of observational validity from the Hopi standpoint. What seem to us to be descriptions of time are, to the Hopi, properties inherent in the observation of phenomena. Whorf expresses the distinction between English time and Hopi validity by means of a paradigm involving an objective field, a speaker, and a hearer. He compares a number of situations and concludes that "the timeless Hopi verb does not distinguish between the present, past, and future of the event itself but must always indicate what type of validity the **speaker** intends the statement to have."[9] The Hopi language puts several constraints on the speaker to attend to the actual occurrence within the observational field. Before talking, the Hopi must be sure that his words will be understood as, for example, a report of an event rather than an expectation. This precision compels the Hopi to look most carefully before offering a verbal description. English, although involved with an observational field, tends to place more emphasis on the relation of the speaker to the hearer than on that of the speaker to the observational field. Let us proceed through Whorf's analysis and then add to it in terms of this last statement.

The event we are interested in involves running. We have, in English, a situation in which the speaker could point to a runner and say to a man who also sees the runner "He is running." In Hopi the speaker would say **Wari**, which means "running-as-a-statement-of-fact." Next we have a situation in which both speaker and hearer are looking at an observational field that contains no runner. The English speaker would say "He ran," using the past tense to indicate that running has occurred and was seen by both persons. A Hopi speaker, confronted with the same situation, would use the form **Wari,** again meaning "running-as-a-statement-of-fact." The distinction between present and past, seen as real and essential in English, is unnecessary in Hopi. The fundamental issue for the Hopi is whether or not an event is an objective fact, seen by both speaker and hearer, irrespective of the time in which the event is supposed to have occurred.

Now consider a situation in which the observer and listener are not in the same observational field. For example, the speaker may be on the top of a hill looking at the field while the hearer may be at the bottom of the hill, having no view of it. Again, the speaker points to an observed man running and says in English "He is running." A Hopi would, again, say **Wari.** Note that in both English and Hopi it does not matter, grammatically, whether the hearer sees the objective field **if in fact the observer is immediately attending to the runner.**

However, in a situation where the objective field is blank to the speaker and the speaker and hearer are not attending to the same observational field (as in the last situation), a fundamental difference in the two languages may be seen. In English, the speaker would say "He ran," a response identical to the situation in which both the speaker and the hearer are attending to the same observational field. In Hopi this is not allowed. If the runner is seen by neither speaker nor hearer, and if the speaker and hearer are attending to **different** observational fields, then the Hopi must say **Era wari,** meaning "running-as-a-statement-of-fact-from-memory." Here we can see that Hopi is especially tuned in to the problems of the observational field of the speaker.

In yet another situation the speaker and the hearer are attending to the same observational field containing no runner. The English-speaker says "He will run," a statement that implies that both speaker and hearer will be able to see a runner in the future. In Hopi, the speaker would say **Warikni,** meaning that the running is a statement of expectation. Again, no time dimension is presented to the Hopi. English future is looked upon by the Hopi as a statement of expectation rather than of fact. In English, events occurring in the past, present, or future may all be talked about as if they were of the same factual order vis-à-vis the observational field. However, in Hopi an event "occurring" in the English future has as yet not occurred and therefore must be distinguished by its level of observational validity. In fact, the Hopi expectancy usage may refer to events that have occurred in the English past as well. Thus the Hopi **Warikni** may be translated in this case as "He was going to run."

A final situation may be posited in which the relations between the speaker, hearer, and field are identical to the last situation. Here, however, the English-speaker says "He runs," meaning the person is a runner as a general condition (for example, on a track team). In English, this is interpreted as running-through-time, as running-all-the-time. The Hopi speaker would say **Warikngive,** meaning that the running is a statement of law. Again, this Hopi usage does not imply time. The meaning a Hopi speaker conveys is that the statement does not apply to a particular situation, but is rather an invariant condition of the observational field itself. Such statements afford an interpretation of the structure of the field itself, and not a particular manifestation in the field. The statement in

Hopi is about a kind of validity attributed to the observational field, not a temporal nuance as the English equivalent connotes.

The purpose of undertaking this detailed analysis of certain situations regarding English and Hopi linguistic usages is to prepare the ground for our hypothesis that English, in attending primarily to the speaker-hearer relation, has a propensity to be abstract; while Hopi, in attending primarily to the speaker-field relation, has a propensity to be concrete. We have already shown, with our situational analysis, the Hopi propensity. We have seen the powerful constraints placed on the Hopi speaker by the positioning of the observational field vis-á-vis both himself and his hearer. However, we have as yet not presented our evidence that English provides a differing set of priorities for the relations within the basic unit of speaker, hearer, and observational field, whereby the speaker-hearer relation (that is, the conversation) becomes primary. Before attempting to introduce this evidence, we return to Whorf, who wrote:

> There is no distinction in the reportive between past and present, for both are equally accomplished fact. What we call present tense (not counting our present form which corresponds to the nomic) is for the Hopi simply a report to others concerning a situation shared with them, **this report being either redundant information, or used to call attention to, or tell about some fragment of the situation not fully shared.** Thus the Hopi "he is running" need not be different from "he was running," for, if both the speaker and the listener can see the runner, then the "is" of the former sentence means merely that **the listener can see for himself what he is being told;** he is being given redundant information . . . when he can see for himself that it is. If the speaker can see the runner but the listener cannot, then the . . . situation in that case is one of rapidly relaying the information, which rules out the distinctive past meaning of "was," and again the Hopi find our tense distinction irrelevant.[10]

As Whorf implies, the Hopi sees no need for past and present tenses. What then must an English speaker be conscious of in order to use his time-oriented convention? A full answer to this question would detract us from our purpose. However, a few suggestions might be helpful. The use of the English present, Whorf writes, is "to call attention to, or tell about some fragment of the situation not fully shared."[11] In a sense, use of English tenses requires that the speaker be sensitive to overt meanings communicated through the conversation. The present tense, then, is not primarily employed to cue the listener in to the observational field, but to cue the listener in to the sense of the conversation. To the Hopi, the information conveyed to the listener would be redundant, because his point of view originates in the observational field; but to the English-speaker this redundancy is, from the standpoint of the conversation, one of rhetorical emphasis. In the case of the English past, the structural imperative would seem to be related to the establishment of relations of experience within the conversation itself. Thus the imperative for using the past tense may be rooted in the idea in the mind of the speaker that he possesses a certain experience that the listener does not have that must be communicated. Here again the motivating consideration is conversational; that is, it originates in the experiential relation between speaker and listener rather than between speaker and observational field.

Other discussions by Whorf are consistent with these suggestions. For example, he maintains that Hopi abounds in a linguistic structure he terms a cryptotype, which is described as

a dimly felt relation of similarity between the verb usages in each group having to do with some inobvious facet of their meaning, and therefore itself a meaning, but one so nearly at or below the threshold of conscious thinking that it cannot be put into words by the user and eludes translation. . . . Such an elusive, hidden but functionally important meaning I call a CRYPTOTYPE. . . .

In contrast with the cryptotype, which has no formal mark and whose meaning is not clearly evident, but is rather a submerged meaning shown as an influence, I give the name PHENOTYPE to the categories inceptive, future, projective, etc., i.e., the phenotype is the "classical" morphological category, having a formal mark and a clearly apparent class-meaning.[12]

After examining the problem of the inceptive form in Hopi, Whorf concluded:

In many languages the cryptotype concept would be of little use, but there are languages like Hopi in which much of the influential material of paradigm production lies in this heavily veiled state, just as there are people whose mental life is much less accessible than that of others.[13]

For a full exposition of the cryptotype concept, the reader is referred to Whorf.[14] It is mentioned here to introduce the idea that Hopi abounds with verbal structures that are "essentially vague" or "heavily veiled" and that these usages provide an access to Hopi priorities. An examination of these structures shows they are most concerned with nuances between the speaker and observational field. Thus, the Hopi cryptotypes described by Whorf represent a type of causality (continuing, adjusting, tending) in which the activity-within-the-field is causing the topical activity. This contrasts with causality in English, in which the speaker himself causes the topical activity.

In the Hopi language, "in the talk" there are veiled meanings, but "in the seeing" cryptotypes enable the speaker to attend to concrete subtleties that seem to be missing from everyday discourse in English. Consider that English, in comparison with Hopi, seems to abound with phenotypes: We may say that the structural imperatives of the English language are such that the concrete nuances of nature are glossed over in favor of clarity within conversation. The choice is on the side of cultural clarity in English, while in Hopi this tendency is secondary to the myriad nuances presented by nature (including the body). Heavily veiled talk can only lead the participants to look that much harder to the supposed source of the talk, which in the Hopi case is seen to be the observational field—nature as observed and lived.

A final consideration on the metaphysical grounding of English and Hopi is useful here. Again we cite Whorf:

The metaphysics underlying our own language, thinking, and modern culture (I speak not of the recent and quite different relativity metaphysics of modern science) imposes upon the universe two grand COSMIC FORMS, space and time; static three-dimensional infinite space, and kinetic one-dimensional uniformly and perceptually flowing time; two utterly separate and unconnected aspects of reality (according to this familiar way of thinking). This flowing realm of time is, in turn, the subject of a threefold division; past, present, and future.

The Hopi metaphysics also has its cosmic forms comparable to these in scale and scope. What are they? It imposes upon the universe two grand cosmic forms, which as a first approximation in terminology we call MANIFESTED and MANIFESTING (or, UNMANIFEST) or again, OBJECTIVE and SUBJECTIVE. The objective or manifested comprises all that is or has been accessible to the senses, the historical physical universe, in fact, with no attempt to distinguish between present and past, but excluding everything we call future. The subjective or manifesting comprises all that we call future, BUT NOT MERELY THIS; it includes equally and indistinguishably all that we call mental—everything that appears or exists in the mind, or as the Hopi would prefer to say, in the **heart**, not only the heart of man, but the heart of animals, plants, and things, and behind and within all the forms and appearances of nature in the heart of nature . . . in the very heart of Cosmos, itself.[15]

To the Hopi both values are equally real. The manifested world is real in the sense that it is accessible to the senses, the unmanifested world is real because it is the accomplishment of the heart. In Hopi, our "illusion" or "contrary to fact" does not exist. They say instead that something has been (or will be) lived but has not yet taken form in "this world," so that it remains in the manifesting realm, the Hopi "underworld." The concreteness of Hopi is such that whatever is seen, thought, felt, and so forth—the entire range of living experiences—constitutes and at the same time is held together by what we have been calling the observational field, the immanent presence of nature. Thus the Hopi sees man as limited, with the limits imposed by the dimensionality of nature itself. At the extremes of the two worlds, they are blended in such a way that all one can tell is that he is being presented with "something" involving properties of both worlds. The field is seen to prevail in spite of man's limited knowledge of it. And in the final analysis this field includes all phenomena, both subjective and objective.

Thus we see that the Hopi language is grounded in the concreteness of immediate perception and encourages the speaker to attend to the domain of nature. Involved in this attendance is a constant vigilance and preparedness—a looking for and codifying of "given" signs provided by things as diverse (to an English-speaker) as "islands" and "dreams." We have also seen the importance of **positioning** in such a structure. This is expressed in the constant imperative placed on the speaker to be aware of his position within the observational field. These properties allow us to consider the Hopi language as being a preeminently **appositional** instrument. To the Hopi, whose logic is rooted in nature, culture is a necessary element, which exists only to provide direction toward the eventual solution of the problem of these very roots. But the cultural solution is never an attempt to escape from nature into culture or to include nature within culture, but rather to lead the human being back into his natural roots.

English too involves nature and culture. But here we are confronted with a fundamentally **propositional** instrument. In English, knowledge is rooted in abstraction: That is, the source of knowledge is found in propositions that take space and time to be fundamental. While the Hopi language begins in nature, proceeds into the cultural order, and then leads the speaker back to nature, the English language may do the reverse. In English the journey is such that the logic of English-speaking begins in culture (with propositions, hypotheses, questions, and topics) and detours into nature to find empirical "proof" of the correspondence of such linguistic constructs, only to return once again to culture with a "more developed" way of speaking.

When they are analyzed as we have done, English and Hopi turn out to be representatives of two complementary strategies for knowing the world—one propositional, the other appositional. Certainly it must be the case that the structure of language can affect the structure of inquiry carried out in that language. This by no means implies that all inquiries carried out in English are propositional and that all inquiries carried out in Hopi are appositional. But at the same time language is, as Whorf suggested, a powerful contributing factor in the structure of inquiry, and the use of Hopi facilitates appositional inquiry. What is more, of course, inquiries need not be carried out within language at all. In this sense, Hopi, which orients its speakers toward direct sensory perception of nature rather than toward that more abstract **form of perception** we know as language, again predisposes its users to synthetic inquiries. The Hopi, and the Indian American in general, do not seek theories in their inquiries; they struggle to have visions, to have insights.

SPACE AND HYPERMEDIATION

In Chapter 4 we developed the idea that **intensity** constitutes a principal component of cerebral organization, a vertical dimension which impinges on the horizontal dimension which mediates culture and nature. In writing of this dimension of mind, Lévi-Strauss was quoted as saying that this "natural grid" is "constituted by the visceral rhythms," such that the "the mediation between nature and culture that occurs within every language becomes a hypermediation."[16] Whorf's analysis of the Hopi language emphasized the sensitivity of the language to the topic of "vibratory phenomena"—both external and internal. Thus we might expect a similar characterization of the dimension of intensity to be reported by Whorf. Such an analysis is presented, and is linked to the Hopi conceptualization of space. Whorf wrote:

> As far as space is concerned, the subjective is a mental realm, a realm of no space in the objective sense, but it seems to be symbolically related to the vertical dimension and its poles the zenith and the underground, as well as to the **heart** of things, which corresponds to our word "inner" in the metaphorical sense. Corresponding to each point in the objective world is such a vertical and vital INNER axis which is what we call the wellspring of the future. . . . From each subjective axis, which may be thought of as more or less vertical and like the growth-axis of a plant, extends the objective realm in every physical direction, though these directions are typified more especially by the horizontal plane and its four cardinal points. The objective is the great cosmic form of extension; it takes in all the strictly extensional

aspects of existence, and it includes all intervals and distances, all seria-
tions and number. Its **distance** includes what we call time in the sense of
the temporal relation between events which have already happened.[17]

And later on Whorf added:

So the dim past of myths is that corresponding distance on earth (rather
than in the heavens) which is reached subjectively as myth through the
vertical axis of reality via the pole of the nadir—hence it is placed BELOW
the present surface of the earth. . . .
   It may now be seen how the Hopi do not need to use terms that refer
to space or time as such. Such terms in our language are recast into expressions of extension, operation, and cyclic process provided they refer to the
solid objective realm. They are recast into expressions of subjectivity if
they refer to the subjective realm—the future, the psychic-mental, the
mythical period, and the invisibly distant and conjectural generally.[18]

There exist remarkable correspondences between the analyses of Lévi-Strauss
and Whorf regarding Indian Americans. Although both posit a fundamental
vertical axis that focuses on intensity phenomena, an analytic problem occurs
with the compatibility of the two analyses. We have found Whorf's analysis of
the Hopi language most helpful in explicating the intensity component and the
appositional mind. Yet we have carefully avoided endorsement of what is known
as the **Whorf hypothesis.** Whorf's brilliant linguistic analyses took him into the
field of anthropology, and he may have overstated the distinction between language and social structure. Language does contribute to the shaping of our realities, but at the same time changes in social structure of revolutionary proportions can occur with language changing as a **result** of these changes. Moreover,
language can be changing in a society with stagnant institutions. While there is a
connection between language and social structure, the causality is incomplete,
and can work in either direction. As an inquirer into the meaning of social structure (structural anthropology), Lévi-Strauss was able to provide a critique of
Whorf's work that is widely shared among anthropologists. This critique is relevant to our argument. Lévi-Strauss writes:

Whorf has tried to establish a correlation between certain linguistic structures and certain cultural structures. Why is it that his approach is unsatis-
factory? It is, it seems to me, because the linguistic level as he considers it
is the result of a rather sophisticated analysis—he is not at all trying to
correlate an empirical impression of the language, but, rather, the result of
true linguistic work. . . . What he is trying to correlate with this linguistic
structure is a crude, superficial, empirical view of the culture itself. So he
is really trying to correlate things which belong to entirely different
levels.[19]

But Lévi-Strauss's own inquiry ultimately led him into linguistics, and to a
distinction between language and music. While he sees music as language, he sees
a difference between music and speaking or writing as forms of language. For he
writes that language merely mediates culture and nature, while music hypermedi-

ates culture and nature. In stating this case, he too may have made too large a generalization. For just as Lévi-Strauss detects an over extension in Whorf, Whorf's research reveals a similar analytic problem in Lévi-Strauss. Whorf's analysis of Hopi leaves little doubt that a spoken language, Hopi, is capable of hypermediating culture and nature. The Hopi language, for example, is found to abound with cryptotypes that do this. Thus Lévi-Strauss's distinction may be valid for a comparison of his native French (or any Indo-European language) and music, but may be less valid for a comparison of Hopi and music. There may be natural languages that, in the speaking, are nearly musical. For the boundary between speaking and singing is not always clear within a language. Could not a whole language be so laden with heavily veiled usages, cryptotypes, and other semantic utterances without formal marks that the language itself resembles song? Certain Indian American spokesmen have indicated that, before the white man came to America, their people "sang all the time." In fact, a Hopi elder recently made just this statement. Perhaps such a notion should be taken seriously, as it was communicated in a serious mood. In **The Raw and the Cooked** Lévi-Strauss attempts to "musicalize" the French language, dedicates the book to music, and endeavors to organize it in the format of a musical symphony.[20] While this effort may be only a partial success, it does demonstrate that great variations can exist **within** a language.

The works of both Whorf and Lévi-Strauss are invaluable to our present inquiry, though each may become a bit reckless when venturing into the other's field. Yet each corrects the analytic problem in the other, so that their work is complementary. This can be seen in the writings of Merleau-Ponty, who wrote:

> The world, in those of its sectors which realize a structure, is comparable to a symphony, and knowledge of the world is thus accessible by two paths: one can note the correspondence of the note played at the same moment by the different instruments and the succession of those played by each one of them. Thus one would obtain a multitude of laws which permit knowledge.[21]

In this way we can see the perception of structure as a symphony that Lévi-Strauss calls "The Fugue of the Five Senses."[22] Further, we can know about music in form (for example, through sheet music). But this knowledge in form cannot be alone. For Merleau-Ponty adds: "But this sum of coincidences is not the model of all knowledge. If someone knows a fragment of a symphony and the law of the construction of the whole, he could derive the same predictions and, in addition, he would find in the whole the **raison de être** of each local event."[23] Thus in formal language we can be clear about music and the world, but this clarity is not to be found in structure itself, for the actual perception of music is inquiry in structure, and this behavior properly is a rationality for responding to music. Merleau-Ponty wrote: "The notion of response separates into 'geographical behavior'—the sum of the movements actually executed by the animals in their objective relation with the physical world; and behavior properly so called—these same movements considered in their internal articulation and as a kinetic melody gifted with a meaning."[24] Thus he implies that behavior is not merely mediated by physiological and mental relations. Merleau-Ponty was aware that more than mediation is required to connect culture and nature, or form and structure: They must be hypermediated.

● ● ● ● ●

In Chapter 4 the mental order (which can also be called the mind) was described as layered or overlaid in such a way that propositionality is most pronounced in the "outer" layers, in our thoughts of form, while appositionality is most pronounced in the "inner" layers, in our thoughts of structure. Thus our thoughts of "direction" are more propositional than our thoughts of "intensity," and our thoughts of intensity in turn more propositional than our thoughts of "closure." Thus in each layer of the mind, propositionality and appositionality are to some extent shared. In a related statement, Stephen Krashen writes:

> [P]araphrasing Sapir, one can conclude that there are, properly speaking, no language areas in the brain: there are only cortical mechanisms that are useful in the production and comprehension of language. The mechanisms responsible for temporal processing, the use of transformational relationships, the programming of a plan into a sequence of events are no more to be thought of as primary language mechanisms than the lungs, the larynx, the palate, the nose, the tongue, the teeth, and the lips are to be considered the primary organs of speech. Physiologically, language is an overlaid function.[25]

LANGUAGE AS TOOL

Attempts to clarify science are often interpreted as attempts to develop more precise and invariant language. The work of Alfred North Whitehead and Bertrand Russell, for instance, consists of constructing a "metalanguage" in which the propositions of an "object language" can be more accurately expressed.[26] However, this construction does not exhaust the problem of linguistic clarification. The usage and intention of language as well as grammar pose problems in the scientific process. Concreteness is removed from the perceptual level and ascribed to the linguistic constructs, which exist on an analytically distinct level—that of artifact and culture. This is possible only because science implies a perceptual field that provides endless topics in which language can become salient. When this occurs, however, we lose sight of the perceptual contingencies of scientific inquiry. Problems of scientific logic are classically understood to be problems of language, not perception. Within the last thirty years, Merleau-Ponty has attempted to present an alternative program for research that still leaves science to its traditional tasks. Perhaps he sees his program as a form of inverted science when he writes: "We shall no longer hold that perception is incipient science, but conversely that classical science is a form of perception which loses sight of its origins and believes itself complete."[27] Science does not have a monopoly on knowledge. Its activities are constrained to certain analytic levels by its rules of conformation. But within the limits of science, vast panoramas of research opportunities are open to investigators. If science is seen as a "thing among other things" in reference to the ways of knowledge, then science as well as nonscience can emerge as a topic of empirical research.

Our thesis is that propositional knowledge ways, though they involve perception, are primarily rooted in the attendance to language and the clarification thereof, while appositional knowledge ways, though they involve talk, are primarily rooted in the attendance to perception. Once knowledge ways are related to distinct levels of phenomena, an empirical analysis becomes possible, and we may then speak of contrasts and convergences between these knowledge ways and their respective phenomenal levels. The common thread that runs through both these knowledge ways is the attempt to uncover order and meaning. This attempt is a real and desirable possibility, which becomes realized in, through, and as inquiry. The inquiring activity can be identified with rationality, and rationality can emerge, be transformed, and reemerge at several levels. In our case it can appear as propositionality in a life lived primarily on the level of language, or as appositionality in a life lived primarily on the level of perception.

Wittgenstein has had a profound influence on the development of thought in the twentieth century within "propositional" cultures. His studies of language make him a founding father of logical positivism and analytic philosophy.[28] Through his analysis of everyday language Wittgenstein was able to specify the limits of language and to recognize that language activity itself is only one of several levels of phenomena. In his earlier book, **Tractatus Logico-Philosophicus**, Wittgenstein introduces the thesis that the limits and structure of language and the phenomenal world coincide. He stated that "the limits of my language mean the limits of my world."[29] Yet within this highly profound work are certain paradoxes. In the preface to the **Tractatus** Wittgenstein wrote: "The whole sense of the book might be summed up in the following words: what can be said at all can be said clearly and what we cannot talk about we must consign to silence."[30] He seems to be saying that there are indeed things we cannot talk about and, insofar as he identifies knowledge with language, that the limits of knowledge are coincident with the limits of language. He seems somehow to suggest that the classical problem of finding the limits and conditions for thought can be solved by determining what can and what cannot be said. Although we do not accept this solution, for we do not equate knowledge and language, we appreciate Wittgenstein's recognition, in his preface, that there are levels of phenomena that lie outside of "the world" (at least as Wittgenstein conceived it as being limited ultimately by language). To us, the world (as well as knowledge) is at least partially determined by two levels—language and perception. Wittgenstein himself claims, "What **can** be shown **cannot** be said."[31] This comment reveals an awareness of a distinction between a "saying" level and a "showing" level.

A remarkable feature of Wittgenstein's intellectual career is that in his later work, **Philosophical Investigations**, he repudiates much of the **Tractatus**. This rejection of an earlier point of view seems to be rooted in the realization of some fundamental difficulties in ascribing the same logical form to a proposition, which exists on a linguistic level, and a fact, which exists on a perceptual level. Wittgenstein concluded that it was untenable to believe a fact has any logical form whatsoever if logic is thought of in its classical meaning. Instead of a notion of language involving propositions that are mirrors of the logical structure of the factual world (the **Tractatus**), we are presented with the notion of "language games" of which proposing is just one of countless types. Justus Hartnack has chronicled this basic change.

In the **Tractatus** a meaningful proposition was said to be one made up of the names of objects, and to serve as a picture of a fact; language depicted the world. In the **Philosophical Investigations** language is no longer said to act like this. Picturing or depicting the world is discarded as a meaningless notion; there are many different language games, some of which serve to describe, to assert, to report. The countless other language games that do not describe, assert or report are still languages; and the countless other sentences that do not describe, assert or report are still sentences. In the **Tractatus** a word is meaningful if, and only if, it is a name. In the **Philosophical Investigations,** a word is **not** a name, a word can be **used** as a name, but it can be used in numerous other ways as well.[32]

Once the notion of language games exists, we are no longer presented with the idea of an underlying single language which functions as a communicator or descriptor or mirror of reality. Rather, there now exist many language games which have nothing in common functionally. Wittgenstein introduces the idea that language is comparable not to a picture of reality, but to a.tool. He writes: "Think of the tools in a tool box: there is a hammer, pliers, a saw, a screwdriver, a rule, a glue-pot, glue, nails and screws. The functions of words are as diverse as the functions of these objects. (And in both cases there are similarities.)"[33] From this point of view, the extreme propositionality displayed by science, whereby a linguistic usage is determined to be true or false insofar as it reflects or expresses a structure of observable facts, stands as only a peculiar linguistic game. Innumerable possibilities are born **within** the level of language itself. It is possible to conceive of language games that can be described as appositional: those that are not intended to function solely as literal accounts or reports of facts (that is, propositions), although they involve linguistic usages. Conceivably, languages can be said to exist that accomplish differentiation and discrimination on the levels of nature and perception, as well as on the levels of culture and verbal communications. Hopi may constitute one such language. What is especially significant is that Wittgenstein saw fit to discard an earlier absolute notion on language, which in turn opens the question of knowledge to more than linguistic considerations. To borrow from Merleau-Ponty, "indirect communication and the voices of silence" become as analytic a form of knowing as the direct communication of talk characteristic of propositional activity.

It is informative here to turn to Lévi-Strauss's analysis of primitive thought. He has been able to characterize this form of thought as "the science of the concrete" and has been able to locate a real difference between this science and the science of the abstract found in "civilized" societies. Significantly, he has explicated his analysis by the use of a similarity he sees between primitive thought and the activity of the **bricoleur.** As defined by Lévi-Strauss, the **bricoleur** "is still someone who works with his hands and uses devious means compared to those of a craftsman."[34] The translator adds the note: "The 'bricoleur' has no precise equivalent in English. He is a man who undertakes odd jobs and is a jack-of-all-trades or a kind of professional do-it-yourself man, but, as the text makes clear, he is of a different standing from, for instance, the English 'odd job man' or handyman."[35] He is also different from the engineer, which to Lévi-Strauss characterizes the science of the abstract. There may exist a connection between Lévi-Strauss's **bricoleur** (as a model of primitive thought) and Wittgenstein's later notions on language. For when Wittgenstein asks the reader to think of words like objects in a toolbox, he is in a sense prodding the reader to think in a strange way, from the point of view of a particular cultural context. And this strange way of thinking about language is strikingly similar to the thinking of the **bricoleur**. Lévi-Strauss writes:

> The characteristic feature of mythical thought is that it expresses itself by means of a heterogeneous repertoire which, even if extensive, is nevertheless limited. It has to use this repertoire, however, whatever the task in hand because it has nothing else at its disposal. Mythical thought is therefore a kind of intellectual "bricolage.". . . The analogy is worth pursuing since it helps us to see the real relations between the two types of scientific knowledge we have distinguished i.e., the science of the concrete and the science of the abstract. The "bricoleur" is adept at performing a large number of diverse tasks; but unlike the engineer, he does not subordinate each of them to the availability of raw materials and tools conceived and procured for the purpose of the project. His universe of instruments is closed and the rules of his game are always to make do with "whatever is at hand," that is to say with a set of tools and materials which is always finite and is also heterogeneous because what it contains bears no relation to the current project, or indeed to any particular project, but is the contingent result of all the occasions there have been to renew or enrich the stocks or to maintain it with the remains of previous constructions or destructions. The set of the "bricoleur's" means cannot therefore be defined in terms of a project (which would presuppose besides, that, as in the case of the engineer, there were, at least in theory, as many sets of tools and materials or "instrument sets" as there are different kinds of projects). It is to be defined only by its potential use, or putting this another way and in the language of the "bricoleur" himself, that . . . "they may always come in handy." Such elements are specialized up to a point, sufficiently for the "bricoleur" not to need the equipment and knowledge of all trades and professions, but not enough for each of them to have only one definite and determinate use.[36]

This general discussion of language as tool brings us to the point at which analysis of the two kinds of inquiry can begin.

NOTES

1. Benjamin Lee Whorf, "Science and Linguistics," **Technology Review**, vol. 42, 1940, p. 231. Also see pp. 229–231.

2. Benjamin Lee Whorf, "Linguistic Factors in the Terminology of Hopi Architecture," **International Journal of American Linguistics**, vol. 19, 1943, pp. 141–145.

3. Benjamin Lee Whorf, "The Relation of Habitual Thought and Behavior to Language," in Leslie Sapir, ed., **Language, Culture and Personality: Essays in Memory of Edward Sapir**, Menosha, Wis.: Sapir Memorial Publications Fund, pp. 75–93.

4. Ibid., p. 81. The theory of the principal components of scalable variables shows that all variables (universes of content) for which ranks can be assigned with perfect internal consistency have an infinity of solutions to the problem of underlying metric. The first principal component is in this sense the best solution, and the second component the second solution.

Given this, it is possible to imagine concepts for variables that use just one solution. For example, time is clearly a single variable that can be measured by a metric (e.g., minutes, days, and so on), and therefore has an infinity of principal components. English is a language that measures time by its first component, direction, a "line running from left to right." Whorf suggested that the English language measures time in just this way, as "a smooth continuum which proceeds at an equal rate out of a future, through a present, into a past: or, in the stream of duration continuously away from a past and into a future." Whorf described the Hopi concept of time as containing no past, present, and future, and no reference to an abstract concept of time, either explicitly or implicitly. Since the first component of time does not appear in the Hopi language, time is compressed into a vertical line, with a zero point and varying levels of intensity. Whorf wrote:

> Time is mainly reckoned "by day" (taLk,-tala) or "by night" (tok), which words are not nouns but tensors, the first formed on a root "light, day," the second on a root "sleep." The count is by ORDINALS. This is not the pattern of counting a number of different men or things, even though they appear successively, for, even then, they COULD gather into an assemblege. It is the pattern of counting successive reappearances of the SAME MAN or thing, incapable of forming an assemblage. The analogy is not to behave about day-cyclicity as to several men ("several days"), which is what we tried to do, but to behave as to the successive visits of the SAME MAN. One does not altar several men by working upon just one, but one can prepare and so alter the later visits of the same man by working to affect the visits he is making now.

In comparing the "timeless" and "spaceless" Hopi language to English, Whorf added:

> A sense of cumulative value of innumerable small moments is dulled by an objectified, spatialized view of time like ours, enhanced by a way of thinking close to the subjective awareness of duration, of the ceaseless "latering" of events. To us, for whom time is a motion on a space, unvarying repetition seems to scatter its fact a row of units of that space, and be wasted. To the Hopi, for whom time is not a motion but a "getting later" of everything that has ever been done, unvarying repetition is not wasted but accumulated. It is storing up in an invisible charge that holds over into later events. As we have seen, it is as if the return of the day were felt as the return of the same person a little older but with all the impresses of yesterday, not as "another day," i.e., like an entirely different person.

See Whorf, "The Relation of Habitual Thought," pp. 87–88.
5. B. L. Whorf, "The Punctual and Segmentative Aspects of Verbs in Hopi," **Language**, vol. 12, 1936, p. 131.
6. Ibid., p. 128.
7. Ibid., p. 127.
8. Ibid., pp. 128–130.
9. Whorf, "Science and Linguistics," p. 248.
10. Benjamin Lee Whorf, "Some Verbal Categories of Hopi," in **Language**, vol. 14, 1938, p. 277 f., emphasis added.
11. Ibid., p. 276f.
12. Benjamin Lee Whorf, "Discussion of Hopi Linguistics," in John B. Carrol, ed., **Language, Thought, and Reality: Selected Writings of Benjamin Lee Whorf**, Cambridge, Mass: MIT Press, 1965, pp. 104–105.
13. Ibid., p. 110, emphasis added.
14. Benjamin Lee Whorf, "An American Indian Model of the Universe," **International Journal of Linguistics**, vol. 16, 1950, pp. 67–72.
15. Ibid., pp. 68–69.
16. Lévi-Strauss, **The Raw and the Cooked**, p. 27.
17. Whorf, "An American Indian Model," pp. 70–71.
18. Ibid., pp. 71–72.
19. Claude Lévi-Strauss, **Structural Anthropology**, trans. Claire Jacobson and Brooke Grundfest Schoepf, New York: Basic, 1963, pp. 72–73.
20. Lévi-Strauss, **The Raw and the Cooked**.
21. Merleau-Ponty, **The Structure of Behavior**, p. 132.
22. Lévi-Strauss, **The Raw and the Cooked**, p. 147.

23. Merleau-Ponty, The Structure of Behavior, p. 132.
24. Ibid., p. 130.
25. Stephen Krashen, Language and the Left Hemisphere, Los Angeles: UCLA Working Papers in Phonetics, No. 24, October 1972, p. 43. Edward Sapir, Language, New York: Harcourt Brace Jovanovich, 1921.
26. Bertrand Russell and Alfred North Whitehead, Principia Mathematica, London: Cambridge University Press, 1925.
27. Merleau-Ponty, Phenomenology of Perception, p. 57.
28. Justus Hartnack, Wittgenstein and Modern Philosophy, Garden City, N. Y.: Doubleday, 1965.
29. Ludwig Wittgenstein, Tractatus Logico-Philosophicus, New York: Harcourt Brace Jovanovich, 1922, p. 115.
30. Ibid., p. 3.
31. Ibid., p. 51.
32. Hartnack, op. cit., pp. 69–70.
33. Ludwig Wittgenstein, Philosophical Investigations, p. 6.
34. Lévi-Strauss, The Savage Mind, pp. 16–17.
35. Ibid., p. 17.
36. Ibid., pp. 17–18.

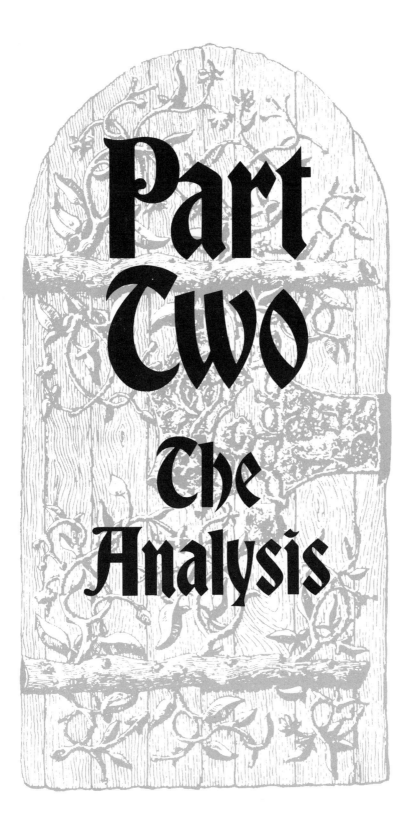

Part Two

The Analysis

Chapter
6

Scientific and Synthetic Rationalities

The idea that the sciences do not have a monopoly on knowledge, though perhaps a commonsense truism, is a proposition that has engendered increasing concern within the scientific community itself. A traditional scientific stance toward nonscientific knowing sometimes involves labeling such enterprises as vague, illusory, mystical, or superstitious. Science, on the other hand, is seen as clear, true, logical, and rational. Apart from these polemics, few traditionalists attempt to specify their beliefs by research into both scientific and nonscientific ways of knowing.

SCIENTIFIC RATIONALITIES
Comparative analyses of scientific and nonscientific inquiries have not been carried out in large measure because scientists simply do not take other forms of inquiry seriously and do not define them as appropriate subjects for study. Furthermore, scientists view their own practices as sufficient for the study of **any** topic. Many scientists express concern about methodological difficulties, yet, ultimately, their belief in the superiority of science as a method is retained. In the social sciences, for example, it is paradigmatic that the sociologist's activities are methodological, while the subject's or respondent's activities are merely

"social action." Garfinkel's term hits the nail on the head: To the sociologist, the person he studies has the status of a "judgmental dope."[1] The prevailing sociological model pictures social reality as essentially the result of the automatic responses of actors to their value orientations. It is as if the actor, though conscious, does little thinking. The sociology of Talcott Parsons and his coworkers sets rationality equal to economic behavior, and irrationality equal to normative (social) behavior; Parsons sees the traditional concern of sociology to be the irrational. Essentially the task of sociology would be "to be rational about the irrational," or "to be scientific about the nonscientific."

In his essay, "The Rational Properties of Scientific and Common Sense Activities," Garfinkel proposes an alternative program for sociology involving just this question of rationality. His program rests on the observation that order is "known" to an actor as common sense, and that common sense itself must be described as rational. He writes:

Commonly, sociological researchers decide a definition of rationality by selecting one or more features from among the properties of scientific activity as it is ideally described and understood. The definition is then used methodologically to aid the researcher in deciding the realistic, pathological, prejudiced, delusional, mythical, magical, ritual, and similar features of everyday conduct, thinking, and beliefs.

But because sociologists find with such overwhelming frequency that effective, persistent, and stable actions and social structures occur despite obvious discrepancies between the lay person's and the ideal scientist's knowledge and procedures, sociologists have found the rational properties that their definitions discriminated empirically uninteresting. They have preferred instead to study the features and conditions of nonrationality in human conduct. The result is that in most of the available theories of social action and social structure rational actions are assigned residual status.

With the hope of correcting a trend, it is the purpose of this paper to remedy this residual status by reintroducing as a problem for empirical inquiry (a) the various rational properties of conduct, as well as (b) the conditions of a social system under which various rational behaviors occur.[2]

An interesting aspect of Garfinkel's paper is his proposal that rationality designates many different ways of behaving. Garfinkel presents an inventory of descriptions, each of which may be considered ex post facto as a criterion for deciding rationality. These include such familiar activities as categorizing and comparing, tolerable error, search for "means," analysis of alternatives and consequences, and strategy. These criteria constitute the commonsense rationalities. Thus Garfinkel presents us with the opportunity to examine activities that have before this time been considered irrational as alternative forms of rationality.

In Garfinkel's essay it is clear that the "scientific rationalities," although real, are particular forms of rationality. They do not possess the sole claim to intelligibility. Rather, scientific rationalities are a "thing among other things." Science includes the rationalities of common sense and four rationalities that do not occur in commonsense discourse. The four scientific rationalities are (1) compatibility of ends—means relations with principles of formal logic, (2) semantic clarity and distinctness, (3) clarity and distinctness "for their own sakes," and (4) compatibility of the definition of a situation with scientific knowledge.[3]

The incompatibility of these uniquely scientific rationalities with common sense activities can be demonstrated by invoking them in an ordinary conversation. For example, if clarification is demanded for its own sake when talking informally with someone, hostility and a breakdown of the conversation are likely to ensue. While it is necessary to pursue clarity for its own sake in the context of a scientific investigation, to do so in the everyday world is inappropriate.

That science is primarily a propositional enterprise is rooted in its reliance on language activity as the beginning and end of its project. Each of the four properties associated with scientific rationality is grounded in certain aspects of language. Thus we will refer to them as **rationalities for formulation** in science. Rationality 1 requires that a researcher's activity conform to certain established linguistic rules that compose "formal scientific logic." A researcher may proceed without adhering to formalities, but the problem cannot be considered solved nor the research accepted by the scientific community unless the procedure is compatible with formal rules. The scientist begins on the level of formal logic by stating the problem in the form of an hypothesis. The natural world can then be investigated to test an hypothesis, but to afford a solution it is necessary to return to a world composed of formal linguistic rules. To do science means to be a member of a cultural community of a particular kind—one that takes language to be a basic requirement.

Rationality 2 further expands science's reliance on language. Until a scientist offers a feasible description of a research experience, the task is not complete. Therefore, it is necessary to assign maximum value to the construction of feasible descriptions. Semantic clarity and distinctness become high correlates or even components of knowledge itself. It is quite possible that a scientist may select mystery as his topic, but it is not at all permissible to **talk of** such a topic in a mysterious way.

This leads us to rationality 3, clarity and distinctness for their own sakes. In the program of science the task of clarification is a project in its own right. In scientific writing, all terms, concepts, and procedures must be carefully defined, described, and explicated. Garfinkel contrasts this "clarification for its own sake" with "clarification that is sufficient for present purposes," that is, in informal, commonsense discourse, and in nonscientific writing.

Scientific rationality 4 requires a scientist to embed findings in a larger body of findings recorded as scientific publications. Again the priority of scientific investigation is determined by linguistic considerations in accord with a recorded body of established data. Tied into this rationality is the prohibition against a scientist's use of feelings as criteria for the acceptance of a given proposition. Garfinkel writes, "There is nothing that prohibits a scientific investigator from being passionately hopeful that his hypothesis will be confirmed. He is prohibited, however, from using his passionate hope **or** his detachment of feeling to recommend the sense or warrant of a proposition."[4]

SYNTHETIC RATIONALITIES

The Garfinkel inventory of rationalities for formulation in science poses a problem. Our investigation into synthetic systems suggests they might be as intricate and elaborate as are scientific systems. However, according to Garfinkel's conception, they could be classified as common sense because they do not seem to contain the activities constituting the scientific rationalities. But to regard nonscientific ways of knowing as common sense would not be accurate. These systems are highly articulated structures that share with science an intricacy and depth as methodologies for discovering the world. Furthermore, our argument that scientific and synthetic ways of knowing are mirror images implies that synthetic inquiries have rationalities in addition to those shared with common sense. It should be possible to transform the scientific rationalities in a consistent way so that they would mirror the synthetic rationalities and thus transcend common sense.

The following list is a transformation, mapping, or mirroring of Garfinkel's inventory of scientific rationalities.

> Transformation A:
> (1) Compatibility of ends–means relationships with principles of formal logic.
> (1') Compatibility of means–ends relationships with layers of structural perception.
> Transformation B:
> (2) Semantic clarity and distinctness.
> (2') Semantic veiledness and complexity.
> Transformation C:
> (3) Clarity and distinctness "for their own sakes."
> (3') Veiledness and complexity "for their own sakes."
> Transformation D:
> (4) Compatibility of the definition of a situation with scientific knowledge.
> (4') Compatibility of the perception of a situation with synthetic knowledge.

Through these transformations, we have exchanged terms for their opposites: ends/means, formal logic/structural perception, principles/layers, clarity/veiledness, distinctness/complexity, scientific/synthetic, and definition/perception.

We hypothesize that for each statement describing rationality in scientific inquiry there is a corresponding statement obtained by replacing every concept by its opposite concept. If scientific and synthetic rationalities are mirror images of each other, then the statements generated from the substitution procedure must characterize actual rational processes. The Garfinkel inventory provides the opportunity to carry through such transformations. Our theory demands that the transformed statements be meaningful descriptions of actual practice within synthetic inquiries.

With this orientation, we can now proceed to examine the hypothesized synthetic rationalities. They will be discussed in the order C, B, A, D.

Transformation C: Veiledness and Complexity "For Their Own Sake"

An explication of the meaning of clarity and distinctness will be deferred until the next section. Here we examine the transformed statement 3', "Veiledness and complexity 'for their own sake.' " This is done by attempting to show that veiledness and complexity are rationalities in the contexts of the three synthetic inquiries used as case studies. To an extent, the purpose of these discussions is explication of the synthetic rationalities rather than critical evaluation of their hypothesized presence.

In the discussion of the **Tarot**, we examined selected aspects of the first three arcana. The Magician, the first arcanum, depicts a man in active position with the four suits of the Minor Arcana lying upon a table, symbolizing the four elements in nature—fire, earth, air and water. Some **Tarot** decks call him the Juggler—a manipulator par excellence. The High Priestess holds in her arms the **Torah,** which is conceived in Kabbalist tradition as the divine law of the universe. But note that she veils the divine law: The word "Torah" is partially covered by her blue veil, leaving an incompletely exposed formulation. The background of the card, in dramatic contrast to the Magician, is characterized by its complexity. Here we have a reversal of the first arcanum, in that the movement is from the one to the many, instead of from the many to the one. The High Priestess sits, her legs in front of the two columns beyond which lies the "swarm" of the perceptual order. In the **Tarot** knowledge is veiled because it is rooted in perception. Therefore, any knowing is singularly incomplete. The message is that insofar as knowledge is to be found in perceiving, it must remain partially hidden. Clarity is to be found only in culture, whereas nature is recast as resources that are "on the table" for the manipulations of the abstract cultural projects. But to the **Tarot** this is not in itself knowledge. As in other synthetic systems, knowledge must be based on the realities of natural observation, even if these realities never permit clear and definite solutions.

We are reminded of Lévi-Strauss's observation that, so far as the primitive is concerned, "one may readily conclude that animals and plants are not known as a result of their usefulness; they are deemed to be useful or interesting because they are first of all known."[5] In this statement we detect that primitive inquiry begins with the recognition of an object and then proceeds to make this perceived object interesting and useful. This is movement from the one to the many. The primitive, in grasping the sense of the operation, executes it in a manner that is interesting and that suggests complex alternatives. In propositional thought, on the other hand, what is interesting is what leads to a clear solution. Although there can be many possibilities, decisions are to be made among them; a singular solution represents an ideal in clarity.

● ● ● ● ●

Let us now turn to the **I Ching.** Appended to the text is a collection of fragments and treatises that stand as commentary to the **I Ching** itself. These writings are referred to as the "Ten Wings." In the Fifth Wing are several chapters that refer to the veiled nature of the inquiry. The first statement is derived from **Ta Chuan,** The Great Treatise:

> In it [the **I Ching**] are included the forms and the scope of everything in the heavens and on earth, so that nothing escapes it. In it all things every-

where are completed, so that none is missing. Therefore by means of it we can penetrate the tao of day and night, and so understand it. Therefore the spirit is bound to no one place, nor the Book of Changes to any one form.[6]

A full appreciation of this statement is beyond the scope of our discussion. However, several of its ideas are important to our investigation. The first is that the book is able to contain everything "in the heavens and on earth." The second is that nothing escapes it, and therefore "we can penetrate the tao of day and night and so understand it." The third is the relation of the Book to **tao**, which indicates that the Book, like **tao** itself, is bound to no one place nor to any single form.

For now, it is adequate to conceive of **tao** as Wilhelm does. "Tao . . . is something that sets in motion and maintains the interplay of these forces. As this something means only a direction, invisible and in no way material, the Chinese chose for it the borrowed word tao, meaning 'way,' 'course,' which is also nothing in itself, yet serves to regulate all movement."[7] The **I Ching**, at its deepest level, is not constrained to "any one form." The intelligibility of the **I Ching** is not one that produces a single and clear solution to any problem. Instead, it presents veiled possibilities within a problem. The emergence of a hexagram does not provide an answer, but rather an occasion where a definite problem may be exposed to complexities that were overlooked prior to the throwing. The hexagrams are not merely answers, but are frames of reference in which problems may be exposed to further investigation. The hexagram is not the end of thought, but a beginning of thought on a disciplined level. The rationality of the **I Ching** seems to be in accord with Wittgenstein's statement, "when the answer cannot be put into words, neither can the question be put into words. The **riddle** does not exist. If a question can be framed at all, it is possible to answer it."[8]

A hexagram frames a question, giving a sense of gestalt to it. Although the hexagram does not give an answer, it makes finding an answer possible. Thus the **I Ching** introduces a complexity, a picture veiled in its meaning. To the inquirer seeking an answer to a problem, the **I Ching** provides instead what can be termed an "intervening problem." The hexagram is substituted as the problem for thought, characterizing in its particular form the original problem. Undisciplined thought about one's problem is transformed into thought about one's problem in terms of the hexagram. The intervention of a frame that may be as problematical as the original question may seem to be a strange strategy for inquiry. It makes sense only within the context of a rationality in which veiledness and complexity are pursued for their own sake. Through the form of a particular hexagram, thought is drawn into the complexity posed by a situation.

● ● ● ● ●

The **tao** is defined as direction, as nature, or as order. It would be most reasonable, from our theoretical standpoint, to define **tao** as order, which includes direction as its outermost layer, and nature in its inner layers. In Archie Bahm's translation of Lao Tzu's **Tao Teh King**, tao is translated as nature, and it is written,

Nature is the formless source of all forms, and yet it remains unaffected by its forms.[9]

The formlessness of **tao** simply means that it is, as a principle of order, invisible. Lao Tzu wrote: "Nature is something which can be neither seen nor touched."[10] In its formlessness **tao** resembles the ally in don Juan's system of sorcery. Recall Castaneda's description.

An ally's condition or formlessness meant that it did not possess a distinct, or vaguely defined, or even recognizable form; and such a condition implied that an ally was not visible at any time. . . . A sequel to an ally's formlessness was another condition expressed in the idea that an ally was perceived only as a quality of the senses, that is to say, since an ally was formless its presence was noticed only by its effects on the sorcerer.[11]

An ally is associated with definite objects in nature (for example, certain plants), yet is in itself formless. Tao is associated with a definite form (the particular hexagram that comes up in a consultation with the oracle), but is itself formless and invisible. The **tao** is the direction or the way a situation is going and as such it is **perceivable** but formless and invisible. Like an ally, it represents a quality of a certain level of experience apart from its objective referents. The **tao**, then, may be associated with Merleau-Ponty's description of the world.

The world itself, which (to give a first, rough definition) is the totality of perceptible things and the thing of all things, must be understood not as an object in the sense the mathematician or the physicist gives to this word— that is, a kind of unified law which would cover all the partial phenomena or as a fundamental relation verifiable in all—but as the universal style of all possible perceptions.[12]

Like an ally, **tao** is a quality of perception—more correctly **the** quality of perception. Its properties are found in perception itself. A second statement from the Fifth Wing gives us some of its properties. "It manifests itself as kindness but conceals its workings. It gives life to all things, but it does not share the anxieties of the holy sage. Its glorious power, its great field of action, are of all things most sublime."[13]

Tao is described as having no form, yet it is the source of form. An ally and **tao** are **qualities** in perception. Since there is a relation between quality and structure, it can be said that quality is in structure, or that qualities are properties **of** structure. Color is an example of a quality of structure, which can be used to pursue this line of reasoning. Wittgenstein wrote:

Something red can be destroyed, but red cannot be destroyed, and that is why the meaning of the word "red" is independent of the existence of a red thing—Certainly it makes no sense to say that the color red is torn up or pounded to bits.[14]

Color is a property of a perceived object, as are form, texture, and density. While **tao** may be formless, it may be the organizing principle of both form and structure. While clay may be shaped in the form of a pot, the structure of the clay is independent of this form, and pounding the pot to bits does not alter certain structural properties of clay. We could say that order is veiled to our perceptions, because while we can perceive properties of order, order itself transcends immediate perception. There is order in the world that we cannot see, touch, hear, or feel; and yet we sense its presence.

Perception is concealed in its workings and is—as the I Ching suggests—possibly the most sublime of all things. Perception can never be distinct in the sense of the written equations and laws in science, in which terms are carefully defined by distinct rules, or is regarded as an elementary sign. Perception is sublime, essentially concealed, and unclear in the sense that a formal argument is clear. It is veiled in the sense that each percept is basically ambiguous: Some of the elements are "here," but at the same time some are "there." Again we quote Merleau-Ponty, who wrote:

> Perception is . . . paradoxical. The perceived thing itself is paradoxical; it exists only in so far as someone can perceive it. I cannot even for an instant imagine an object in itself. As Berkeley said, if I attempt to imagine some place in the world which has never been seen, the very fact that I imagine it makes me present at that place. I thus cannot conceive a perceptible place in which I am not myself present. But even the places in which I find myself are never completely given to me; the things which I see are things for me only under the conditions that they always recede beyond their immediately given aspects. Thus there is a paradox of immanence and transcendence in perception. Immanence, because the perceived object cannot be foreign to him who perceives; transcendence, because it always contains something more than what is actually given. And these two elements of perception are not, properly speaking, contradictory. For if we reflect on this notion of perspective, if we reproduce the perceptual experience in our thought, we see that the kind of evidence proper to the perceived, the appearance of "something," requires both this presence and this absence.[15]

Thus veiledness and complexity, while not appropriate rationalities in the context of a scientific inquiry, may be appropriate objectives for an inquiry into the perceptual.

Transformation B: Semantic Veiledness And Complexity

Research into the two hemispheres of the brain shows that the left hemisphere usually determines certain verbal abilities, and that the right hemisphere also has verbal activities. We have encountered a natural language, Hopi, that can be described as appositional—focusing on higher-order layers of mind. Recall that Hopi is characterized by Whorf as displaying a property of veiledness. "In many languages the cryptotype concept would be of little use, but there are languages like Hopi in which much of the influential material of paradigm production lies in the heavily veiled state, just as there are people whose mental life is much less accessible than that of others."[16]

In science semantic clarification and distinctness is attained by treating semantics as language-written-down,[17] so that it can exist as an object before the scientist.[18] "Primitives" and speakers of languages that are not written experience semantics from the point of view of speech rather than objectified language. As such, "semantics" is a problem of perception of the concrete speaking act, and it is to this experience that thought is related. It is important to note that primitives do have formalized systems that involve semantics. For example, Australian churingas and Native American petroglyphs are records of clan and personal experiences and are often the subject of protracted discussions regarding meaning. Unlike formal systems containing propositions, however, these forms are not rules or norms of particularized language objects. Instead, they provide occasions for speaking. They do not prescribe **how** one should talk or even **what** one should talk about. But they do "lend" themselves to talk and it is in the talking that they come to have meaning. In this function they contribute to the production of culture. Insofar as the **Tarot** and the **I Ching** are realized in concrete settings as occasions for speaking about problems, within a frame of reference provided by an array of cards or a given hexagram, they function much like churingas and petroglyphs.

In providing an occasion for speech, an arrangement of **Tarot** cards or a hexagram invokes meanings. But as these structures are discussed—in the reading or the throwing—additional features come to be perceived which were not recognized prior to the speaking. Thus a relation exists between speech and the structure spoken about: They transform each other. Speech comes to be experienced not as an object in the situation but as a perception in itself. The power of talking is that the speaker is able to see things in the figures that were not available in silent perception. The preeminently cultural objects—the speech and the array of cards or the hexagram—are posited in a situation where they mutually effect continual transformations in the perception of a situation. Both the speech and the cards or hexagram are essentially incomplete: It is always possible to "see" new things in the arcana, and discussion about the situation portrayed by cards or a hexagram is potentially endless.

This perceptual instability in the practice of synthetic ways of knowing contrasts sharply with scientific formulation, which is stable and invariant with respect to perception. The meanings of an array of cards or a hexagram are fundamentally veiled, as is the talk about them. The whole meaning is hidden; efforts to grasp a meaning that transcends visual fragments capture just part of the meaning. Speech in these situations is not really distinct, but rather provocative of deeper complexities. Each new semantic utterance adds to the complexity of the situation until the speaking abruptly ends, often not as a result of solving the problem or making a well-defined decision, but rather through losing oneself in the complexities. In this way such systems produce an expansion from the one to the many, rather than a reduction from the many to the one. Operationally, these systems work by increasing the production of views of a situation to such an extent that experiences of inquiry in culture lead to grasp of a situation in nature. That is, culture is returned to its natural roots through boundlessly reproducing itself until formulations come to rest on grounds of primary perception, nature, and the grasp of inner structure.

● ● ● ● ●

The following passage, taken from the Ten Wings of the I Ching, illustrates the expansion from the one to the many and the attempt to grasp the inner structure and the complexities of the situation.

> The names employed sound unimportant, but the possibilities of application are great. The meanings are far-reaching, the judgments are well ordered. The words are roundabout but they hit the mark. Things are openly set forth, but they contain also a deeper secret. This is why in doubtful cases they may serve to guide the conduct of men and thus to show the requital for reaching or for missing the goal.[19]

That words can be "roundabout" but "hit the mark" seems to convey the essence of semantic veiledness. Although the words of the I Ching (excluding the Wilhelm commentaries) have been committed to writing, they have the style of cryptic pronouncements. The text of the I Ching resembles a record of speech that is not primarily experienced as read, but rather as heard. By convention, the text of the book is read aloud by one or more participants in the context of a throwing of the coins.

It has always been a principle of the I Ching that the words do not exhaust the meaning of the hexagrams, but rather, coupled with the images in the lines, are suggestive of a perception of one's situation. As forms of perception, the words and lines are incomplete. It is tao, not the forms that are posited to pertain to it, that may be characterized as complete. Thus, we find the passage "The Master said: Writing cannot express words completely. Words cannot express thoughts completely."[20] Referring to the holy sages, the mythical scholars who developed the I Ching, the text continues:

> They speak of the most confused diversities without arousing aversion. They speak of what is most mobile without causing confusion. . . .
> This comes from the fact that they observed before they spoke and discussed before they moved. Through observation and discussion they perfected the changes and transformations.[21]

The Book of Changes is an attempt to penetrate the meaning of concrete situations through an interplay between the Judgments and the Images. The Judgment for a hexagram corresponds to a formal pronouncement on the linguistic level, whereas the Image corresponds to a structure on the perceptual level. Through this interplay meaning is revealed. Rooted in the perceptual level (nonverbal observation), the I Ching attempts to show transformation and change: Things come into view, reveal ever-changing facets, and pass out of view or go out of focus. Semantic aspects are veiled insofar as they refer to a field of observation that is constantly changing.

The interplay between the Judgment, the Image, and persons in the situation can be shown through an example. Suppose the coins are thrown and the hexagram Limitation occurs. The construction of the hexagram is carried out according to formalized rules, but there are no rules for interpreting it. The hexagram appears first as this six-lined figure, corresponding to the Chinese "word" Chieh:

 Chieh, or

According to Wilhelm, **Chieh** can be translated into the English word **limitation**. However, in James Legge's version of the **I Ching** the hexagram is not named at all,[22] and John Blofeld's version names it Restraint.[23] The semantic meanings of hexagrams are not clear, and the Chinese characters for the hexagrams do not translate easily into English. There is no Chinese word for the word **word**.

In Limitation, the upper trigram is the Abysmal, water, and the lower trigram is the Joyous, lake. Instead of a six-lined whole, we now have two three-lined figures, one above and one below, each with its distinctive properties. To a practitioner who has achieved some degree of competency in the system, this elementary beginning is already pregnant with meaning. He may immediately see a relation between the two trigrams: On the linguistic level, they are both "water signs." One practitioner offered this description of the hexagram Limitation:

> Above is the stream. See. (He pointed to the trigram ☵.) The two outside lines are yin and represent the banks of the stream. The inside line passes through the banks, and the stream itself is a yang line. It reminds me of the Grand Canyon. Water is between steep earth cliffs; [it] conjures up a vision of falling and danger. You can almost fall into the trigram. See the depth! And what happens when you dam up a stream? (He took out a pencil and drew the stream as ☵, and then changed the bottom line from yin to yang by filling in the space in the broken line, forming the trigram **Tui,** ☱.) You get a lake![24]

Then this practitioner read us the Judgment aloud:

> Limitation. Success.
> Galling limitation must not be persevered in.[25]

These words are recognized by practitioners as having something to do with the lines. In this illustrative reading, the practitioner continued:

> There is something frustrating in the situation—a sort of conflict. See the nuclear trigrams. (He points to lines 2, 3, 4 and lines 3, 4, 5, which form the trigrams ☳ **Chên,** thunder; and ☶ **Kên,** mountain.) See the mountain—hollow inside, sealed and lofty outside. A perfect mountain. Thunder moves upward but is blocked by the mountain which has the attribute of Keeping Still. Deep in the situation, below what we are immediately conscious of, is a blockage. This is why the **I Ching** speaks of a "galling limitation."[26]

In this talk we become increasingly aware of complexities within complexities, veiledness within veiledness. The words before us invoke new views to be seen in the situation, and in turn these views change the sense of the original words. We end our example, as at this point the practitioner said, "I've seen enough." We

asked him for his accounting of the accuracy of the throwing vis-à-vis the question, and he replied that it was "appropriate." This word is common among
practitioners; a throwing is never "true" or "false," or "right" or "wrong." It is,
however, either "appropriate" or "inappropriate." Such evaluations seem to
express a sense of veiledness and complexity that the words and images in the
situation display in their changes and reinterpretations. Truth and falsity as
evaluations are possible only in situations in which semantic clarity and distinctness can be guaranteed through fundamental rules that can be formally stated. In
the I Ching, and in the other synthetic inquiries, no such body of rules exists.
Codes, signs, and frames of reference that may aid in interpretation do exist, but
do not supply the interpretation of any given case. The pronouncements in the
text cannot be clear in the sense of an equation. Like the Hopi cryptotypes, they
have no real formal mark and are impossible to translate directly. The meanings
of the pronouncements may be grasped, but they cannot be explained exhaustively. In this sense they resemble music and myth, in that they are not directly
translatable, although they are understood. The words do not merely stand in a
mediated one-to-one correspondence with definite things. Instead, they stand on
the edge of the relation between conscious thought and other dimensions of
awareness, and they hypermediate the speech and the vision of serious practitioners. At this level of involvement in the methodology of the I Ching, what is
seen is not vision quale and what is heard or spoken is not acoustic quale. Synaesthetic perception is the rule. The intercommunication of the senses within the
inquiry leads, in the words we have cited from Merleau-Ponty, to the "inner
structure" of the situation, to a synthetic unity of the senses.[27]
    The words as well as the images in the I Ching are fundamentally per-
ceptual—they are signs rather than concepts. As such they display the property
of opaqueness that Merleau-Ponty found fundamental to language.

> There is thus an opaqueness of language. Nowhere does it stop and leave a
> place for pure meaning; it is always limited only by more language, and
> meaning appears within it only set in a context of words. Like a charade,
> language is understood only through the interaction of signs, each of
> which, taken separately, is equivocal or banal, and makes sense, only by
> being combined with others.[28]

●　●　●　●　●

The Tarot is believed by practitioners to provide—through some sublime process—an answer to a question. A Tarot reading can be even more veiled and complex than an I Ching throwing. For a Tarot reading involves not six lines, but as
many as fifteen cards from the deck, and the cards are associated with varying
aspects of a situation—what is coming, what is passing, what is manifesting, and
so forth.[29] The interplay between speech and the hexagrams resulting in mutual
and hypermediative change can also be observed in the reading of an array of
cards in the Tarot. In the Tarot this interplay produces ever-greater densities of
meaning as attention to the speech and the cards proceeds. In a sense the cards
become denser in that the situation transforms from a universe of content (the
question) to a multiverse of content. So, for example, particular details of a

given card (the snake that composes the belt of the Magician) are bracketed out of the background and come to constitute new signs that recursively affect speech, vision, and the other senses. The cards are experienced as having a depth (like our preceding hexagram), as having a density equivalent to that of a natural perceptual field. Like the hexagram, there seems to be no end to what may be discovered therein. As practitioners unravel the dense weave of the cards, the original question is explored and suggestions are revealed. The situation never is absolutely clear on the perceptual level. In fact, the method of the **Tarot** is conceived by Waite, one of its foremost commentators, as "The Veil."[30] In the **Tarot**, as in the **I Ching**, semantic veiledness is a conscious property of the method.

● ● ● ● ●

Both the **Tarot** and the **I Ching** may be considered from the point of view of a method of philosophy. Eliphas Levi described the **Tarot** as

> a truly philosophical machine . . . a lottery of thought as exact as numbers, perhaps the simplest and grandest conception of human genius. . . . An imprisoned person, with no other books than the **Tarot**, if he knows how to use it, could in a few years acquire universal knowledge and would be able to speak on all subjects with unequalled learning and inexhaustible eloquence.[31]

While Levi may have a slight tendency toward exaggeration, it is nonetheless true that one can learn from the **Tarot**.

Waite noted, "The true **Tarot** is symbolism; it speaks no other language and offers no other signs."[32] It can be argued that a language of symbolism is one that is both veiled and complex. Charles Morris, a scholar greatly influenced by George Herbert Mead, has devoted much of his career to the study of signals, signs, and symbols. Morris defines a sign process as "a five term relation—v, w, x, y, z—in which v sets up in w the disposition to react in a certain way, x, to a certain kind of object, y (not then acting as a stimulus) under certain conditions, z. The v's, the cases where this relation obtains, are signs."[33]

A symbol is conceived by Morris as a special type of a sign—a sign that produces an interpretation by its juxtaposition with another sign that is in a synonymous relation. As Merleau-Ponty noted above, signs in themselves are insignificant, but when combined with other signs a tentative meaning emerges in the relationship not observed in the isolated sign itself. A symbol, then, may be said to be the relationship between signs.

And symbols have additional properties. Lévi-Strauss describes symbols as "meaningful equivalents of things meant which belong to another order or reality," and adds that "the effectiveness of symbols would consist precisely in this 'induction property,' by which formally homologous levels of life—organic processes, unconscious minds, rational thought—are related to one another. Poetic metaphor provides a familiar example of this inductive process."[34]

Symbols, then, can be characterized as special sign relations that effect a hypermediation. They mediate culture and nature and also hypermediate the two. Scientific language, on the other hand, starts on the level of intelligibility through formal and unidimensional concepts and in a sense **mediates** cultural potentialities and natural actualities. This means that symbols can intensify perceptions of different levels, and can relate these levels in novel and radical ways. The presence of symbolic relations between signs in perception and sensation permits changing and producing forms that are antecedent to the introduction of the symbol. We have seen this "culture producing" function in the **I Ching.** A hexagram is studied intensely on many levels, and the discovery of these levels transforms the perceptions of a situation that occasioned the throwing. Thus symbols are relations between signs on different phenomenal levels.

While symbols are available on the cultural level, their full meanings are never exhausted by that level. It is to the levels of perception and sensation that one must ultimately turn to grasp the meaning of a particular symbol. The meaning of a symbol, like the perception of an object, always remains somewhat hidden. Unlike a word with a formal mark—such as a name for a thing—that mediates a natural object, the meaning of a symbol is not available by mere pointing. (We cannot point to several levels at the same time.) This limitation prevents us from knowing symbols **clearly** and talking about them **distinctly.** Symbols pertain to a multiplicity of levels, and for this reason symbolic language is not clear and distinct; like poetic or metaphorical language, it is veiled and complex. We can inquire into the meanings of symbols, but such investigations never enable us to **point out** exactly what they mean. Symbols may then be seen to resemble philosophical constructs and Wittgenstein's language game because they are not subject to ostensive definition, and they are of philosophical interest. Thus the **Tarot** is appropriately called a "philosophy machine." Its symbols generate philosophically interesting situations—situations in which the problems of meaning cannot be solved by pointing to this sign or that. Instead they involve interpretations that are necessarily incomplete but that are capable of producing intensive communication on many levels of reality at once.

Practitioners of the **Tarot** refer to their cards as arcana. This name further illustrates the property of veiledness found in the poetic speech of those who interpret the cards and their symbols. On this, Sadhu writes:

> In Hermeticism, INITIATION is based on what are known as AR-CANA, or mysteries. . . . 'Arcanum' (in English also called Trump) is a mystery, necessary for the cognition of a definite kind and number of things, laws or principles; a mystery without which one cannot operate, since the necessity of that cognition has been born in us; a mystery accessible to a mind strong and curious enough to see that knowledge. . . . 'Mysterium' is the magnificent system of Arcana and their secrets which are used as a synthesis by a definite occult school. . . . 'Secretum' (its equivalent in English is simply 'secret') means something which a number of men agree to hide, for some practical reason or even a caprice. . . . [O]ne of the most important matters for us to study will be the first term **arcanum.** It can be expressed in words, written in any usual language, or SYMBO-LIZED.
>
> The ancient initiatory centers chose this third way for the transmission of the highest ideas which were born in their minds, that is they recorded them in SYMBOLS.[35]

Sadhu, like Waite, views the **Tarot** as a system of knowing that involves symbols. Furthermore he associates these symbols with mystery and secrecy. Veiledness in the **Tarot** appears to enchance, rather than detract from, the value and significance of the interpretations of the symbols.

● ● ● ● ●

Similarly, veiledness is seen to have positive value in the practice of sorcery. Some of the materials from **The Teachings of Don Juan** indicate that clarity, though recognized as an occurrence, is not to be sought after and is not particularly desirable. Don Juan instructs Castaneda that there are four enemies of a man of knowledge, one of which is clarity. He explains:

"Once a man has vanquished fear, he is free from it for the rest of his life because, instead of fear, he had acquired clarity—a clarity of mind which erases fear. But then a man knows his desires; he knows how to satisfy those desires. He can anticipate the new steps of learning, and a sharp clarity surrounds everything. The man feels that nothing is concealed.

"And thus he has encountered his second enemy: Clarity! The clarity of mind, which is so hard to obtain, dispels fear, but also blinds.

"It forces the man never to doubt himself. It gives him the assurance he can do anything he pleases, for he sees clearly into everything. And he is courageous because he is clear, and he stops at nothing because he is clear. But all that is a mistake; it is like something incomplete. If a man yields to this make-believe power, he has succumbed to his second enemy and will fumble with learning. He will rush when he should be patient, or he will be patient when he should rush. And he will fumble with learning until he winds up incapable of learning anything."

"What becomes of a man who is defeated in that way, don Juan? Does he die as a result?"

"No, he doesn't die. His second enemy has just stopped him cold from trying to become a man of knowledge; instead, the man may turn into a bouyant warrior, or a clown. Yet the clarity for which he has so dearly paid will never change to darkness and fear again. He will be clear as long as he lives, but he will no longer learn, or yearn for, anything."

"But what does he have to do to avoid being defeated?"

"He must do what he did with fear; he must **defy his clarity** and use it only to see, and wait patiently and measure carefully before taking new steps; he must think, above all, that his clarity is almost a mistake. And a moment will come when he will understand that his clarity was only a point before his eyes. And thus he will have overcome his second enemy, and will arrive at a position where nothing can harm him any more. This will not be a mistake. It will not be only a point before his eyes. It will be true power."[36]

Transformation A: Layers of Structural Perception

One difference in the practice of scientific and synthetic inquiries is that of working with form (formulating theory) or with structure. Science is an activity involving the manipulation of forms and objects under investigation. Insofar as scientific observations are controlled—presided over by canons of proper methodological procedure—they are observations in and of form. For instance, in a laboratory experiment natural structures come to be known by virtue of being constrained to culturally imposed forms. Laboratory animals might be classified as rats-in-a-control-group and rats-in-an-experimental-group, these groups being defined a priori in terms of a formulation the scientist wants to test. Thus the activities of science are basically formal. Numbers, items, data, sets, tables, theories, and so forth are objects in culture. They have been produced by man-in-culture and it is to these forms that the scientist addresses his thought.

One can inquire into structure only to the extent to which one is in structure. To perceive and grasp phenomena is possible only because one is incarnate in a body that exists as the virtual instrument of discovery. Yet this instrument is not of the same order as a measurement gauge is an act of mediation between the gauge and the object being measured. The instrument of discovery (the gauge) and the object being investigated are both phenomena of the same order—they are phenomena being investigated and experienced as a spectacle of forms. If one's body is considered as an instrument of scientific investigation, it is perceived as another mediated form.

In synthetic inquiries, means and ends are compatible with layers of structural perception—ways in which the world becomes available through the body in ever more complex ways. Within these inquiries, experience is the primary focus; the formalization of experience into communicatable-to-others systems is only secondary. It is rare indeed for an artist or a practitioner of synthetic inquiry to be able to speak clearly, or even without confusion or difficulty, of what is done in the work.

At this point it is necessary to outline the layers of structural perception. Our tentative list of relationships of the body and the world is a preliminary effort to organize a topic, and is not intended to be exhaustive. The objective is merely to show that the phrase "layers of structural perception" has a meaningful interpretation.

The following chart provides two features for each layer of structural perception: the **style of work** of the body in realizing the principle, and the **quality of the world** that is manifested in such work.

LAYERS OF STRUCTURAL PERCEPTION

	Style of Work	Qualities of the World
1	looking	mechanical-formal
2	pointing	topical-formal
3	touching, grasping	sensual-formal
4	interenveloping	sensual-structural
5	throwing	social structure
6	dying	— — — —

Looking. The body in the work of looking can be said to be least involved in its world. The world in this position does not seem to contain the body—the world is experienced as an external spectacle. The quality of such a world may be said to be mechanical-formal. It is a world populated by things experienced primarily as formal objects. Movement in such a world is never movement-with-the-body but movement of forms outside the body that seem to be propelled by their own laws, motives, and so forth. Such movement is **mechanical** insofar as it resembles the workings of a machine, automatic and nonreflexive on the looker and in a sense detached from the observer. In such a world of forms the body of the looker is not present. This world is premediative in that what is going on outside in no way bears on one's personal possession. One is not forced to relate his thoughts and words to what is sensed.

Pointing. In the work of pointing, the body becomes involved, and the quality of the world comes to be seen not as mechanical and formal, but as an object of interest. By pointing, the body begins to involve itself in the world, although in a restricted and constrained manner. A subject is added to the initial looked-at object, and this subject must position himself in the work of pointing in an ordered way. For the first time the world has become problematic. The problem is one of mediating two domains: the subjective intention of the pointer and the immanence of objects. The work of pointing requires mediating the domains of culture and nature. In developing commonsense perception, or perception at the level of inquiry, this crude bodily pointing is supplemented by formalized devices such as questions or descriptions. But insofar as these devices are referents of the object, they stand as formalized means of pointing.

In pointing, the body and the world become mediated: They become involved in an order constituted by both and each influences the other. It is in the pointing that the body begins to learn of itself **as a form.** This occurs in the most dramatic way in the relation of the body to a mirror. What emerges in this type of pointing is that the body is given a picture of itself; it is given what might be termed a body image. It is possible in such a relationship for the body to take this two-dimensional image to be **the** representation of itself. Insofar as this is so the body learns to experience itself as a form, so that thought can conceive of its body as a form among other forms. In front of a mirror the body can **perform** for itself, can make itself a topic of interest of the same order as any other external form, and can launch an investigation **of** itself. This body image can then obtain the status of a form: It can evaluate itself, point out aspects of itself, mediate its inner thoughts with something of itself that remains forever available on the outside. It is in this mediation that the body may be said to begin its enculturation.

Touching and Grasping. The style of work characterized by touching and grasping is the first instance of hypermediation between the body and the world. When the hand touches an object lying on a table, everything possible in pointing is already accomplished. But here the body reaches a new level of experience—the level of sensation. The touched or grasped object is outside the body, but it is experienced within the body. The grasper draws the object closer, endowing the external world with a quality of depth. What we can touch and grasp is not only close to us; it is literally experienced inside the body. The world contains "objects" only to the extent that minds are able to grasp or comprehend their presence. Touching or grasping dynamically connects different levels in reality, that is, hypermediates them.

The body is the instrument of discovery of the world. In this sense the body constitutes a toolbox. Poet Charles Olson once put it this way:

> The difficulty of discovery (in the closed world in which the human is because it is ourselves and nothing outside us, like the other) is, that definition is as much a part of the act as is sensation itself, in this sense, that life is preoccupation with itself, that conjecture about it is as much of it as its coming at us, its going on. In other words, we are ourselves both the instrument of discovery and the instrument of definition.[37]

In the **Book of Changes** the holy sages are credited with this thought: "What has bodily form they called a tool."[38]

Tools are forms in the sense that they can be operated through touch or grasp, and set to work by the body. Thus the bodily form, as tool, can be put to work by the mind to the use of other tools.

Interenveloping. In the work of grasping, the body and the world beyond its edges become properties with depth and thickness. With the emergence of depth, the potentiality for experience that transcends culture comes into being.

Merleau-Ponty's comment regarding the spatiality of the body sets the stage for explicating the concept of interenvelopment.

> If my arm is resting on the table I should never think of saying that it is beside the ash-tray in the same way in which the ash-tray is beside the telephone. The outline of my body is a frontier which ordinary spatial relations do not cross. This is because the parts are inter-related in a peculiar way: they are not spread out side by side, but **enveloped** in each other.[39]

Grasping introduces us to the experience of sensations. Nevertheless, form prevails even though grasping imbues form with sensation. However, in the work we call **interenvelopment** sensation becomes dominant and form is limited.

One example of the work of interenveloping is found in sexual being. If one person's body has an enveloped spatiality, then two persons in a sexual embrace are interenveloped. This is not merely touching and grasping in which the partners constitute objects so that "sex roles" can be performed. Although sexuality exists on this level, such experience of sexual behavior falls short of attaining the work of interenvelopment. For sexual being can transcend the grasping of a "love object," and can instead bring into being a suprapersonal structure in which the component substructures communicate through a melody of gesture. The movement of lovemaking, when it exists at a level transcending performance, is not the property of two separate bodies in coordination, but of a single, suprapersonal structure that is so highly integrated that there can be no "error" in the movement, no individual "skill" in it, but rather a melody of movement that belongs to no one.

We describe the quality of the world constituted by the work of interenvelopment as sensual—structural. The quality of such a world is formless; it defies being constrained on the perceptual level to this form or that. The quality of this world is dynamic; complex motions provide the "background" in which the suprapersonal envelopment of the bodies is contained. When a leg trembles in sensation, it is the perception of the trembling that is primary; the leg is perceived only ex post facto. In this work we surrender to these motions—they sweep our body image away, and we are engulfed in perceptions of intense sensory experience. The relation of the body and the world becomes one in which structure comes to the forefront of awareness. One may enter a form or object, but one is enveloped in embrace.

In interenvelopment, the problem of the body is not one of putting itself in motion in accord with some externally projected point to bring its form into adjustment with its context. Instead, the problem of the body is releasing itself into motion and permitting the hypermotion within which it suddenly finds itself. In an enveloped space the body is not pointed toward something outside itself; there are no outside and inside axes. One finds oneself enveloped all around, involved in a motion without goals, a motion for itself. Motion at this level is an involvement with another body. In interenveloping, motion, sensation, and perception are not in-and-out, but rather in-all-around, a "going forward and backward without ceasing."[40] Interenvelopment is a primal case of construction, for it is work with structure, with sensory arrays, and with life itself.

Culture generally disapproves and represses inquiries into structure. This is certainly the case with respect to inquiry involving sexual practices. In the West, the Judeo-Christian religions defined sexuality as necessary, but not as a vehicle for attaining enlightenment. In the East, within the ways of Hinduism and Buddhism, a goal of meditative disciplines is the establishment, not of pleasure and ecstasy, but rather of enstasy, which is "a non-discursive, quasi-permanent condition . . . tantamount with supreme insight or wisdom."[41] This state, according to orthodox Hindu and Buddhist views, "was to be reached through a long tedious process of conformity to canonical instruction and discipline only; on the Hindu side, through rigid observation of the nitya and naimittika rituals and through the performance of the meditations laid down in the canonical texts."[42] Even the classical Yoga, which involves concentration on nondiscursive internal processes, "stipulated the eradication of the sensuous personality."[43] There is, however, an opposing tradition called Tantra, which defies orthodox practices and consequently has a "bad name" in India and much of Buddhist Asia as well as the West. On this, Agehananda Bharati writes, "The tantras do not teach to subdue the senses, but to increase their power and then to harness them in the service of the achievement of lasting enstasy, the target of these methods thus being the same as that of the orthodox."[44]

Tantra, which developed about A.D. 300–400, has become part of Indian and Tibetan philosophical systems. It constitutes an alternative to asceticism, as Metzner writes, "by affirming and glorifying the role of the body and of sense experiences, and by teaching that although ordinarily they were obstacles to realization, when transformed through the esoteric practices of tantric yoga they become the very vehicles of liberation . . . from the subtle web of illusion (māyā) spun by sense experience."[45]

In Tibetan Buddhist iconography, the integration of the male/female opposition is portrayed by the father/mother, or yab/yum, deities locked in an embrace, within which the bodies fuse to the point of indistinguishability. This symbolic sexual union is made explicit in some variants of Tantra (see Figure

Figure 17. Tibetan Yab-Yum.
Source: Los Angeles County Museum of Art, **P'yag na Rdo Rje** (Vajrapāṇi and his consort), bronze sculpture, ca. A.D. 1400, from the Nàsli and Alice Heeramaneck Collection.

17). In certain instances of such practices, an adept or guru and his or her disciple ritually interenvelope, the man sitting in a meditative position and the woman sitting on his lap, in a situation that would under ordinary circumstances be described as copulation. In this practice enstasy is reached through learning to immobilize the "three jewels": the breath, the seminal fluid, and the mind. Control of these bodily processes occurs in stages. First, through chanting mantras (words of power) the breath is reduced. Then the adept learns to do this in sexual union with his or her partner. Next, control of seminal ejaculation is attained, as Bharati puts it, "in the laboratory setting of tantric ritual copulation."[46] And third, the highest step involves preventing the mind from apprehending any object external to the suprapersonal structure containing the guru and the disciple. Practitioners of tantric inquiry appear—to orthodox seekers of enstatic consciousness who employ "conformity to instructions" and "performance of meditation" as their methods—to be libertines, but in fact they are not.

Throwing. In the work of interenveloping, it is possible to give our bodies to a suprapersonal structure, and it is also possible to throw our bodies into this structure. This throwing includes the power of creating certain forms of behavior and of appropriating a certain world. The work of throwing the body is the work of **gesturing**—of the creation of forms through participation with other persons. Through gesture, the body is extended into the world, which has an indefinite number of views (that is, is haunted by populations of men and animals looking out at it)—a world that affects sensations in the body, but in addition **demands** that the body make its presence felt in a definite way. In the style of work of throwing, the body experiences the world as a **practical** affair. And insofar as this work occurs **with** others—which, in addition to being resources for the body, impose demands on it—this is the work of **social structure.**

Speech, perhaps more than any other expression, provides us access to others. On this, Merleau-Ponty wrote:

> In understanding others, the problem is always indeterminate because only the solution will bring the data retrospectively to light as convergent, only the central theme of a philosophy, once understood, endows the philosopher's writing with the value of adequate signs. There is, then, a taking up of others' thought through speech, a reflection in others, an ability to think **according to others** which enriches our own thoughts. Here the meaning of words must be finally induced by the words themselves, or more exactly, their conceptual meaning must be formed by a kind of deduction from a **gestural meaning** which is immanent in speech. And as, in a foreign country, I begin to understand the meaning of words through their place in a context of action, and by taking part in a communal life—. . . I begin to understand a philosophy by feeling my way into its existential manner, by reproducing the tone and the accent of the philosopher.[47]

The early Wittgenstein saw the essence of language as **naming**—as a mediative relation between the language and the facts, where language depicts the logical structure of the facts. This view was repudiated by Wittgenstein himself when he saw that gesture did indeed play an important part in language. Hartnack writes:

> The story of how Wittgenstein came to doubt and then reject the picture theory is this. A Cambridge colleague was the Italian economist Piero Sraffa, with whom Wittgenstein often discussed philosophy. One day when Wittgenstein was defending his view that a proposition has the same logical form as the fact it depicts, Sraffa made a gesture used by Neapolitans to express contempt and asked what the logical form of that was. According to Wittgenstein's own recollection, it was this question which made him realize that his belief that a fact could have a logical form was untenable.[48]

To overcome his initial view of language as ostensive definition, he introduced the concept of language games, where ostensive definition is one game among innumerable others. "Here the term 'language-**game**' is meant to bring into prominence the fact that **speaking** of language is part of an activity, or form of life."[49] Later Wittgenstein wrote:

It is sometimes said that animals do not talk because they lack the mental capacity. And this means: 'they do not think, and that is why they do not talk.' But—they simply do not talk. Or to put it better: They do not use language—if we accept the most primitive forms of language—Commanding, questioning, recounting, chatting, are as much a part of our natural history as walking, eating, drinking, playing.[50]

Wittgenstein's insight is that speech is a natural human activity and can be described in terms of the bodily work that the human does in realizing its existence. From this point of view, the problem of language is not that of finding grammatical rules that govern usage, but rather describing how usage is tied into the particular types of work the body has to do to share its view with others. In speaking, words are not usually defined, but are **conveyed** by such things as the gestures and tones of the body.

In Wittgenstein's later investigations, he described language in terms of the bodily sensations. Wittgenstein saw that words do not describe sensations but express them. More precisely, words are gestures that extend the body's experience into the world—a particular mode by which the body can throw feeling into the world effectively and practically. As Wittgenstein stated, the ability to replace a primitive sensation (crying, for example) with a word enables the person to express the body's sensation in new ways and thus to extend the range of possible behaviors.

How do words **refer** to sensations?—There doesn't seem to be any problem here; don't we talk about sensations every day, and give them names? But how is the connexion between the name and the thing named set up? This question is the same as: how does a human being learn the meaning of the names of sensations?—of the word "pain" for example. Here is one possibility: words are connected with the primitive, the natural, expression of the sensations and used in their place. A child has hurt himself and he cries; and then adults talk to him and teach him exclamations and, later, sentences. They teach the child new pain-behaviour.

"So you are saying that the word 'pain' really means crying?"—On the contrary: the verbal expression of pain replaces crying and does not describe it.[51]

● ● ● ● ●

The body and the world are both topical to inquiries into structure. A concern for the fundamental importance of the body in synthetic investigations appears in both the **I Ching** and the **Tarot**. In the Great Treatise on the **I Ching** we encounter the following passage:

The Changes is a book vast and great, in which everything is completely contained. The tao of heaven is in it, the tao of earth is in it, and the tao of man is in it. It combines these three primal powers and doubles them; this is why there are six lines. The six lines are nothing other than the ways (tao) of the three primal powers.[52]

To this passage Wilhelm adds: "Here the places are divided according to the three primal powers. The first and second lines are the places of the earth, the third and fourth those of man, and the fifth and top lines those of heaven."[53] Thus in the I Ching we are given a view of the world according to a tripartite division of power in which man occupies a middle position between the powers of earth below and of heaven above. The hexagram suggests an image of man standing with his feet on the earth, marking the boundary of the world below, and his head marking the boundary of the world above. Man is characterized in this situation by the unique nature of his body. Above and below are available as powers only because the body has the capacity to create an above-below axis by virtue of its upright stance. In a hexagram, man occupies the place of the third and fourth lines. This position is made possible by the support of the first and second lines, which occupy the earth's place. Man, in turn, is in a position of support of the heavens; he regulates earthly affairs in accordance with the heavenly cycles of the seasons and the stars—of time.

● ● ● ● ●

Although the language is different and the treatment of problems varies somewhat between the I Ching and the Tarot, both systems attach fundamental importance to the problem of the body. Perhaps the most perplexing aspect of the Tarot to persons committed to the principles of science is the constant reference of Tarot practitioners to "the bodies." Competing versions of the Tarot often allude to three, five, or seven bodies belonging to man. In light of this inference, it appears that a concern with the body (or bodies) as a topic is fundamental to Tarot inquiry. Sadhu, in the introduction to his treatise on the Tarot, presents a definition of the terms his analysis requires. One term that is given a longer treatment than the term arcana is astrosome, which "as used in the Kabbalah means the whole complex which remains when the physical body is taken out of consideration, and refers to the astral and mental bodies confined."[54] Processes associated with the term include "**exteriorization** of the astral element or astrosome: this term is used for the voluntary and temporary abandonment of the physical body by an advanced occultist (no one else can perform such an operation) while retaining full consciousness and awareness of what then happens."[55] Finally there are the terms **Tourbillions**, or **Vortexes**.

> [These are] astral creations of force which are the bases of all astro-mental realizations. Tradition ascribed the funnel like forms to them. Knowledge of the laws ruling over the Tourbillions and their construction, is one of the foremost principles of magic . . . under the veil of Kabbalistic structures. The most guarded secrets of Hermetic magic are: **finding the point of support** for the Tourbillion on the physical plane, and the **formula of transition** from the astral to the physical world.[56]

● ● ● ● ●

Don Juan makes reference to the body as presented to a sorcerer who **sees.** An end of his system was to lead an apprentice to seeing the human body in this extraordinary way. The body then must be considered as a prevalent topic, for don Juan's description of it provides Castaneda with his most persistent example of what a man of knowledge sees.

"Men look different when you **see**. The little smoke will help you to **see** men as fibers of light."
"Fibers of light?"
"Yes. Fibers, like white cobwebs. Very fine threads that circulate from the head to the navel. Thus a man looks like an egg of circulating fibers. And his arms and legs are like luminous bristles, bursting out in all directions."
"Is that the way everyone looks?"
"Everyone. Besides, every man is in touch with everything else, not through his hands, though, but through a bunch of long fibers that shoot out from the center of his abdomen. Those fibers join a man to his surroundings; they keep his balance; they give him stability. So, as you may **see** some day, a man is a luminous egg whether he's a beggar or a king and there's no way to change anything; or rather, what could be changed in that luminous egg?"[57]

Transformation D: Perception of the Situation
Science demands that the definition of an inquirer's situation be compatible with a corpus of materials, rules, and so on that compose scientific knowledge. Synthetic inquiries are primarily concerned with the organization of thought without the necessary constraints of communication of knowledge to a critical professional group: The perception of an inquirer's situation must be made compatible with synthetic knowledge. Clear and distinct definitions of a situation are not an organizing norm in synthetic inquiries; inquiries do not operate to provide opportunities for formal definitions of a situation. Providing perception of a situation means that a practitioner reaches an understanding of his subject and knows the practices and sensual components of a situation. That one has a perception of a situation and is free to remain silent about it is a choice open in synthetic inquiries. That one senses is sufficient; telling and formalizing are of secondary importance. In science, sensing is secondary; the telling, the formalizing, to others is primary.

An emphasis in nonscientific inquiries is that the perception of a situation must be compatible with personal knowledge. That is, the personal experience of an inquirer provides a source of authority for knowledge. It is not incumbent upon a synthetic inquirer to harmonize his or her sense of a situation with the canons of an external body of knowledge known as "the literature." A synthetic inquirer **may** place himself or herself in accord with a traditional line of interpretation (for example, the Wilhelm instead of the Blofeld version of the **I** Ching), but this is not necessary. Within these systems, the authority of a knowing is ultimately dependent upon the personal relation between the inquirer and the practice.

The elements that constitute the perception of a situation have been covered in Transformation C. Now, in support of the claim of the "primacy of the personal" as a characteristic of synthetic rationalities we can draw on relevant materials from the **Tarot**, the **I** Ching, and don Juan.

An approach to this problem can begin with a consideration of **intuition**. The logical empiricist school within the philosophy of science has maintained that intuition is not a fundamental component of scientific inquiry, and that the work of intuition stands in irreconcilable opposition to science. Nevertheless, intuition is a component of knowledge and enters into even the most scientific of inquiries. Edmund Husserl, in his phenomenology of ideas, saw that intuition may well be the foundation of mathematical work and calls his program a "science of intuition."[58] The problem of intuition, though a disturbing and unmanageable discovery in the sciences, is a recognized beginning point in the **Tarot** and the **I Ching**. These systems view knowledge as fundamentally, though not exclusively, intuitive and seek to develop the capacity for intuition as a prevailing concern and means of production.

● ● ● ● ●

Sadhu writes in the introduction to his book on the **Tarot**:

> Now, I would like to stress, that the Tarot in itself does not expound any definite SPIRITUAL DOCTRINE, but rather has the purpose of expanding the abilities of the student, that is to teach him an infallible method for developing and using his mental faculties. From the occult point of view the man of average intelligence is not well prepared for the realization and solving of the deep problems of the microcosm and macrocosm. No doubt some people have brilliant flashes of mental understanding and even intuition, but all such are only of a sporadic character and could hardly be called controlled abilities, or **guided intuition**. . . . The mental machine of the Tarot tries to fill this gap and to help every earnest seeker, who cannot as yet follow any DIRECT SPIRITUAL PATH, as taught by the great Teachers of humanity, but who feels an urgent need to examine everything for himself and to reconcile his mind to the supposed highest aims of human attainment.[59]

Throughout his treatment of the **Tarot** Sadhu emphasized that intuition is ranked as a "higher power than mind" and sees the function of the **Tarot** as that of training or guiding this power.[60]

The **Tarot** as a "guided intuition" can be related to the idea that the practice of intuition may be a description of magic and that such a practice has as a feature the production and development of personal knowledge. The perception of a situation is primarily made available through the exercise, not of a "mere" intuition but of a highly organized, or "guided," intuition. In the brain research terminology, this refers to the functioning of the right cerebral hemisphere, of what Bogen calls the appositional mind.

In other treatments of the **Tarot** one can observe further evidence of the operation of the rationality considered here. Papus writes: "Each man contains in himself an Adam, source of the Will, i.e., the Brain; and Eve, source of Intelligence, i.e., the Heart, and he should balance the heart by the brain, and the brain by the heart, if he would become a center of divine love."[61] Although the physiology in this argument cannot be taken seriously, it is interesting that to Papus intelligence is understood as intuition. He writes: "Intelligence is here taken in the sense of Intuition, and not in the sense usually attributed to it by the Philosophy of the Universities,"[62] to which he refers. Our earlier discussion of the brain indicates that neither left- nor right-hemisphere thought can properly be referred to as "higher" than the other and that neither can properly be defined as constitutive of "intelligence."[63]

In his discussion of the fortune-telling aspect of the **Tarot**, Papus maintains that intuition is the great secret behind the practice and that it operates **irrespective** of the particular system used to guide it. This places ultimate authority and responsibility in the person who uses the system. In the interpretation given by Papus we have an extreme case of the personal insights involved in the **Tarot**.

> We have learnt that intuition and practice are necessities in the art of fortune-telling by cards, now that the art has losts its scientific principles (Astronomy) and launched into empiricism. . . . Our readers are therefore able to select whichever system they prefer, and whichever they find most successful. We must repeat that intuition is the great secret of all the divining arts, and that fortune-telling by cards, in water, in earth, or coffee-grounds, is precisely the same thing.[64]

Turning to Waite's commentary on the **Tarot** we find a similar stance vis-à-vis intuition.

> The value of intuitive and clairvoyant faculties is of course assumed in divination. Where these are naturally present or have been developed by the Diviner, the fortuitous arrangement of cards forms a link between his mind and the atmosphere of the subject of divination, and then the rest is simple. Where intuition fails, or is absent, concentration, intellectual observation and deduction must be used to the fullest extent to obtain a satisfactory result. But intuition, even if apparently dormant, may be cultivated by practice in these divinatory processes. If in doubt as to the exact meaning of a card in a particular connexion, the Diviner is recommended, by those who are versed in the matter, to place his hand on it, try to refrain from thinking of what it ought to be, and note the impressions that arise in his mind. At the beginning this will probably resolve itself into mere guessing and may prove incorrect, but it becomes possible with practice to distinguish between a guess of the conscious mind and an impression arising from the mind which is sub-conscious.[65]

Waite recognized the reciprocal relation that exists between intuition and the arrangement of the cards in the deck for the purpose of divination. Intuition may be cultivated or developed through practice in these divinatory processes, in which the cards and intuition seem to instruct each other. We may conclude from Waite's description that intuition is a type of knowledge that can distinguish itself in practice from mere guessing.

● ● ● ● ●

In the **I Ching** we find a similar attitude in operation. Jung stated in his appraisal of the practice: "Clearly the method aims at self-knowledge, though at all times it has also been put to superstitious use."[66] Jung's view is in accord with a certain aspect of the **I Ching**, but it does not exhaust the meaning of the method as one involving personal knowledge. The aspect that is relevant to the rationality discussed here is expressed in the following passage and in Wilhelm's commentary on it. Jung, being committed to a psychological perspective, interpreted the **I Ching** as a method for attaining the realization of the higher aspects of being which he has termed self-knowledge. The psychological aspect of the **I Ching** can be seen from the following passage in the text:

> Since in this way man comes to resemble heaven and earth, he is not in conflict with them. His wisdom embraces all things, and his tao brings order into the whole world; therefore he does not err. He is active everywhere but does not let himself be carried away. He rejoices in heaven and has knowledge of fate, therefore he is free of care. He is content with his circumstances and genuine in his kindness, therefore he can practice love.[67]

Wilhelm added the comment:

> Here we are shown how with the help of the fundamental principle of the Book of Changes it is possible to arrive at a complete realization of man's innate capacities. This unfolding rests on the fact that man has innate capacities that resemble heaven and earth, that he is a microcosm. Now, since the laws of heaven and earth are reproduced in the Book of Changes, man is provided with the means of shaping his own nature, so that his inborn potentialities for good can be completely realized.[68]

However attractive this claim may be, there is still a deeper dimension to the **I Ching** than that of developing moral perfection. Later in the same chapter we encounter the final passage:

> That aspect of it which cannot be fathomed in terms of the light and the dark is called spirit.[69]

Wilhelm added:

> In their alternation and reciprocal effect, the two fundamental forces [heaven/earth; light/dark; yang/yin] serve to explain all the phenomena in the world. Nonetheless, there remains something that cannot be explained in terms of the interaction of these forces, a final why. This ultimate meaning of tao is the spirit, the divine, the unfathomable in it, that which must be revered in silence.[70]

Thus, within the **I Ching** is an aspect that underlies the entire system, but which Wilhelm contends is to be met in silence. We have seen earlier in our discussion of this transformation that silence is an acceptable option open to practitioners of systems like the **Tarot** and the **I Ching**. This silence is related to the essential veiledness that characterizes these systems of knowledge. What seems to be veiled in silence is the working of a "something" in the method that is inexplicable in terms of the analytic units given in the system, but which the system serves to instruct, develop, and express. We have met this "something" in the

Tarot; it is the aspect of personal knowledge that can be termed intuition. Intuition can be identified with the spirit whose manifestation is not guaranteed solely by working with any set of rules, principles, or signs that are contained in the method. This position finds support in R. G. H. Siu's writings on the I Ching.

> The prime point to bear in mind in the use of the I Ching as a guide to one's dealings with his fellow men is the philosophy of forming the basis for its counsel. Its central emphasis is on the intuitive grasping of the totality. Specific facts and figures are not constants to be searched out for their own sakes. The whole is ever in continuous flux. No single constituent is without impact on the others and vice versa.[71]

Thus the psychological aims of the I Ching are subsumed in its methodological organization. The working of a rationality involving personal knowledge can be interpreted in this context as the provision within the method whereby "specific facts and figures" are not constant in the system; the specifics provide the format whereby intuition may operate and develop itself. This predicates the option of silence in that intuition is first and foremost a manner of thinking and need not be limited by the constraints of communication. Personal knowledge can mean that one has developed a method of "intuitive grasping" that he or she is aware of but cannot specify clearly at all times to others. The I Ching is a method that directs a practitioner to the development of this kind of knowledge. It includes self-knowledge, but it is also a method whereby knowledge of others can be analyzed. The I Ching can be seen as a procedure for analyzing what Polanyi terms "personal knowledge" and the "tacit dimension." What is tacit in our civilization's prevailing philosophy is topical in these systems, and vice versa. Jung wrote:

> The manner in which the I Ching tends to look upon reality seems to disfavor our causalistic procedures. The moment under actual observation appears to the ancient Chinese view more of a chance hit than a clearly defined result of concurring causal chain processes. The matter of interest seems to be the configuration formed by chance events in the moment of observation, and not at all the hypothetical reasons that seemingly account for the coincidence. While the Western mind carefully sifts, weighs, selects, classifies, and isolates, the Chinese picture of the moment encompasses everything down to the minutest nonsensical detail, because all of the ingredients make up the observed moment.[72]

Note the essential qualification in the last two lines of the following passage.

1. The Changes is a book
From which one may not hold aloof.
Its tao is forever changing—
Alteration, movement without rest,
Flowing through the six empty places;
Rising and sinking without fixed law,
Firm and yielding transform each other.
They cannot be confined within a rule;

It is only change that is at work here.
2. They move inward and outward according to fixed rhythms.
   Without or within, they teach caution.
3. They also show care and sorrow and their causes.
   Though you have no teacher,
   Approach them as you would your parents.
4. First take up the words,
   Ponder their meaning,
   Then the fixed rules reveal themselves.
   But if you are not the right man,
   The meaning will not manifest itself to you.[73]

● ● ● ● ●

In don Juan's practice, seeing is an example of intuition. Seeing is carefully distinguished from looking—to see an object is to grasp its inner structure—that is, to obtain an intuitive insight. This inner nature of seeing, of "getting through things" to the essence, is described by don Juan.

"An average man can 'grab' the things of the world only with his hands, or his eyes, or his ears, but a sorcerer can grab them also with his nose, or his tongue, or his will, especially with his will. I cannot really describe how it is done, but you yourself, for instance, cannot describe to me how you hear. It happens that I am also capable of hearing, so we can talk about how we hear. A sorcerer uses his will to perceive the world. That perceiving, however, is not like hearing. When we look at the world or when we hear it, we have the impression that it is out there and that it is real. When we perceive the world with our will we know that it is not as 'out there' or 'as real' as we think."
"Is will the same as **seeing**?"
"No. Will is a force, a power. **Seeing** is not a force, but rather a way of getting through things. A sorcerer may have a very strong will and yet he may not **see**; which means that only a man of knowledge perceives the world with his senses and with his will and also with his **seeing**."[74]

● ● ● ● ●

In this investigation it has been argued that a set of four synthetic rationalities parallel four rationalities of the scientific method presented in Garfinkel's inventory. For each of three synthetic types of inquiry—the **Tarot**, the **I Ching**, and "primitive" inquiry including the **Teachings of don Juan**—the nonscientific rationalities are present. At the empirical level our results are hopeful but not conclusive. Moreover, while Garfinkel lists four scientific rationalities, there may be other scientific rationalities. There is always the possibility that rationalities exist in one domain that are **not** mirrored in the other. The rationalities for formulation in science may not exhaust the rational bases of science that are beyond common sense.

NOTES

1. Harold Garfinkel, **Studies in Ethnomethodology**, Englewood Cliffs, N. J.: Prentice-Hall, 1967, p. 67.
2. Ibid., pp. 262–263.
3. Ibid., pp. 267–268.
4. Ibid., p. 268.
5. Lévi-Strauss, **The Savage Mind**, p. 55.
6. Wilhelm, **I Ching**, p. 296.
7. Ibid., pp. 297–298.
8. Wittgenstein, **Tractatus**, p. 109.
9. Bahm, **Tao Teh King**, p. 21.
10. Ibid., p. 26.
11. Castaneda, **Teachings**, p. 214.
12. Maurice Merleau-Ponty, **The Primacy of Perception**, ed. with intro. by James M. Edie, Evanston, Ill.: Northwestern University Press, 1964, p. 16.
13. Wilhelm, **op. cit.**, p. 299.
14. Wittgenstein, **Philosophical Investigations**, p. 28.
15. Merleau-Ponty, **The Primacy of Perception**, p. 16. If tao is a quality of perception, and perception has a paradox of immanence and transcendence, then **tao** should also be described in this way. Chang Chung-yuan writes that "even the notion of unity or synthesis of parts into a whole is still far from conveying the deepest meaning of **Tao**. For Tao is immanent and yet transcendent." See Chang Chung-yuan, **Creativity and Taoism: A Study of Chinese Philosophy, Art, and Poetry**, New York: Harper & Row, 1963, pp. 33–34.
16. Whorf, **Language**, p. 110.
17. For a discussion of written notational systems see Saussure's "Graphic Representation of Language" in Ferdinand de Saussure, **Course in General Linguistics**, ed. Charles Bally and Albert Sechebaye in collaboration with Albert Riedtinger, trans. with an introduction and notes by Wade Baskin, New York: McGraw-Hill, 1966, pp. 23–32.
18. Maurice Merleau-Ponty, **Signs**, trans. Richard C. McCleary, Evanston, Ill.: Northwestern University Press, 1964, p. 86, distinguishes between language "as mine" and language as "object of thought."
19. Wilhelm, **op. cit.**, p. 345.
20. Ibid., p. 322.
21. Ibid., p. 304.
22. Legge, **I Ching**, p. 197.
23. Blofeld, **I Ching**, p. 202.
24. Personal communication.
25. Wilhelm, **op. cit.** p. 231.
26. Personal communication.
27. Merleau-Ponty, **Phenomenology of Perception**, p. 228.
28. Merleau-Ponty, **Signs**, p. 42.
29. Metzner, **op. cit.**, p. 80.
30. Waite, **op. cit.**, p. 3.
31. Sadhu, **op. cit.**, p. 11.
32. Waite, **op. cit.**, p. 4.
33. Charles Morris, **Signification and Significance: A Study of the Relations of Signs and Values**, Cambridge, Mass.: MIT Press, 1964, p. 2; Also see George Herbert Mead, **Mind, Self and Society**, Chicago: University of Chicago Press, 1934.
34. Lévi-Strauss, **Structural Anthropology**, p. 197.
35. Sadhu, **op. cit.**, p. 33.
36. Castaneda, **Teachings**, pp. 80–81, emphasis added.
37. Charles Olson, "Human Universe," in Robert Creeley, ed., **Selected Writings of Charles Olson**, New York: New Directions, 1951, p. 51.
38. Wilhelm, **op. cit.** p. 318. Also, the text reads: "What is above form is called tao; what is within form is called tool." Ibid., p. 323.
39. Merleau-Ponty, **Phenomenology of Perception**, p. 98, emphasis added.
40. Wilhelm, **op. cit.**, p. 318.

41. Agehananda Bharati, **The Tantric Tradition**, Garden City, N. Y.: Doubleday, 1965, p. 288.

42. Ibid., p. 289.

43. Ibid.

44. Ibid., p. 290.

45. Metzner, op. cit., pp. 30–31.

46. Bharati, op. cit., p. 296.

47. Merleau-Ponty, **Phenomenology of Perception**, p. 179.

48. Hartnack, op. cit., p. 62.

49. Ibid., p. 67f.

50. Wittgenstein, **Philosophical Investigations**, p. 12.

51. Ibid., p. 89.

52. Wilhelm, op. cit., pp. 351–352.

53. Ibid., p. 352.

54. Sadhu, op. cit., p. 25.

55. Ibid., p. 27.

56. Ibid., p. 29.

57. Castaneda, **Separate Reality**, pp. 33–34.

58. Edmund Husserl, **Ideas: General Introduction to Pure Phenomenology**, trans. W. R. Gibson, London: Collier-Macmillan, 1962, pp. 74–76.

59. Sadhu, op. cit., p. 22.

60. Ibid., p. 86.

61. Papus, op. cit., p. 209.

62. Ibid., p. 209f.

63. In this sense, tests such as the Street Gestalt Completion Test can be regarded as measures of appositional performance, just as standard intelligence quotient tests measure propositional performance. If appositional performance is, as both the neurological theory and the theory presented here imply, as intricate and complex as is propositional thought, it is an intelligence in its own right. To define the verbal skills as intelligence, a common practice in psychology, represents a value judgment and little more. From a logical point of view, it makes as much sense to say that appositional performance should be defined as intelligence. We feel there is no conclusive evidence that what is called intelligence is inheritable. See TenHouten, **Cognitive Styles and the Social Order**.

64. Papus, op. cit., p. 333.

65. Waite, op. cit., pp. 310–311.

66. Carl Jung, "Forward," in Wilhelm, op. cit., p. xxxiv.

67. Wilhelm, op. cit., p. 295.

68. Ibid., p. 295.

69. Ibid., p. 301.

70. Ibid.

71. R. G. H. Siu, **The Men of Many Qualities: A Legacy of the I Ching**, Cambridge, Mass.: MIT Press, 1968, pp. 5–6.

72. Jung, in Wilhelm, op. cit., p. xxiii.

73. Wilhelm, op. cit., pp. 348–349.

74. Castaneda, **Separate Reality**, p. 181.

Chapter
7

Enemies in Scientific Inquiries

Don Juan instructs his apprentice, Carlos Castaneda, that in questing after a vision and becoming a "man of knowledge" four enemies must be overcome. These enemies are **fear, clarity, power,** and **old age**. We concur with don Juan's penetrating analysis of his own practice and hypothesize that these four enemies are present in **any** synthetic inquiry. In the **I Ching** and the **Tarot** it is first necessary to overcome the fear of pursuing nonordinary realities. It is next necessary to abandon the notion that the practice can be reduced to talk about the hexagrams and arcana and then to resist attachment to the power that one can gain through such inquiry. Finally, as with sorcery and the struggle to see, when these three enemies are vanquished only fatigue stands in the way.

We further hypothesize that there are enemies of the practice of science standing in a mirror image relation to the enemies of synthetic inquiries. They are, in corresponding order, **belief, veiledness, weakness,** and **immaturity**. These enemies can be traced in the career of an individual scientist, as well as in the history of a scientific discipline.

BELIEF
In order to get "into" a work of art, it is necessary to **suspend disbelief** in the expressed vision of the artist. The same argument can be extended to all syn-

thetic inquiries. In order to appreciate a kind of inquiry as having value, or to work toward becoming a practitioner, it is necessary to suspend disbelief. For example, in the three books that Castaneda has so far written about his apprenticeship to a sorcerer, it is nowhere hinted that Castaneda literally believes in the actuality of the nonordinary reality he perceives. He asks don Juan, for example, if he "really" flew through the air, and if he "really" talked with a coyote. Castaneda is not informed about sorcery by don Juan, but instructed in it, and this emphasis on structure rather than form is appropriate for a practice constituting an inquiry into structure. Castaneda's research shows the value of an anthropologist's taking seriously the knowledge in a nonmodern culture. When this knowledge is taken seriously, disbelief in it is suspended, and this suspension immediately produces a fear of confronting an unknown reality, inhabited by potentially dangerous entities that are apt to appear without invitation.

Belief is an enemy of science, because when our world is given to us, externally, by a belief system, our minds are to some extent closed. On this, Arthur Koestler writes: "By a closed system I mean a cognitive matrix, governed by a canon. . . . Its canon is based on a central axiom, postulate, or dogma, to which the subject is emotionally committed, and from which the rules of processing reality are denied. The amount of distortion involved ranges from the scientist's involuntary inclination to juggle with data as a mild form of self-deception, motivated by his commitment to a theory, to the delusional belief system of clinical paranoia."[1]

Thus, while synthetic inquiries require the suspension of disbelief, scientific inquiries require the suspension of belief. To suspend belief does not mean to disbelieve; to suspend disbelief does not mean to believe. Neither mode of inquiry demands that anything either be believed or disbelieved; on the contrary, inquiry presupposes an open mind.

In ancient and medieval times, decadent religions persecuted science and its practitioners. It is known that innumerable scientists have been mistreated for their efforts to overcome the first enemy of their practice and to suspend belief in philosophical and religious dogma specifying the ultimate nature of man and the cosmos. While science has overcome this obstacle to some extent, the victory is less than total. Scientists continue to be denied resources where they dare to challenge philosophical and political doctrines. In advanced technological societies, science is subordinated to the state and to the economic system. In the physical sciences, theories are no longer repressed, but the application of theories remains firmly in the grasp of political and economic elites.

At the same time, modern science remains immersed in its belief in objectivity. Charles Frankel writes: "Objectivity in thought and judgment, generally speaking, is a social achievement, the product of long cooperative processes of controlled questioning, communication, and mutual criticism."[2] Charles Novak asserts that "objectivity is a highly selective, highly developed, subjective state. It is the selection of one set of values in preference to others, the shaping of perception and other mental operations along specified lines, and the establishment of social means of verification."[3] He adds:

Objectivity, in short, has the logical status of a myth: it builds up one sense of reality rather than others. It is a myth whose attainment and maintenance demands of its subjects a rigorous and continual asceticism. . . . [S]tudents who wish to give their lives to this myth through careers in science or technology are often taught that they must learn to censor flights of fancy, dreams, impulses, wishes, preferences, instincts, and spontaneities of many sorts, to do so not only occasionally but habitually, and not only in their immediate professional activities but for long supporting stretches of their lives as well. Science and technology ask of their practitioners a whole way of life for which young people must be socialized by many years of schooling.[4]

But this inculcation does not develop **real** science. On this, Michael Novak notes: "Insofar as the objective mind is thought to be impersonal, detached, analytic, verbal, precise, and clear, the theory of objectivity represents only a part of human judgment."[5] In the vocabulary developed here, it can be said that the belief in objectivity stultifies the development of the practice of science, stopping the practitioner in his tracks. For, above all, to do science is to suspend belief, to question everything. Novak writes:

> The drive to question operates through every stage of awareness: through dreams, images, experiences, perceptions, orientations, conceptions, theorizing, decisions, and actions. Insofar as these moments of awareness can be ordered among themselves in various ways, the drive to question may also be directed to different sequences and complex combinations.[6]

A scientist vanquishes his first enemy the moment it is realized that everything can be questioned, that nothing can be an article of belief. Novak sees this capacity to question as "the necessary condition for the experience of nothingness. . . . Whatever the presupposition of a culture or a way of life, questions can be addressed against them and other alternates can be imagined."[7]

> [T]he experience of nothingness casts doubt . . . on the reasons and methods of sociology (and every other science or philosophy), . . . [and is] beyond the limits of reason. . . . It is terrifying. . . . The person gripped by the experience of nothingness sees nearly everything **in reverse image.** What other persons call certain, he sees as pretend; what other persons call pragmatic or effective, he sees as a most ironical delusion. . . . The experience of nothingness is an awareness of the multiplicity and polymorphousness of experience.[8]

VEILEDNESS
Once practitioners of science vanquish the value assumptions and beliefs that exclude possible topics and restrict mental capacities to the propositional mind, they have an enhanced capacity for vision and theoretical insight. And here the scientist encounters the second enemy—veiledness. Scientists attain insight or vision only through protracted struggles to see. Whatever might have been previously believed is dispelled, and it is possible to develop the courage to pursue the vision.

It is a fundamental challenge in the practice of science to convert a vision— the idea for a theory—into a clear verbal expression. The vision must be condensed into a point before the eyes. **The vision must be defied and the character** of its order must be changed from entwined ideas at the edge of words to a linear order in which the ideas are unraveled and set forth in the form of a propositional argument. The ideas need to be brought within written language and ranged one before another in a relation of order or spatial succession.

In the vision quest of don Juan, clarity—which is just such a point before the eyes—is an enemy. But for scientists the creation of clarity before the eyes is the essence of the practice. The need to be clear imposes discipline on the inquiry. This discipline comes about through rendering verbal accountings of phenomena compatible with principles of propositional formulation.

Thus we see that the practice of science involves both the **construction** of the idea for a theory, and its eventual **formulation**. Setting down a vision in a clearly written form, such that the laws of the theory are **about** the inner structure of phenomena, is not a problem in formal logic. In theory construction— which is work with structure—the logic-in-use may involve the synthetic rationalities of appositional thought working with propositional thought and the senses. Thus theory building is creativity of a nonlinear order. The formulated theory is the product of this inquiry, and yet the logic contained in it does not exhaustively describe the rationality involved in constructing the idea for the theory and formulating it. In this process, the scientist uses the synthetic rationalities and his enemies are fear, clarity, power, and old age.

This analysis establishes a distinction between **theory construction** and **theory formulation**. Theory is constructed in the appositional mind, or as a result of an inter**play**, or **work**ing together, of the two sides of the brain and the mental order as a whole. The logic contained in the published version of a theory—the end product—does not exhaust the rationality of construction and formulation. A theory may be reduced to logic in the sense that it can be seen in its purely formal aspect, but the theory also is about inner structure, the layers of the perceived world we know only indirectly.

Clarity Through Language
Scientific theories are often presented in formal analytic language—logic or mathematics—or in some combination of formal language and natural language, so used that clarity of presentation is an end in itself. Hence, in writing of language used in scientific inquiries, attention must focus on highly propositional forms. Since scientific inquiries often demand a level of clarity not attainable in natural language, it is necessary to use invented, or artificially constructed, languages. Wittgenstein wrote: "To invent a language could mean to invent an instrument for a particular purpose on the basis of laws of nature (or consistent with them); but it also has the other sense, analogous to that in which we speak of the invention of a game."[9] In a natural language that members of a culture speak or write, the inventors of the language give it properties of concreteness and abstraction. But languages can be distinguished from one another by the **emphasis** given these features. Hopi emphasizes the first usage; English and Wittgenstein's native German emphasize the second. The scientific rationalities, which demand presentations that are clear and distinct, and compatible with principles of formal logic, require languages that emphasize rules and have the structure of games. That is, scientists are able to overcome veiledness, to speak and write clearly, in artificially constructed languages such as those provided by symbolic logic and mathematics.

The above argument does not imply that natural languages such as English and German are veiled. In these languages, it is possible to determine whether properly formed statements are consistent with one another and whether certain statements can be deduced from others. It is also possible to determine whether properly formed statements are internally consistent. But problems of veiledness do exist. Rules for making such determinations are never invented by one person; they are continually modified and expanded by invention. The formulation of a scientific theory, for example, can result in the addition of hundreds of new words to a language and the explication or modification of existing terms. In addition, at any given moment of time the "rules" for forming statements may not be shared by users of a language. These problems can be magnified if a scientific community is international and papers pertaining to a given topic are formulated in different languages.

Artificial, invented languages are abstract insofar as statements within them can be formed and interrelated without attaching significance to the vocabulary of the language. Philosopher Richard Rudner writes that within an abstract language, "if a list of the elements . . . as well as a list of its grammatical rules, is available . . . , then the language may be generated without knowledge of, or without taking into account, the meanings of the words in the language."[10]

Thus the comparisons of English and Hopi can be expanded to include abstract languages. There are languages that hypermediate culture and nature: Hopi, which abounds in cryptotypes without formal marks, is an instance of such a language; singing renders any language closer to this. There are natural languages that, though capable of hypermediating culture and nature, function primarily to mediate culture and nature. These languages tend to exclude internal subjective experience. And there are languages that do not mediate culture and nature, but instead exist as nearly "pure culture" in the sense that they are based on a set of rules and can be construed as games.

Veiledness and the Foundations of Logic

In the late nineteenth century, intensive inquiries into abstract mathematical and logical forms—that is, inquiries into the morphology of mathematical structures such as David Hilbert's work on geometry[11]—contributed to the development of formal logic. In logic, general rules of deduction used in natural language are translated into a formal system consisting of elementary signs, sequences of signs (formulas), and sequences for formulas (proofs) that are constructed by rules of formation. The rules of formation in symbolic logic make it possible to create a system in which deduction takes place according to the rules of inference embodied in the system.

In a language, the rules of formation are called the grammar or syntax of the language. The concept of rule is related to an attribute of propositional thought—the outer layer of the mental order, called direction. Wittgenstein wrote: "Following a rule is analogous to obeying an order. We are trained to do so; we react to an order in a particular way."[12] And he added: "When I obey a rule, I do not choose. I obey the rule **blindly**."[13] Thus a set of rules commands how we must speak, and this means that only certain orderings of semantic units are permissible. Of course, we can speak informally and even nongrammatically and still be within a language. As Wittgenstein noted: "Orders are sometimes not obeyed. But what would it be like if no orders were **ever** obeyed The concept 'order' would have lost its purpose."[14]

In an effort to place logic on a clear basis and to demonstrate that it constitutes a foundation for mathematics, Alfred North Whitehead and Bertrand Russell published, in 1910, a monumental work entitled **Principia Mathematica**.[15] This book shows that the axioms of algebra can be reduced to arithmetical expressions, and that arithmetic can in turn be deduced from a small number of axioms or postulates. But this reduction of the "uncertain" in logical inference did not eliminate the problem of incompleteness, for at the heart of all mathematics there loom statements that must be assumed in order for mathematics to proceed. Such statements are called metamathematical.

The magnitude of this problem was revealed in a most extraordinary paper written in 1931 by a 25-year-old mathematician named Kurt Gödel.[16] This paper astounded mathematicians and philosophers interested in the foundations of logic and science. For Gödel's paper proves that formal logic—which lies at the foundation of mathematics—is incomplete. His paper shows, as Ernest Nagel and James R. Newman write, that "the resources of the human intellect have not been, and cannot be, fully formalized, and that new principles of demonstration forever await invention and discovery."[17] Philosophers have insisted that this does not imply that mystical or occult systems should be taken seriously. For example, Nagel and Newman caution that the Gödel paper does not imply that "a 'mystic' intuition (radically different in kind and authority from what is generally operative in intellectual advances) must replace cogent proof. . . . It would be irresponsible to claim that these formally indemonstrable truths established by meta-mathematical arguments are based on nothing better than bare appeal to intuition."[18]

This caution is well-advised; it would indeed be irresponsible to attempt to discard science and mathematics on the ground that their logical foundations are somehow incomplete. Yet for all the assertions about what such knowledge could **not** be, the question of what these truths **could** be has received limited attention. If there exist ways of knowing that are not formal, and yet are not "bare" or "mystic" intuition, could they not be some other kind of intuition? If this way of knowing is not something that we should **not** take seriously, then it is something that should indeed be taken seriously.

Gödel's paper is abstruse and difficult. Nagel and Newman have described the essentials of the argument clearly, but the outright complexity of the paper cannot be avoided. The paper shows that while collections of statements assumed true (axioms) can be used to generate innumerable other true statements (theorems), there will always be still other statements which are true, but which cannot be shown to be either true or false within the system itself. Thus these truths are not **in** formal logic, as all sentences in a formal logical system must have "truth values" (T = true, or F = false) assigned to them. Nagel and Newman write:

> What is more, [Gödel] proved that it is impossible to establish the internal logical consistency of a very large class of deductive systems—elementary arithmetic, for example—unless one adopts principles of reason so complex that their internal consistency is as open to doubt as that of the systems themselves. In the light of these conclusions, no final systematization of many important areas of mathematics is attainable, and no absolutely impeccable guarantee can be given that many significant branches of mathematical thought are entirely free from internal contradiction.[19]

Gödel took for his example of an abstract system the logic presented by White-head and Russell. The formulas in this system are constructed out of elementary signs, which constitute the fundamental vocabulary for the logic. A set of formulas constitute the axioms of the system, and the theorems are deduced from the axioms by a set of rules of inference (called transformation rules).[20]

Gödel established a method of associating a unique number with all elementary signs, formulas, and proofs in arithmetic. The elementary signs are **logical constants** and **variables.** The constant signs include the sign for negation, $\sim$, the signs for parentheses, ( ), the comma, and so on. The variable signs are of three types. One represents numerical variables that can take on a range of values, denoted **x, y,** and so on; a second type represents sentences, denoted **P, Q,** . . . the third type represents predicate variables, denoted **S, T,** . . . and used for concepts such as "is the brother of," "is prime," or "is T-related."

Gödel attached the numbers 1 through 10 to this list of constant signs, prime numbers to numerical variables, squared prime numbers to sentential variables, and cubed prime numbers to predicate variables. He then devised a method of associating a unique number with each formula. Nagel and Newman present a good example, "$(\exists x)\ (x = sy)$," which means "there exists a number **x** that is the successor of the number **y**," or "every number has a successor." The numbers associated with the signs are:

$$
\begin{array}{cccccccccc}
(& \exists & x &) & (& x & = & s & y &) \\
\downarrow & \downarrow & \downarrow & \downarrow & \downarrow & \downarrow & \downarrow & \downarrow & \downarrow & \downarrow \\
8 & 4 & 11 & 9 & 8 & 11 & 5 & 7 & 13 & 9
\end{array}
$$

To reduce the entire formula to a single number, the first ten successive prime numbers are raised to a power equal to the number for the elementary sign, so that the huge single number representing the entire equation is:

$$2^8 3^4 5^{11} 7^9 11^8 13^{11} 17^5 19^7 23^{13} 29^9$$

This number represents all equations with this form, so that the variables **x** and **y** can be replaced by numbers without changing the value of the "Gödel number" which serves as its mirror image. By such procedures, and by more elaborate numbering devices for sequences of formulas, Gödel was able to imagine assignment of a unique number to every expression in Whitehead and Russell's logic, or in any formal logic. In this way he attained a reduction of the entire system to a collection of numbers. Nagel and Newman write that Gödel "showed that all meta-mathematical statements about the structural properties of expressions in the calculus can be adequately **mirrored** within the calculus itself."[21] Note that it is metamathematics that is mirrored in this process: Gödel's mirror shows structure as the image of form. For this reason Nagel and Newman are able to write that this mapping "facilitates an inquiry into structure."[22]

Gödel showed that it is possible to construct a formula **G** representing the metamathematical statement: "The formula **G** is not demonstrable." It is shown that **G** is demonstrable if, and only if, its formal negation **not-G**, is also demonstrable. But if a formula and its negation can both be demonstrated, then the arithmetic is not consistent. Thus if the arithmetical calculus **is** consistent, the truth or falsity of **G** cannot be determined within it. Gödel then showed that while **G** is both true and outside the system, then the axioms are incomplete: The outermost layer of order, where abstract form is most concentrated, is not free of structure and does not exhaust order itself. Gödel went on to prove that arithmetic must always be incomplete, no matter how many signs, formulas, axioms, and so forth are added to it. Moreover, he constructed a number representing the statement, "Arithmetic is consistent." Then he proved that the statement "Arithmetic implies the formula **G**" is formally demonstrable. That is, arithmetic implies true things that cannot be demonstrated within it. Therefore, the consistency of arithmetic cannot be represented by an argument in formal logic. As a result of this amazing argument, we are, as Nagel and Newman assert, "compelled to recognize a fundamental limitation in the power of the axiomatic method. Against previous assumptions, the vast continent of arithmetical truth cannot be brought into systematic order by laying down once and for all a set of axioms from which **every** true arithmetical statement can be formally derived."[23] And the final conclusion reached by Gödel is this: Arithmetic may or may not be consistent. If it is consistent, this consistency cannot be established by any metamathematical reasoning within the formal deduction of arithmetic, although metamathematical proof of consistency is possible.

Thus inquiry in form cannot express everything that is true. In order to inquire, formal logic is an invaluable tool, but it does not exhaust the potentiality of the toolbox. There is also inquiry in structure, which is carried out with rationalities appropriate to perception and sense experience. Gödel's argument points to a type of intuition, or a way of knowing, that is partially described by the rationalities of synthetic inquiries.

Since synthetic rationalities are directed to the knowing of inner structure, we can know about them through form, but this knowledge must remain tacit. There may be laws of nature embodied in theories, but since laws are form, these laws are **about** but not **in** the structures to which they pertain. We can be clear about the meaning of form, but the meaning of structure is veiled. Gödel seems to have proved that there can be no final victory over the enemy veiledness. Newman and Nagel conclude that Gödel's conclusions are "now widely recognized as being revolutionary in their broad philosophical import."[24]

● ● ● ● ●

It can be agreed, by means of logic alone, that the sentence "All squares are rectangles" is true. To do so is to analyze the predicate out of the subject, so that the meaning of the predicate is contained in the subject. Such a sentence is true a priori, because it is necessarily true. Thus it is **analytic a priori**. Philosophers have not proved that there either are or are not sentences that are **synthetic a priori**. But consider the sentences "Being red includes being colored" and "Being red excludes being blue." These sentences seem not to be analytic, and may be instances of the synthetic a priori. In discussing the synthetic a priori with these and related examples, philosopher Roderick Chisholm carefully argues:

> There are sentences which seem to express what is known a priori, and which, up to now, have not been shown to be logically true. This fact may be **some** presumption in favor of the view that there is a synthetic a priori.

And if there is a synthetic a priori, then this fact, in turn, might be taken to have important bearing upon the nature of the human mind (it would imply, for example, that our a priori knowledge is not restricted to knowledge of 'formal' truths).[25]

It would be too much to claim that the Gödel paper demonstrates the synthetic a priori, but it certainly does lead to the same conclusions.

WEAKNESS

When a scientist or a community of scientists are beyond the first two enemies of the practice and have set forth a vision in a clearly formulated theory, the third enemy—**weakness**—is encountered. For a formulated theory may prove not to be true, and the vision, however promising and imaginative, must be adjudged to be in error. A scientific community must have the **power** to reject a theory found inconsistent with data gathered to test it. To the extent that this power is lacking, **weakness** is present.

Second, hypotheses derived from the general statements, or laws, of a theory must be consistent with empirical observation, so that it can be determined to what systems, if any, the theory applies. If hypotheses are consistent with observations, it is said that the theory is externally valid and that it is empirically true.

Assuming a theory is logically consistent, there are two types of errors that can be made regarding its external validity:

Type I: A true theory can be falsely rejected;
Type II: A false theory can be falsely not rejected.

There are difficulties in attaching a numerical probability to a theory, and these problems have been dealt with in the philosophy of science.[26] At the conceptual level, we can call the probability of making a Type I error α and the probability of making a Type II error β. The complement of α, $1-\alpha$, is defined as the **confidence** we can have in the test of the theory. The complement of β, $1-\beta$, is called the **power** of the test of the theory—which is the probability that it will be found out that the theory is false. Consistent with this, the probability, β, that the false theory will not be rejected can be defined as **weakness**.

The history of science contains numerous examples of Type I errors. Martin Gardner describes a few instances of

> novel scientific views which did not receive an unbiased hearing, and which later proved to be true. . . . The opposition of traditional psychology to the study of hypnotic phenomena . . . is an outstanding instance. In the field of medicine the germ theory of Pasteur, the use of anesthetics, and Dr. Semmelweiss' insistence that doctors sterilize their hands before attending childbirth are other well known examples of theories which met with strong professional prejudice.
>
> Probably the most notorious instance of scientific stubbornness was the refusal of eighteenth century astronomy to believe the stones actually fell from the sky. . . . Even the great Galileo refused to accept Kepler's theory, long after the evidence was quite strong, that planets move in ellipses.

Fortunately there are always, in the words of Alfred Noyes, "The young, swift-footed, waiting for the fire," who can form the vanguard of scientific revolutions.[27]

There is some defense for this inherent conservatism in science, as Gardner recognizes.

A certain degree of dogma—of pig-headed orthodoxy—is both necessary and desirable for the health of science. It forces the scientist with a novel view to mass considerable evidence before his theory can be seriously entertained. If this situation did not exist, science would be reduced to shambles by having to examine every newfangled notion that came along.[28]

Thus, while Type I errors are to be avoided, theories whose time has come, no matter how odd or radical they may seem to the orthodox practitioner, will in time receive a fair hearing.

On the other hand, a Type II error poses a more fundamental enemy of science. Philosopher Karl R. Popper's analysis of theory testing illustrates the priority of overcoming the weakness of Type II errors.

All tests can be interpreted as attempts to weed out false theories—to find the weak points of a theory in order to reject it if it is falsified by the test. This view is sometimes considered paradoxical; our aim, it is said, is to establish theories, not to eliminate false ones. But just because it is our aim to establish theories as well as we can, we must test them as severely as we can; that is, we must try to find fault with them, we must try to falsify them. Only if we cannot falsify them in spite of our best efforts can we say that they have stood up to severe tests. This is the reason why the discovery of instances which confirm a theory means very little if we have not tried, and failed, to discover refutations. For if we are uncritical we shall always find what we want: we shall look for, and find, confirmations, and we shall look away from, and not see, whatever might be dangerous to our pet theories. In this way it is only too easy to obtain what appears to be overwhelming evidence in favour of a theory which, if approached critically, would have been refuted. In order to make the method of selection by elimination work, and to ensure that only the fittest theories survive, their struggle for life must be made severe for them.[29]

New theories often need reworking and clarification. Laws may have to be added or deleted. The conditions under which a theory can be expected to hold—the domain of the theory—can be explored. Sometimes, after protracted efforts to overcome weaknesses in a theory by changing its internal structure in an effort to bring its hypotheses into closer correspondence with observation, the entire enterprise will have to be abandoned. The land of science-past is haunted by theories that were, in their time, widely accepted, but that are now labeled "error," and with occasional exceptions, this labeling is justified. Thomas S. Kuhn has some interesting thoughts on this matter.

[S] cience does not develop by the accumulation of individual discoveries and inventions. Simultaneously, these same historians (of science) confront growing difficulties in distinguishing the 'scientific' component of past observations and beliefs from what their predecessors had readily labelled "error" and "superstition." The more carefully they study, say, Aristotelian dynamics, phlogistic chemistry, or caloric thermodynamics, the more certain they feel that these once current views of nature were, as a whole, neither less scientific nor more the product of human idiosyncrasy than those current today. If these out-of-date beliefs are to be called myths, then myths can be produced by the same sorts of methods and held for the same sorts of reasons that now lead to scientific knowledge. If, on the other hand, they are to be called science, then science has included bodies of belief quite incompatible with the ones we hold today. Given these alternatives, the historian must choose the latter. Out-of-date theories are not in principle unscientific because they have been discarded. That choice, however, makes it difficult to see scientific development as a process of accretion.[30]

Disconcerting amounts of what is now held to be valid may be headed for the junk heap, but while Kuhn correctly points out that science is not cumulative for all the formulations that come to be accepted within scientific communities, some of it may survive indefinitely. Many present theories will be incorporated in more complex theoretical formulations that will account for phenomena in a more satisfactory manner. Modern mathematics—the theory of abstract form and structure—for example, is hardly apt to be discarded. It is more reasonable to anticipate that it will—while perhaps shedding inconsistencies as it expands—become embedded in theories that are far more powerful, and that explore even more of the possible manifestations of abstract form and its relation to structure. It is even possible that it could develop into a theory of order. If our analysis of form and structure as the outer and inner layers of order is justified, we might speculate that the concept of order will come to play a larger role. In the social sciences the prospects for current formulations are not bright. A substantial portion of what is now believed to be true by modern behavioral science may some day come to be rejected or to undergo major structural change.

The power of science to develop theory has been associated with unprecedented investments by nations in scientific manpower. Science has become a major segment of the economics in modern technological societies. Derek J. de Solla Price observes: "The large-scale character of modern science, new and shining and all powerful, is so apparent that the happy term 'Big Science' has been coined to describe it."[31]

IMMATURITY

As scientists develop their theories it is centrally important to inform themselves regarding what has been discovered, what is hypothesized, what is known, and what is rejected. The problem is enormous, for science has expanded into a vast enterprise containing scientists working intensively on theoretical topics, publishing their work in innumerable books and journals. At the frontiers of scientific disciplines, elite communities of scientists (de Solla Price calls them "invisible colleges"[32]) exchange written descriptions of their work with each other for information and criticism. At times theories develop so rapidly that nearly every practitioner engaged in a particular topic will read versions of the most advanced thought and its experimental support long before it comes to be preserved in academic journals and eventually described in textbooks. Students in advanced training for careers in science often have access to only these formal records of the practice and have difficulty inferring the actual practice and its logic-in-use from these published accountings and their logic, reconstructed so that it all appears perfectly clear and orderly, as if only propositional thought were involved in the enterprise. Even the most competent practitioners are continually in danger of not adequately keeping up with current investigations, of knowing what has been done, of repeating error, and in general of proceeding with insufficient information. An overall grasp of a scientific discipline as a whole, together with a sense of its history and prospects, comes only with protracted effort and enables the practitioner to deal with the enemy **immaturity.** While many discoveries come as a surprise, others are expected, so that several people may be working simultaneously on the edge of the same discovery. The result is frantic activity on the frontier of a scientific discipline, with practitioners apt to dispute one another for the credit for an idea whose time is here.[33]

● ● ● ● ●

Immaturity is also a problem for a scientific discipline as a whole. It is well known that the behavioral and social sciences are immature in comparison with the biological and physical sciences. Most formulations within behavioral and social science are not clear enough to be considered theories, and the few formulations that clearly are theories often do not contain sufficient explication of the concepts and the domain of the theory so that they can be tested empirically. The reasons for the relative immaturity of the social sciences is a most interesting topic, which awaits an adequate explanation. Philosophers in the logical empiricist tradition have found that social, biological, and physical sciences do not differ fundamentally in their basic methodologies, so the explanation might lie elsewhere. It is clear that the reason must have something to do with the values of a civilization convinced that its problems can be solved by technology, by machines, and by applied physical science. It is further clear that the myth of objectivity constrains both the physical and social sciences but that the greater effect has been felt within social sciences. For if applied physical and biological sciences are defined as potentially capable of solving problems of behavior and society, then the investment will naturally focus on these disciplines. On the other hand, because of its belief in science per se, the economic and political systems are compelled to provide some level of support for the social sciences, even at the risk of a nagging criticism provided without invitation by politically oriented practitioners. In other words, social and behavioral sciences remain unable to vanquish their final enemy, immaturity, in part because they have been hampered, on at least two counts, by their first enemy, belief. At present the direction of Western civilization cannot be predicted or its present circumstances explained, but the conclusion seems inescapable that belief in the reduction of phenomena to the material level is invalid. Problems of social structure obviously are not merely problems in human engineering. The reconstitution of social institutions appears to require a more highly developed knowing of **these** structures. There is apt to be a close relation between revolutions that discard theories and revolutions in sociopolitical and economic institutions. A civilization that relies on science is not immune to the consequences of the social science it produces.

NOTES

1. Arthur Koestler, **The Ghost in the Machine,** New York: Macmillan, 1968, p. 263.
2. Charles Frankel, **The Love of Anxieties and Other Essays,** New York: Dell, 1967, pp. 24–25, cited in Michael Novak, **The Experience of Nothingness,** New York: Harper & Row, 1970, p. 34.
3. Novak, op. cit., p. 37.
4. Ibid., p. 37.
5. Ibid., p. 38.
6. Ibid., p. 46.
7. Ibid., p. 14.
8. Ibid., pp. 12–13.
9. Wittgenstein, **Philosophical Investigations,** p. 137.
10. Richard S. Rudner, **Philosophy of Social Science,** Englewood Cliffs, N. J.: Prentice-Hall, 1966, p. 13, emphasis in text.
11. David Hilbert and Wilhelm Ackerman, **Grundzüg der Theorischen Logik,** Berlin: Springer, 1928; David Hilbert and Paul Bernays, **Grundlager der Mathematik,** 2 vols., Berlin: Springer, 1934.
12. Wittgenstein, **Philosophical Investigations,** p. 82.
13. Ibid., p. 85.
14. Ibid., p. 110.
15. Bertrand Russell and Alfred North Whitehead, **op. cit.**
16. Kurt Gödel, "Über Formal Unentscheidbare Sätze der Principia Mathematica und Verwandter Systeme I," **Monatsnefte für Mathematik und Physic,** vol. 38, 1931, pp. 1173–1198.
17. Ernest Nagel and James R. Newman, **Gödel's Proof,** New York: New York University Press, 1958, p. 101.
18. Ibid., p. 101.
19. Ibid., p. 6.
20. Ibid., p. 39, 47–48, 50.
21. Ibid., pp. 76–77.
22. Ibid., p. 77.
23. Ibid., p. 94.
24. Ibid., p. 4.
25. Roderick M. Chisholm, **Theory of Knowledge,** Englewood Cliffs, N.J.: Prentice-Hall, 1966, p. 88.
26. See, for example, Rudolf Carnap, "On Inductive Logic," **Philosophy of Science,** vol. 7, 1945, pp. 72–97.
27. Martin Gardner, **Fads and Fallacies in the Name of Science,** New York: Dover, 1957, revised and expanded edition, p. 9.
28. Ibid., p. 11.
29. Karl R. Popper, **The Poverty of Historicism,** New York: Harper & Row, 1964, pp. 133–134.
30. Thomas S. Kuhn, **The Structure of Scientific Revolutions,** vol. 2, number 2, **International Encyclopedia of Unified Science,** 1962, p. 2.
31. Derek J. de Solla Price, **Little Science, Big Science,** New York: Columbia University Press, 1963, p. 3.
32. Ibid., p. 62.
33. Thomas S. Kuhn, "Historical Structure of Scientific Discovery," **Science,** vol. 136, 1962, p. 760; de Solla Price, op. cit., p. 66.

Chapter
8

Synthetic Inquiry: Appositional Thought in the I Ching

This chapter analyzes synthetic inquiries and explicates the meaning of appositional thought. Just as appositional thought functions with a scope comparable to propositional thought, so synthetic inquiries may be as intricate as scientific inquiries.

Giorgio de Santillana and Hertha von Dechend set themselves a similar task in their treatise on the origins of science. Although they write from an historical perspective, and their arguments are not entirely persuasive, they provide a number of useful insights. In dealing with their materials—composed mainly of classical myths—they encounter a basic methodological difficulty that seems unavoidable in constructing a model of nonscientific inquiry.

> Most frustrating, we could not use our good old simple catenary logic, in which principles come first and deductions follow. This was not the way of the archaic thinkers. They thought in terms of what we might call a fugue in which all notes cannot be constrained into a single melodic scale, in which one is plunged directly into the midst of things and must follow the temporal order created by their thoughts.[1]

We are reminded of Lévi-Strauss's treatment of primitive myth. His entire analysis is organized in terms of music, which seems to resemble the structure of mythic experience; he describes that experience as "The Fugue of the Five Senses."[2]

In our analysis of synthetic inquiries, we are guided by two principles. The first is that appositional thought is not governed by principles. The second is that the relation of appositional thought to the natural world—to structure—is not one of cause to effect. In its most simple conception, we can see that the model of appositional thought consists of three organizing layers, (1) the sign particulars, (2) the interpretive codes, and (3) the invariant frames. The notion of layering, which is essential to the model of appositional thought, needs explication before we attempt a description of the layers in relation to materials in the Tarot and the I Ching.

LAYERED STRUCTURES

Lévi-Strauss concludes his analysis of myth in The Raw and the Cooked with this observation: "Mythic thought only accepts nature on condition that it is able to reproduce it. By so doing, it limits itself to the choice of these formal properties by which nature can signify itself and which consequently are appropriate for metaphor."[3] Concomitantly, Lévi-Strauss characterizes myth as organized in a "layered structure," allowing us "to look at myth as a matrix of meanings which are arranged in lines and columns, but in which each level always refers to some other level, whichever way the myth is read. Similarly, each matrix of meanings refers to another matrix, each myth to other myths."[4] Two significant points are raised here. First, the type of thought Lévi-Strauss describes (which may be seen as identical to appositional thought) stays close to nature in that it organizes itself in the way that nature presents itself to the perceiving subject. In this type of thought, the relations between organizational units are modeled after the relations that are recognized as existing in nature. Furthermore, mythic thought produces in the minds of practitioners the direct experience of nature. This involves emphasizing the particular natural relation that is in a practitioner's problematical situation. The purpose of this parallel organization—of relations in nature and relations between units of appositional thought—is succinctly stated by Lévi-Strauss:

> And if it is now asked to what final meanings these mutually significative meanings are referring—since in the last resort they must refer to something—the only reply to emerge from this study is that myths signify the mind that evolves them by making use of the world of which it is itself a part. Thus there is a simultaneous production of the myths themselves, by the mind that generates them and, by the myths, of an image of the world which is already inherent in the structure of the mind.[5]

Lévi-Strauss suggests that the mind can think in a way that is isomorphic to the way nature presents itself: as a set of relations that exist between perceived objects. Thought could be so close to perception that the relations among percepts govern the rational operations of a type of mind.

There is a second point raised by Lévi-Strauss's description of mythic thought. If appositional mind is close to the perceptual as the source of an "image" of the world, such thought closely resembles perception in the immediacy of sensory experience. If mythical thought contains a layered structure, as Lévi-Strauss observes, then it should be possible to describe perception itself as a layered structure. To develop a model of perceptual experience as a multilayered "depth" experience of the world, we turn to Merleau-Ponty, who wrote: "Sense experience is the vital communication with the world which makes it present as a familiar setting of our life. It is to it that the perceived object and the perceiving subject owe their thickness."[6]

A fundamental objective in synthetic inquiries is to provide an image or reproduction of the concrete experience of perceiving the natural. Insofar as perception produces the experience of depth, synthetic systems evoke a semblance of depth. These systems are inquiries into concrete perceptions by means of appositional thought. Since depth is a definitive feature of perception, some understanding of the meaning of depth in perception can contribute to a description of appositional thought. Merleau-Ponty's discussion of the phenomenology of depth perception offers insight into this meaning.

> Depth is a **third dimension** derived from the other two. It will pay us to dwell for a moment upon the third dimension. It has first of all something paradoxical about it. I see objects which hide each other and which consequently I do not see; each one stands behind the other. I see it (the third dimension) and it is not visible, since it goes toward things from a starting point, the body to which I myself am fastened. But the mystery here is a false one. I don't really see it (the third dimension), or if I do, it is only another size (measured by height and width). On the line which lies between my eyes and the horizon, the first (vertical) plane forever hides all the others, and if from side to side I think I see things spread out **in order** before me, it is because they do not completely hide each other. Thus I see each thing to be outside the others, according to some measure otherwise reckoned. . . . We are always on the side of space or beyond it entirely. It is never the case that things **are** one behind the other. The fact that things overlap or are hidden does not enter into their definition, and expresses only an incomprehensible solidarity with one of them—my body. And whatever might be positive in these facts, they are only thoughts that I formulate and not attributes of the things. I know that at this very moment another man, situated elsewhere—or better, God, who is everywhere— could penetrate their "hiding place" and see them openly deployed. Either what I call depth is nothing, or else it is my participation in a Being without restriction, a participation primarily in the being of space beyond every (particular) point of view. Things encroach upon one another **because each is outside of the others.** The proof of this is that I can see depth in a painting which everyone agrees has none and which organizes for me an illusion of an illusion. . . . This two-dimensional being, which makes me see another (dimension), is a being that is opened up . . . —as the men of the Renaissance said, a window.[7]

Depth is, according to Merleau-Ponty, a "participation in a Being without restriction, a participation primarily in the being of space beyond every (particular)

point of view." The primacy of space has already been associated with appositional thought. The body provides vantage points for seeing the world and experiencing it as layers of order. Synthetic inquiries explore the many positions the
body can take in respect to its definitive limits imposed by an absolute space
available as the perception of depth. These inquiries study the transformations
and changes involved in moving from one position to another and then on to
another, coming back perhaps to the first, and on again unceasingly.

Once the dimensionality of perception is recognized, the problem of **ordering the details** that are made present through these dimensions becomes salient.
Again, it is the work of perceiving that provides the model for this ordering. The
organization of percepts must parallel the organization of units of meaning within synthetic inquiries. Regarding the organization of details in perception,
Merleau-Ponty wrote: "To perceive is to render oneself present to something
through the body. All the while the thing keeps its place within the horizon of
the world, and the structuralization consists of putting each detail in perceptual
horizons which belong to it."[8]

At their inner limits, the layers of order constituting the topic of synthetic
inquiry may be seen as "perceptual horizons." Knowledge within these systems
consists of the ability to assign perception to these horizons in such a way as to
produce a meaningful myth. Systems such as the **Tarot** and the **I Ching** provide
horizons in which perceptions may be ordered so as to provide a myth, a cultural
reality, or an answer to a question. The horizons of meaning that compose the
structure of these systems attempt to reproduce the order of nature in culture
by copying them.

The sign-particulars, interpretive codes, and invariant frames are structures
in the mind that provide the precondition for **construction**. Work with structure
(con-struction) is work with these layers. Insofar as structure is nature, these
layers represent structure (the natural) in the mental order. As horizons, they are
relationships imposed on cultural objects, just as perceptual horizons are imposed on natural objects.

While the explication of the model could be carried through with any
synthetic inquiry, economy of space demands that we confine our analysis to
one such inquiry— the **I Ching**. The following remarks on the Chinese mind by
Marcel Granet, a noted Orientalist, aid in an understanding of this synthetic
system.

> The mythical mode of thought—and with it the various techniques that
> aim to order the world—is steeped in the belief that physical things can be
> controlled by their images. The theoreticians of the divining arts, by giving
> to the mythical mode of thought a systematic formulation, succeeded in
> reinforcing this disposition of the Chinese mind. By conceiving of the **Tao**
> as a **principle of Order** that rules both mental activity and the life of the
> universe, one is led to admit that the changes that can be noted in things
> are identical to the substitution of symbols that takes place in the process
> of thought.[9]

The statement "physical things can be controlled by their images" implies that
the essence of a physical thing is its image. If one has possession of an image—a
systematic perception—of a thing, one already has the rudiments of an under-

standing of it. The attitude described by Granet ascribes the proper source of knowledge to an understanding of images that are associated with the perceptual.

Granet ascribes a basic law of identity to the "theoreticians" of Chinese divination. In the order of the world containing mind, the changes that take place in perception are **identical** to the substitutions of symbols that are definitive of the thought process. The relationships that compose thought processes within these Chinese systems parallel the relationships that constitute perception. Granet goes on to observe:

> These ways of thinking did not prevent the ancient Chinese from showing great mechanical abilities: the perfection of their archery and their carriages proves it. But this is how they conceived of the growth of an invention: when one of their philosophers wants to explain the invention of the wheel, he states that the idea was given by the flying seeds whirling in the air.[10]

Granet sees "a principle of Order that rules both mental activity and the life of the universe" as a definition of **tao. Tao** is sometimes defined as the way or direction, or as nature, and this definition is compatible with the argument that direction is the outermost layer of order, and structure (nature) the inner layers.[11]

SIGN PARTICULARS

> In ancient times the holy sages made the Book of Changes thus. Their purpose was to follow the order of their nature and of fate. Therefore they determined the **tao** of heaven and called it the dark and the light. They determined the **tao** of the earth and called it the yielding and the firm. They determined the **tao** of man and called it love and rectitude. They combined these three fundamental powers and doubled them; therefore in the Book of Changes a sign is always formed by six lines.[12]

Thus, the hexagrams in the **I Ching** are conceived as signs. Granet offers an explanation of the notion of signs in Chinese thought.

> What Chinese thought likes to record are not causes and effects but, the order of appearances being of little importance, phenomena conceived of as peculiar, although issuing from the same root: **equally demonstrative, they seem substitutable one for the other.** A river that runs dry, a landslide, a man who changes into a woman—all may announce the approaching end of a dynasty. These are four aspects of the same event: An obsolete order disappears to make room for a new order. Everything deserves to be noted down, as a precursive sign or as confirmation of a sign—or of a series of signs—but nothing encourages the search of an efficacious cause. . . . Instead of considering the stream of events as a series of phenomena that may be measured and then related, the Chinese see in perceptual facts a mass of concrete signals.[13]

Perception, then, is involved with the recording of masses of signs. And since knowledge and thinking are identical to perception, the I Ching addresses itself to the problem of systematization of **particular signs.**

According to the Great Treatise, a hexagram is a sign. But actually it is a special type of sign—a "master sign"—in that its meaning is derived from its capacity to organize a number of particular signs under its heading. A hexagram is composed of a lower and an upper trigram; these trigrams represent the particular signs that are arranged to compose a hexagram. At the same time, the hexagram is the "root" from which the particular signs issue in the particular situation. The relation between the trigrams and the hexagram is that of the relation between the particular and the general. Once these levels have been established, the question of which is the cause of the other is spurious. To the appositional mind it does not matter which comes from which.

Polanyi writes of sign particulars as aspects of knowledge that are tacit in understanding. His analysis suggests that we come to know the meanings of the trigrams through a recognition of the hexagram as a whole, as a gestalt whose comprehension follows from a simultaneous grasping of the sign particulars—the lower and upper trigrams, and the nuclear trigrams intertwined with the primary trigrams. When a practitioner of the I Ching comes upon an understanding of a hexagram, this new awareness is apt to be dramatic. This instantaneous knowing also characterizes recognition of a figure in the Street Gestalt Completion Test, or the recognition of a snake camouflaged as a pile of leaves. Perhaps it is for this reason that the I Ching refers to a hexagram as the Time.

At the outset of an inquiry among practitioners of the I Ching, a question is asked and the coins are thrown. The inquiry begins with the master sign—the hexagram, which can be regarded as a symbol—and **then** moves toward the discovery of what is implicit in the hexagram—the trigrams and lines. The procedure in science is exactly the opposite. The formulation of a theory begins with elementary signs—logical and extralogical—that constitute the symbolic vocabulary of the theory, which can be known only tacitly in form. The analysis then establishes an elaborate theoretical formulation, which is presented as an entire deductive system. The theory itself can be comprehended explicitly; it is what the theory is **about** that remains tacit.

That the I Ching is directed toward the level of the sign particulars rather than toward elaborate networks of concepts is suggested by the fact that the analyses presented in the Wilhelm-Baynes I Ching begin with the presentation of the hexagram, and then explain the hexagram in terms of the trigrams found within it. In our ethnographic studies of practitioners of the I Ching, the following process has been systematically observed: (1) A sign (hexagram) is constructed through an apparently random process—throwing coins or yarrow stalks; (2) The particulars of the sign are then considered, in order to see what can be found as metaphors for the situation described by the question that occasioned the throwing; (3) An indefinite number of views can be posited on the situation, depending only on the particulars represented by the primary trigrams. The particulars of the nuclear trigrams may also be considered, although these trigrams—which are in a way more tacit than the primary trigrams—are less apt to come into the talk about the situation.

The layers of the sign particulars are made available through attending to the role played by the trigrams in any given hexagram. The trigrams are the concrete images upon which a hexagram is based. They represent the concrete manifestation of the situation imbedded in the hexagram. Thus they are the source of the Images for the hexagrams, which metaphorically describe the situation in nature. For example, the Image for the hexagram Waiting (nourishment), states:

> Clouds rise up to the heaven:
> The Image of Waiting.
> Thus the superior man eats and drinks,
> Is joyous and of good cheer.[14]

The linear form of the hexagram is:

The hexagram can be separated into the lower trigram **Ch'ien** (heaven) and the upper trigram **K'an** (water). The situation of clouds rising in the heavens can be represented as two discrete signs—clouds and heaven. These particulars suggest the meaning of the situation as a whole.

> When clouds rise in the sky, it is a sign that it will rain. There is nothing to do but to wait until the rain falls. It is the same in life when destiny is at work. We should not worry and seek to shape the future by interfering in things before the time is ripe. We should quietly fortify the body with food and drink and the mind with gladness and good cheer. Fate comes when it will, and thus we are ready.[15]

The nuclear trigrams **Li** (fire) and **Tui** (lake) are overlapped with the upper and lower trigrams. They represent aspects of the situation that are even more tacit than the primary trigrams with respect to conscious knowing of it, but that also must be fully understood if one is to grasp the meaning of the situation.

Trigrams in a hexagram function in a manner comparable to the elementary signs (concepts) in a scientific theory. Trigrams provide elements from which knowledge is derived. They differ from concepts in that they are not really building blocks of theories, but rather receptors or basins in which sense experience is assigned and collected. The trigrams arrange perceptions into significant groupings. They map the territory of perceptual life so that the significance of percepts of all sorts can be understood. Percepts are deposited in the particulars of a system and thus become recognized as an Image. Work on the layer of the sign particulars involves the assigning of the concrete events of perceptual life to the appropriate concrete image represented by the respective trigrams.

Much of the work with the sign particulars is done by the conventionalized assigning of certain perceptions (or perceptual images) to certain trigrams. These conventions are outlined in the Great Treatise. Each trigram is manifested in three categories of perceptual life: in nature, as Image; in culture, as a member of the family (the paradigmatic cultural unit in ancient China); and in mind, as a psychological attribute. These categories stand as the conventionalized particulars of the sign particulars represented by the trigrams. These conventionalized particulars do not exhaust the area of the sign particulars. Problematic perceptions do occur. However, the conventionalized categorization of sense experience into nature/culture/psyche is adequate for most practical purposes. The conventionalized categories for the eight trigrams were shown in Chapter 3. Practitioners are apt to offer a rationale for the association of the trigrams with their given conventionalized particulars. For example, it is enough for some practitioners to see that **Kên** is the mountain because $\equiv\!\equiv$ resembles the concrete perception of a mountain.

In addition to the conventional categories of nature/culture/psyche in which a given trigram is said to be manifested, there exist chains of conventionalized associations linked to particular hexagrams. For example, each trigram is a metaphor for an animal. "The Creative acts in the horse, the Receptive in the cow, the Arousing in the dragon, the Gentle in the cock, the Abysmal in the pig, the Clinging in the pheasant, Keeping Still in the dog, the Joyous in the sheep."[16] And for each trigram there are myriad other signs. Conventionalized or linked with the Creative, we find that "the Creative is heaven. It is round, it is the prince, the father, jade, metal, cold, ice; it is deep red, a good horse, an old horse, a lean horse, a wild horse, tree fruit."[17]

Of course, the conventionalized particulars do not exhaust the realities of perceptual life. Many percepts do not seem to fit any of the trigrams. Competency in the practice involves the ability to assign an extremely peculiar particular to the sign particular (trigram) to which it belongs. Appropriate assignments are tantamount to **seeing,** which is the end of appositional knowledge. Granet writes:

> We are dealing here only with signals, for which the qualitative estimates of size and frequency are irrelevant. The most useful of precursive signs are, in fact, the most peculiar, the most minute, the rarest, the least obvious. A bird that destroys its nest indicates a breakdown—both physical and moral—in the Empire, since the sentiment of domestic piety is lacking even among the smallest of animals. The purpose of the catalogue is not to discover **sequences;** its aim is rather to reveal solidarities. . . . Far from trying to isolate facts from their time and place references, the Chinese see them only as signs revealing the qualities specific to a given Time and to a given Space.[18]

The trigrams, as sign particulars, provide the means whereby puzzling particulars of perception are given a base. The **I Ching** is used as an oracle when the perception of a situation is so diffuse and disorganized that a solidarity in the situation cannot be seen. Through the trigrams a connection between the particulars of a situation and a system of reliable and omnipresent signs can be revealed. An inquirer is given a definite picture of the situation, and the unique nature of the situation seen to be a special case of one of the hexagrams. Thus, in times of stress, when the world appears to vanish and disorder prevails, the oracle is used to invoke the world—to reveal the solidarity of the stress situations with enduring images. In such situations one may perceive objects but may have lost the world that grounds them, and it is the aim of the **I Ching** to reestablish the world's presence in the mind of an inquirer. In this manner the **I Ching** functions to invoke or establish the concrete in times when a practitioner's thoughts are lost in myriad fleeting sensations and disengaged abstractions. The I Ching can accomplish this only because its signs can be readily pointed out in nature: There is heaven; you are standing on earth; there is a lake. It is through the concrete sign particulars that the practitioner can be certain that any peculiar perception is ultimately a "hidden" particular of the sign particulars that compose the elementary units in the system.

The sign particulars determine within the complex of appositional thought what may be termed the **message.** The intermingling of the particular trigrams communicates to a practitioner the ostensive subject matter that is relevant to the question posed. For example, the image of fire on the mountain, which constitutes the hexagram, the Wanderer, suggests to a practitioner a definite state of affairs. This state of affairs is a metaphor of the situation as a whole. The Image is **about** the particular problem of a practitioner. It provides a thematic device to which the particularity of the problem **must** be referred. Discussion of the problem consists of the continual reference of its particularity to the particularity posed by the Image. The Image provides an immediate contextual message to the practitioner, but only at the cost of stripping the problem of its own isolated uniqueness by converting it to a version of a definite theme.

CODES

The sign particulars may be conceived as "mapping" the territory of a given perceptual problem. They highlight (extend) perception by providing enduring referents (the trigrams) in which the flux of perceptual experience can be deposited. As perceptions are elevated to the level of signs through this process, a new layer of appositional thought emerges. After they are seen in relation to a matrix of signs that are identical to natural, cultural, and psychological reality, their reality must be interpreted.

Signs are seen to function together in definite ways. These ways contribute to the meanings of a sign complex: the special sign relationships that effect a hypermediation, which are called **symbols.** The hexagram the Wanderer consists of the sign particulars mountain and fire. But its sense would be incomplete without the knowledge that fire is **on top of** the mountain, and it is through this relation between the two sign particulars that the symbolic meaning of the hexagram can be grasped.

Since a hexagram contains two trigrams, the meaning of the hexagram will always involve the subjects in the situation (sign particulars) and their relationships as well—which we will call interpretive codes.

The principle of identity mentioned in connection with the sign particulars applies to the interpretive codes as well. The codes themselves correspond to relationships that nature exhibits. The relationships of the I Ching are identical to concrete relationships that can exist in nature between its Images. Hence the rationality of the I Ching is based on the analogy between its relationships and the concrete relationships seen in nature.

Competency in interpretation involves the **seeing** of these relations between subjects. The I Ching provides a multiplicity of such codes that have no clear-cut rules of application. For our purpose, we distinguish between two types of codes, (1) **immediate sensory codes** and (2) **extended ultracodes.**

Immediate Sensory Codes

The positions of the trigrams in the I Ching illustrate our concept of "immediate sensory codes." Wilhelm wrote: "The positions of the trigrams in relation to each other must be taken into account. The lower trigram is below, within, behind; the upper is above, without, and in front. The lines stressed in the upper trigram are always characterized as 'going'; those stressed in the lower trigram, as 'coming'."[19]

A code is here defined as a relationship describing the pattern of function between a number of signs. Immediate sensory codes are those available to a perceiving subject. They are analogous to the most familiar relations existing between objects in everyday perception. They include relations that can be tested by the insertion of the body into the midst of them—hence the descriptions **immediate** and **sensory.** For example, a person can easily ascertain the position of a tree in relation to a stream, for the "test" of such a relation is available in the seeing. An observer atop a mountain might describe the tree as below the stream. It would be possible, however, to move to a position between the tree and the stream, by standing in the stream and pointing up to the tree. The body's ability to interpose itself changes the relation between the two objects.

An immediate sensory code is a relationship that can be changed by the interposition of the body. It is the code of things that have an "earthy" existence in that one can perceive them through the transportation of the body into the center of the relationship. Many immediate sensory codes are present in the I **Ching.** Some of them are listed and elaborated here:

Below/Above. The relation between primary trigrams in any hexagram may be interpreted on a vertical axis of below/above. Wilhelm provided innumerable examples of an interpretation generated from the below/above. Consider his commentary on the hexagram **Lü** (Treading, Conduct).

The name of the hexagram means on the one hand the right way of conducting oneself. Heaven, the father, is above, and the lake, the youngest daughter, is below. This shows the difference between high and low, upon which composure—correct social conduct—depends. On the other hand, the word for the name of the hexagram Treading, means literally treading upon something. The small and cheerful [**Tui**] treads upon the large and strong [**Ch'ien**].[20]

Within/Without. This code is common in the practice of the I **Ching,** defining an important axis of interpretation. Wilhelm provides an example that involves this axis, and below/above as well. The hexagram **Chien** (Development, Gradual Progress) is illustrative of the within/without code.

Wilhelm wrote:

> This hexagram is made up of **Sun** (wood, penetration) above, i.e., without, and **Kên** (mountain, stillness) below, i.e., within. A tree on a mountain develops slowly according to the law of its being and consequently stands firmly rooted. This gives the idea of a development that proceeds gradually, step by step. The attributes of the trigrams also point to this: within is tranquillity, which guards against precipitate actions, and without is penetration, which makes development and progress possible.[21]

Behind/In Front. Primary trigrams may also be related on an axis of behind/in front. This relation is reminiscent of Merleau-Ponty's statement on the horizon. That is, the sense of extension that finds its limits at the horizon is made possible by the fact that objects partially hide other objects—that objects can be arranged so that certain objects "cover" a complete view of other objects. The "covered" objects are behind the complete objects, which are in front. An example of a Wilhelm interpretation based on this code is the hexagram **Kuei Mei** (The Marrying Maiden).

Wilhelm wrote:

> Above we have **Chên**, the eldest son, and below, **Tui**, the youngest daughter. The man leads and the girl follows him in gladness. The picture is that of the entrance of the girl into her husband's house. . . .
> The same is true of all voluntary relationships between human beings. While legally regulated relationships evince a fixed connection between duties and rights, relationships based on personal inclination depend in the long run entirely on tactful reserve. . . .
> The meaning is that a girl entering a family with the consent of the wife will not rank outwardly as the equal of the latter, but will withdraw modestly into the background.[22]

Whereas below/above relations are basic to Wilhelm's interpretations and within/without relations abound, the behind/in front relations—though mentioned—play an inferential role. Such is the case in the example cited above. However, being a frequent relation between objects of perception, it is available as a code for interpretation of hexagrams. In a given situation it may be basic. A competent practitioner will see it as a basic constituting relationship of the sign particulars of the given hexagram.

Coming/Going. The relations we have been considering have a common factor—they are static and can be described as axes. But perception is not exhausted by these static categories, for there is also movement in perceptual life, and the I **Ching** contains codes representing dynamic relations. Birds move across the sky. They come into view and then go out of sight. Their perceptual relationship

vis-à-vis a perceiving subject is that of coming and going. The trigrams in the I
Ching are also interpreted as coming and going. To requote Wilhelm: "The lines
stressed in the upper trigram are always characterized as 'going'; those stressed in
the lower trigram as 'coming'."[23] Thus, in addition to static relations, the I
Ching posits dynamic relations between its sign particulars. The hexagram **Lin**
(Approach), for example, contains a dynamic interpretive code.

Wilhelm commented:

> The Chinese word **lin** has a range of meanings that is not exhausted by any
> single word of another language. The ancient explanations in the Book of
> Changes gives as its first meaning, "becoming great." What becomes great are
> the two strong lines growing into the hexagram from below; the light-
> giving power expands with them. The meaning is then further extended to
> include the concept of approach, especially the approach of what is strong
> and highly placed in relation to what is lower.[24]

Wilhelm's interpretation points out that interpretive codes used for the interpretation of a number of signs **may** be a hybrid of several distinguishable codes
combined for the exigencies of a particular throwing. Again we are reminded of
the **bricoleur,** who must often combine his tools in strange and unique ways to
fulfill the requirements of a particular task. These codes exist within the "toolbox" of a practitioner of the I Ching.

Overlapping, Intermingling, Embedding. In relations between the primary and
nuclear trigrams we encounter certain codes that are both complex and subtle.
Perceptual life always includes relations between percepts that are immediately
sensory while at the same time characterized by a certain ambiguity and a veiledness. Some signs may remain unnoticed, but then suddenly come into view when
the line of interpretation is altered—that is, when the practitioner changes position through the introduction of a new code. One could say that the signs were
always there for the seeing, but had functioned as background prior to the moment of changing the code. Such background relationships become figure when
one considers the nuclear trigrams vis-à-vis the hexagram as a whole.
      On the nuclear trigrams, Wilhelm wrote:

> But it is decidedly necessary to make use of the so-called nuclear trigrams,
> **hu kua.** These form the four middle lines of each hexagram, and overlap
> each other so that the middle line of the one falls within the other. An
> example . . . will make this clear:

The hexagram **Li**, the Clinging, Fire . . . , shows a nuclear trigram complex consisting of the four lines ☲. The two nuclear trigrams are **Tui**, the Joyous, as the upper (☱), and **Sun**, the Gentle, as the lower (☴). . . .

The structure of the hexagrams therefore shows a stage-by-stage over-lapping of different trigrams and their influences. . . .

Thus . . . the beginning and top line are each part of one trigram only. . . . The second and the fifth lines belong each to two trigrams. . . . The third and fourth lines belong each to three trigrams. . . . The result is that the beginning and top line tend in a sense to drop out of connection, while a state of equilibrium, usually favorable, obtains in the case of the second and the fifth lines, and the two middle lines are conditioned by the fact that each belongs to both nuclear trigrams, which disturbs the balance in all except particularly favorable cases.[25]

That percepts may be overlapped, intermingled, and imbedded in each other in the nuclear trigrams presents the possibility of complex relations between signs. First, recognition of the nuclear trigrams requires the introduction of special interpretive codes. There is a basic ambiguity not only in the interpretation of a trigram, but in the seeing of lines as well. The bottom and top lines belong to one trigram each, the 2nd and 5th to two trigrams each, and the 3rd and 4th to three trigrams each. This observation suggests situations in perceptual life that cannot be described only as compositions of isolated elements connected along given axes and vectors. The hexagram, when seen as a gestalt, hides primary trigrams; primary trigrams in turn hide nuclear trigrams that are imbedded in them. Nuclear trigrams intermingle to provide a context for the primary tri-grams. When we focus on lines, the background may contain as many as three trigrams in addition to the hexagram. Such a complex state of affairs often leads to difficulty in interpretation, especially when a line exists (or is contained) in trigrams with contradictory meanings. Codes involving the simultaneous consid-eration of nuclear and primary trigrams are attempts to deal with the ambiguity of certain situations. That a given trigram can overlap, intermingle with, or be imbedded in another implies that certain perceptual situations are complexities that can be inquired into only with the recognition that their meaning is derived from each sign functioning **for** the interpretation of the other signs.

For interpretive purposes, the bottom and top lines of a hexagram, be-cause each is a part of only one trigram, are considered to be the least important. Wilhelm wrote: "As a rule the lowest and the top lines are not taken into ac-count, whereas the four middle lines are active within the time."[26] Thus lines that are most ambiguous play a greater role in interpretation; lines that are not ambiguous (belonging to a single trigram) are given less attention. This is not always the case (in **Fu**, Return, with a firm line in the first position and yielding lines in the other positions, the bottom line is very important), but it serves to indicate that the **I Ching** especially addresses itself to ambiguous situations. If a perceptual situation is not ambiguous there is no reason to consult the oracle. On the other hand, in situations where perceptions are not evident the oracle provides a guide for interpretation. It can do this because the ambiguities within a hexagram are considered significant aspects in generating interpretations. The ambiguity of a perceptual situation is reflectively related to this ambiguity within a hexagram.

The **I Ching** generates interpretations in ambiguity by a complex balancing of individual lines with other lines and with the trigrams to which these lines belong. Analogy and similarity serve as guiding principles in interpretation. For instance, line 2 is related to line 5 in a hexagram because each is a part of two trigrams. At the same time they are middle lines in primary trigrams. An interpretation can be constructed within an ambiguous situation because the lines, ambiguous in themselves, can balance other ambiguous lines. Line 2 and line 5 are related by being ambiguous in similar ways. Similarities can be exploited by a competent practitioner to generate an interpretation in a situation where it would otherwise be impossible.

Overlapped, intermingled, and imbedded codes provide ways of interpreting ambiguous situations. An interpretation can be accomplished by balancing given lines with related lines and the trigrams in which they are imbedded. Consider the hexagram **Chung Fu** (Inner Truth), with a nine in the second place.

The line to be interpreted is in the second place. First, the text reads:

Nine in the second place means:
A crane calling in the shade.
Its young answers it.
I have a good goblet.
I will share it with you.[27]

Wilhelm provided the following interpretation:

This refers to the involuntary influence of a man's inner being upon persons of kindred spirit. The crane need not show itself on a high hill. It may be quite hidden when it sounds its call; yet its young will hear its note, will recognize it and give answer. When there is a joyous mood, there a comrade will appear to share a glass of wine.

This is the echo awakened in men through spiritual attraction. Whenever a feeling is voiced with truth and frankness, whenever a deed is the clear expression of sentiment, a mysterious and far-reaching influence is exerted. At first it acts on those who are inwardly receptive. But the circle grows larger and larger. The root of all influence lies in one's own inner being: given true and vigorous expression in word and deed, its effect is great. The effect is but the reflection of something that emanates from one's own heart. Any deliberate intention of an effect would only destroy the possibility of producing it. Confucius says about this line:

The superior man abides in his room. If his words are well spoken, he meets with assent at a distance of more than a thousand miles. How much more than from near by! If the superior man abides in his room and his words are not well spoken, he meets with contradiction at a distance of more than a thousand miles. How much more than from near by! Words go forth from one's own person and exert their influence on men. Deeds are born close at hand and become visible far away. Words and deeds are the hinges and bowstring of the superior man. As hinge and bowstring move, they bring honor or disgrace. Through words and deeds the superior man moves heaven and earth. Must one not, then, be cautious?[28]

Time, Space, and Immediate Sensory Codes. Immediate sensory codes have been defined as those codes available as perceptions that can be operationally validated through interposing the body into the midst of the perceptual field the codes bring into being. Interpretation of a hexagram by means of these codes provides a sort of "snapshot"—an encapsulated moment of perceptual life. Relations that are posited by these codes are primarily spatial. The hexagram stays in place—as a virtual map of a given moment—while the practitioner generates interpretations by moving from one code to another. Wilhelm maintained: "The situation represented by the hexagram as a whole is called the time."[29] Immediate sensory codes generate interpretations by relating happenings in time with happenings in space. A given situation can be analyzed as a position on a space–time continuum. The spatial relations given by immediate sensory codes are necessary for understanding the situation as a whole.

In the **I Ching,** time is the problem and space is the resource employed to provide a solution. The complex problems confronting an inquirer regarding the temporal situation are resolved by an answer that lies in the domain of spatial relations. Certainty of a temporal situation can be achieved to the extent that its spatial determinants can be ascertained. Codes that are based on spatial relations can transpose temporal uncertainties into concrete perceptions which can in turn be interpreted. It is neither a simple nor automatic process, because the perceptual is dense. Signs distribute themselves in definite horizons or arrangements. These arrangements are made present to the body, and the body experiences itself in a space. But since there exist an indefinite number of horizons, space itself becomes complex. The problem of time is resolved by structuring the possible spatial arrangements available to perception. Any given time is seen to be "resolved" by understanding the "space" to which it belongs.

Granet comments on the problem of time and space:

The Chinese concept of the Universe is neither monistic nor dualistic nor even pluralistic. It is derived from the idea that the Whole distributes itself into hierarchical groups, where it is contained entirely. These groupings are differentiated only by the power of the Efficacious that is specific to each one. Tied to **Space-Time** units that are hierarchically ranked as well as incommensurable they differ by their content and even more by their tension: they are seen as realization, more or less complex, more or less diluted, more or less concentrated, of the Efficacious. Knowledge has for its first and last object a plan of organization of the Universe, which seems to be realized, thanks to a hierarchical arrangement of concrete nomenclatures. In the same way that they abstain from thinking conceptually by gender and species, the Chinese have no taste for syllogism—of what use anyway would syllogistic deduction be for a thought that refuses to derive Space and Time from their concrete character?[30]

The idea that "the Whole distributes itself into hierarchical groups" describes the dialectical way in which perceptual life is organized. The I Ching begins with perceptual life, which is recognizable as a whole or "global" phenomenon. There is no end to the synthesis of the perceptions generated by the senses. We never "pass out" of sensory experience but rather move from one typical arrangement to another. In this way, the whole that constitutes our perceptual life comes to be distributed in "hierarchical groups." Each impinging detail is assigned to a particular group of sensations, and each sign is recognized as significant through its unity with other signs. These multiple arrangements of signs are identical to perceptual horizons. They are "spaces" that are constructed by the way signs are distributed among the layers of order.

Granet says that these groupings are differentiated only by "the power of the Efficacious that is specific to each one." In other words, perceptual life is possible because the body can be presented with arrangements of signs in multiple ways. The difference in arrangements, according to Granet, is a difference in the "power of the Efficacious." The Efficacious can be seen to be the body, for it is through the body that a person affects the world in which he finds himself. The immediate sensory codes are a type of perceptual arrangement in which the power of the efficacious is maximum. In such arrangements, the body is capable of producing an affect—of inserting itself as an absolute criterion. This type of perceptual distribution provides a situation where the body-as-instrument could be transported to the problematic scene in order to obtain an immediate solution; the power of the body within such arrangements is such that it need not be compelled to wait for its results.

Extended Ultracodes

There are also perceptual arrangements in which the body does not have the power to intervene. Instead, it must stay fixed in a given position and await the passing of signs. Furthermore, its normal sensory capacity is limited and signs are available only through a single sense. Codes involving such relations—which we shall call **extended ultracodes**—are present in the I Ching. They are "extended," because they represent arrangements of signs that are beyond "normal" perceptual space (where the power of the body is at a maximum) and "ultra" because they function as "checks" of produced interpretations and ways for deciding the ultimate meaning of the particular time designated by a hexagram. Such codes provide for the practitioner the capability of knowing the possible order that will develop out of the given time.

Immediate sensory codes primarily involve terrestrial "inner" space—that is, arrangements of signs in which the body contains the arrangements. In the I Ching there exist interpretive codes that are founded on celestial phenomena. Such codes are common in mythic systems, in which celestial events are significant to terrestrial events. In Sadhu's analysis of the **Tarot** and the Hermetic tradition in which it is grounded, for example, we find the statement: "What is below is similar to what is above, and what is above is similar to what is below in order

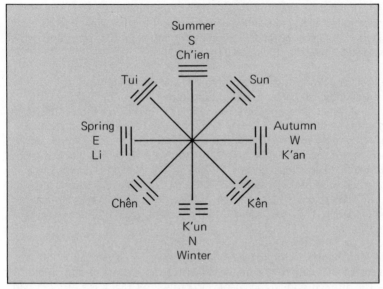

Figure 18. Sequence of Earlier Heaven, or Primal Arrangement. Note that the Chinese place south at the top.
Source: Richard Wilhelm and Cary F. Baynes, trans., **The I Ching or Book of Changes**. Princeton, N. J.: Princeton University Press, Bollingen Series 19, 1967, Figure 1.

to ensure the perpetuation of the miracles of the Unique Thing."[31] Lévi-Strauss has shown that astronomical codes have an important place in primitive mythological systems.[32]

Two celestial-based codes within the I Ching are examples of extended ultracodes. They are not absolute sources of interpretations generated by other codes. Since within the system there is a basic identity between subjective and objective states, these ultracodes provide recurrent corroboration of relations existent but not necessarily evident in "inner" space. They can accomplish this because they are grounded in a space of a different distribution—celestial "outer" space. Practitioners can turn to celestial space for answers when terrestrial spatial arrangements yield none. The sign-particulars (trigrams) exist in heaven and on earth. Furthermore, and perhaps more important, the complex relations between the sign-particulars and the body exist as the coordinates of both spaces. What is explicit in one space is implicit in the other, and vice versa.

Turning to the **Shuo Kuo**—Discussion of the Trigrams—we encounter this statement: "They determined the tao of heaven and called it the dark and the light."[33] These dark and light conditions of celestial space have been "mapped" to produce two arrangements which are introduced at the beginning of the treatise. The first map is called the "Sequence of Earlier Heaven," or "Primal Arrangement"; the second map is called the "Sequence of Later Heaven," or "Inner World Arrangement" (Figures 18 and 19).

These maps have two important features. First, they are conceived as sequences. The respective trigrams are organized into particular cycles, each sign representing a change in an aspect of the night sky or day sky. The idea of time

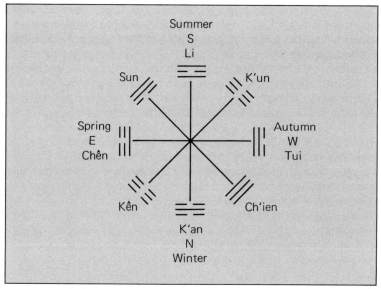

Figure 19. Sequence of Later Heaven, or Inner World Arrangement.
Source: Richard Wilhelm and Cary F. Baynes, trans., **The I Ching or Book of Changes.**
Princeton, N. J.: Princeton University Press, Bollingen Series 19, 1967, Figure 2.

is derived from these relationships of celestial change. The fact that the heavens are perceived as in continual change provides the basis for understanding time in the **I Ching.** In this respect, Wilhelm commented on the Image of Heaven, the first hexagram:

> Since there is only one heaven, the doubling of the trigram **Ch'ien** of which heaven is the image, indicates the movement of heaven. One complete revolution of heaven makes a day, and the repetition of the trigrams means that each day is followed by another. This creates the idea of time. Since it is the same heaven moving with untiring power, there is also created the idea of duration both in and beyond time, a movement that never stops nor slackens, just as one day follows another in an unending course.[34]

Time is the primordial synthetic concept and it is to the problem of its creation that the **I Ching** is addressed. As a general term, it is the result of the synthesis of all the sign particulars (trigrams). A hexagram is the result of the synthesis of two trigrams and is a representation of a **specific** time. Synthetic interpretation of a particular time presupposes the existence of a synthesis of all trigrams in a sequence, which serves as a model of time in general. Insights into any trigram can result from a consideration of arrangements or sequences of trigrams and, of course, from the sequencing of the hexagrams themselves.[35] Thus the Primal and Inner World arrangements can have a bearing on any hexagram. Perceptually, the cognition of such a synthesis is not immediately available. In order to observe these changes and to accomplish their synthesis the body must adopt a fixed vantage point. Its power of effect is at a minimum. It must restrict its sensory inputs to the activity of a single sense—the visual. The perception of the changing heavens is gained only through the fixing of the instrument that is the body and enduring in the chosen spot.

In the map for the Primal Arrangement, **Ch'ien** is in the south, and **K'un** in the north. "**Ch'ien**, heaven, and **K'un**, earth, determine the north-south axis."[36] **Ch'ien** has been associated with celestial movement. **K'un**, on the other hand, may be said to be associated with terrestrial solidarity and fixity.

> Just as there is only one heaven, so too there is only one earth. In the hexagram of heaven the doubling of the trigram implies duration in time, but in the hexagram of earth the doubling connotes the solidity and exten- sion in space by virtue of which the earth is able to carry and preserve all things that live and move upon it.[37]

The association of fixity with the north is further corroborated when we consid- er that the North Star is also the pole star. That is, to an earthbound observer the stars are seen to move from east to west, **except** for the North Star, which remains in fixed position. Perceptually, the entire celestial domain rotates around this fixed point. If an observer fixes his body with his head facing north and his feet to the south, his body figuratively "becomes" the north-south axis. From this fixed vantage point the heavens appear to move around the body. The moon, planets, zodiacal constellations, and eventually the sun, will pass by. In the innumerable positions that the body may assume, this position is the only one in which the significant movements of the heavens registered in the **I Ching** may be observed. In order to perceive the relationships that constitute the ex- tended ultracodes, the body must "reproduce" the yielding properties of the earth. It must minimize its involvement with terrestrial things in order to see what otherwise would remain hidden. In the stillness of bodily movement the essence of time is revealed: objectively, as the movement of the heavens, and subjectively, as the duration and transmutation of bodily moods and conscious states. Of the north, Wilhelm wrote: "The north [symbolizes] the place where [a person] reports on what he has done. At this time he must be alone and ob- jective. In this sacred hour he must do without companions, so that the purity of the moment may not be spoiled."[38] The reference here is to a sacred time in which a man leaves his terrestrial attachments and faces the cosmos alone.

Turning to a second feature of the maps we find that the Sequence of the Earlier Heaven is known also as the Before-the-World Sequence,[39] while the Sequence of the Later Heaven is known also as the Inner World Arrangement. The former sequence refers to the night sky and the latter to the day sky. At night the movements of myriad celestial bodies are observable, while during the day the sun is usually the only celestial body that is visible. Quite literally, at night the earth is a phantom presence of shadows while the heavens stand out in clear perspective. The night presents a strange situation in which the area that provides the ground for the body is visually an elusive shadow world while the area farthest from the body is perceptually distinct. At night the "outer world" is distinctly seen. The **I Ching** refers to this arrangement as Before-the-World. What is implicitly **seen** at night are perceptual relations that become explicit when the sun rises. As the day begins, the terrestrial space is transmuted from a shadow world to a world inhabited by myriad and distinct objects in relation. At night the world is not perceptually evident—only the extremities that mark the boundary of the world are seen. In the day the situation is reversed. The celestial bodies are obliterated and the "inner world" space is revealed. The nature of the obliteration is also reversed—at night the terrestrial is obliterated by darkness; in the day the celestial is obliterated by light. Thus the I Ching chronicles two kinds of space available to perception—an outer space seen at night and an inner space seen in the day. These spaces correspond in turn to our two types of interpretive codes—the ultracodes to outer celestial space, and the immediate sensory codes to inner terrestrial space.

Accompanying the Primal Arrangement is the following passage:

> Heaven and earth determine the direction. The forces of mountain and lake are united. Thunder and wind arouse each other. Water and fire do not combat each other. Thus are the eight trigrams intermingled.
>
> Counting that which is going into the past depends on the forward movement. Knowing that which is to come depends on the backward movement. This is why the Book of Changes has backward-moving numbers.[40]

In the Primal Arrangement, a particular point of view is expressed. We might term this "nature's point of view." The arrangement of trigrams is one that might be perceived by a transcendental subject who is posited to be above and outside the boundaries of outer space. Such an ideal vantage point results in the perception of miraculous relations. For instance, "water and fire do not combat each other." That is, oppositions that would cause destruction when intermingled in terrestrial "inner" space are seen as compatible. This is a contradiction to ordinary terrestrial sense. But if we imagine a transcendental vantage point, opposites could intermingle without mutual destruction. Moreover there is a cognitive referent that accounts for the arrangement as well. If we consider outer space to be the opposite of inner space, we would expect **terrestrial** fire and water to nullify each other, and **celestial** fire and water to intermingle without nullification. From "nature's point of view," relationships that would be impossible on earth exist in the heavens. In nature all is included; a miracle in one space is commonplace in another. This point of view is expressed throughout the I Ching.

> The Master said: What need has nature of thought and care? In nature all things return to their common sources and are distributed along different paths; through one action, the fruits of a hundred thoughts are realized. What need has nature of thought, of care?
>
> When the sun goes, the moon comes; when the moon goes, the sun comes. Sun and moon alternate; thus light comes into existence. When cold goes, heat comes; when heat goes, cold comes. Cold and heat alternate, and thus the year completes itself. The past contracts. The future expands. Contraction and expansion act upon each other; hereby arises that which furthers. . . .
>
> Whatever goes beyond this indeed transcends all knowledge. When a man comprehends the divine and understands the transformations, he lifts his nature to the level of the miraculous.[41]

The relationships of the Primal Arrangement that determine one set of ultra-codes are organized as pairs of opposites.

> Within the Primal Arrangement the forces always take effect as pairs of opposites. Thunder, the electrically charged force, awakens the seeds of the old year. Its opposite, the wind, dissolves the rigidity of the winter ice. The rain moistens the seeds, enabling them to germinate, while its opposite, the sun, provides the necessary warmth. Hence the saying: "Water and fire do not combat each other." Then come the backward moving forces. Keeping Still stops further expansion; germination begins. Its opposite, the Joyous, brings about the joys of the harvest. Finally there come into play the directing forces—the Creative, representing the great law of existence, and the Receptive, representing shelter in the womb, into which everything returns after completing the cycle of life.[42]

Two relationships can be derived from this basic arrangement of paired opposites. Each of these relationships serves as a code for interpretation of a given hexagram. Opposites interrelate as **complements,** in which their influences intermingle in an advantageous way. On the other hand, opposites may be considered as **conflictants,** in which the relationships are those of mutual destruction and misfortune. To exemplify these interpretative codes, the last two hexagrams in the sequence—After Completion and Before Completion—can be considered.

After Completion, ☰☷, has the following Image:

> Water over fire: the Image of the condition
> In After Completion.
> Thus the superior man
> Takes thought of misfortune
> And arms himself against it in advance.[43]

Wilhelm offered an interpretation of the situation using a code in which water and fire are in conflict. Hence there are warnings of misfortune and the advice of caution:

> When water in a kettle hangs over fire, the two elements stand in relation and thus generate energy (cf. the production of steam). But the resulting tension demands caution. If the water boils over, the fire is extinguished and its energy is lost. If the heat is too great, the water evaporates into the air. These elements here brought into relation and thus generating energy are by nature hostile to each other. Only the most extreme caution can prevent damage. In life too there are junctures when all forces are in balance and work in harmony, so that everything seems to be in the best of order. In such times only the sage recognizes the moments that bode danger and knows how to banish it by means of timely precautions.[44]

The hexagram Before Completion, ☰☰ , which is the opposite and mirror

image of After Completion, has the following Image:

> Fire over water:
> The image of the condition before transition.
> Thus the superior man is careful
> In the differentiation of things,
> So that each finds its place.[45]

Wilhelm's interpretation is most interesting. He starts with the idea that the opposites are also moving in opposite directions so that they remain unrelated. However, the task of a man in achieving an effect is to ascertain a way in which they can be related. The connotation here is that if one is careful, opposite forces can be related in a productive way. This interpretation is made possible through the exercise of a code based on the possibility of complementary relationships between paired opposites. Wilhelm commented:

> When fire, which by nature flames upward, is above, and water, which flows downward, is below, their effects take opposite directions and remain unrelated. If we wish to achieve an effect, we must first investigate the nature of the forces in question and ascertain their proper place. . . . They will have the desired effect, and completion will be achieved. But in order to handle external forces properly, we must above all arrive at the correct standpoint ourselves, for only from this vantage can we work correctly.[46]

The relationship of paired opposites is the primary basis of the rationality of the **I Ching**. The hexagrams are ordered in pairs, so that the pair members are generally mirror images. This type of logic has been described by Granet as the basis of the Chinese mind: "If two aspects seem tied together, it is not by way of cause and effect; rather, they seem to be **paired** as are inside and outside, or to use a metaphor as early as the period of **Hi Ts'en**—as paired echo and sound, or shadow and light."[47]

● ● ● ● ●

The Inner World Arrangement is presented with these words by Wilhelm:

> God comes forth in the sign of the Arousing; he brings all things to completion in the sign of the Gentle; he causes creatures to perceive one another in the sign of the Clinging (light); he causes them to serve one another in the sign of the Receptive. He gives them joy in the sign of the Joyous; he battles in the sign of the Creative; he toils in the sign of the Abysmal; he brings them to perfection in the sign of Keeping Still. . . .
> All living things come forth in the sign of the Arousing. The Arousing stands in the east.

They come to completion in the sign of the Gentle. The Gentle stands in the southeast. Completion means that all creatures become pure and perfect.

The Clinging is the brightness in which all creatures perceive one another. It is the trigram of the south. That the holy sages turned their faces to the south while they gave ear to the meaning of the universe means that in ruling they turned toward what is light. This they evidently took from this trigram.

The Receptive means the earth. It takes care that all creatures are nourished. Therefore it is said: "He causes them to serve one another in the sign of the Receptive."

The Joyous is midautumn, which rejoices all creatures. Therefore it is said: "He gives them joy in the sign of the Joyous."

"He battles in the sign of the Creative." The Creative is the trigram of the northwest. It means that here the dark and the light arouse each other.

The Abysmal means water. It is the trigram of due north, the trigram of toil, to which all creatures are subject. Therefore it is said: "He toils in the sign of the Abysmal."

Keeping Still is the trigram of the northeast, where beginning and end of all creatures are completed. Therefore it is said: "He brings them to perfection in the sign of Keeping Still."[48]

In the Primal Arrangement, a point of view we termed "nature's point of view" was expressed. The relationships presented concern mystical and miraculous events—the point of view was definitely transcendental. This arrangement is said to come from "mythic" time and is attributed to the mythical figure Fu Hsi, an ancient Chinese culture hero. Wilhelm wrote of the Primal Arrangement: "Here, in what is probably a very ancient saying, the eight primary trigrams are named in sequences of pairs that, according to tradition, go back to Fu Hsi—that is to say, it was already in existence at the time of the compilation of the Book of Changes under the Chou dynasty."[49] Thus another meaning of the Before-the-World Sequence is derived from a temporal dimension, pertaining to a time before historical record.

On the other hand, the Sequence of the Later Heaven may be seen as a knowledge that is historically derived from an actual historical figure (King Wên). Here we are presented a point of view from "below." Instead of nature's point of view, we are given man's point of view. The trigrams are removed from their supernatural arrangements of nonseclusive opposites and placed in a natural progression based on the movement of the sun through the heaven in a day and in a year. The complexity of the night sky gives way to a complexity of daytime terrestrial life. Although it is the celestial body, the sun, that determines this terrestrial complexity, the Inner World Arrangement is a map of life on earth—of the earthly changes made possible by the sun but still having a life of their own. Of this change in point of view between the two arrangements of trigrams, Wilhelm wrote: "The trigrams are taken out of their grouping in pairs of opposites and shown in the temporal progression in which they manifest themselves in the phenomenal world in the cycle of the year."[50]

The Inner World Arrangement is a mediation between the "extreme" ultra-codes presented in the Outer World Arrangement and the immediate sensory codes that pertain to terrestrial events. The arrangement is analogous to the sun's movements through the heavens, which may be seen as sketching the boundary between the two worlds—celestial and terrestrial. As such a mediator, the Inner World Arrangement corresponds to the third and fourth lines of a hexagram. These are the lines associated with man in the tripartite earth/man/heaven interpretation of hexagrams. Like those lines in hexagrams that belong to the three trigrams, the arrangement is the most ambiguous and the most involved of the interpretive codes.

The Inner World Arrangement is interpreted by seeing a certain situation in the development of specific states in the day or year as represented by the trigrams. Thus, temporal aspects are established. A practitioner may see, in a hexagram that represents the midsummer state of the year, a picture of things to come or an explanation of passed conditions. Interpretations generated from these codes are not complex in themselves. In practice they often serve as "checks" of interpretations produced from other codes. The hexagram **Hsieh** (Deliverance), makes use of this arrangement:

The Judgment reads:

> Deliverance. The southwest furthers.
> If there is no longer anything where one has to go,
> Return brings good fortune.
> If there is still something where one has to go,
> Hastening brings good fortune.[51]

To this Wilhelm added:

> This refers to a time in which tensions and complications begin to be eased. At such times we ought to make our way back to ordinary conditions as soon as possible; this is the meaning of "the southwest." These periods of sudden change have great importance. Just as the rain relieves atmospheric tension, making all the buds burst open, so a time of deliverance from burdensome pressure has a liberating and stimulating effect on life. One thing is important, however: in such times we must not overdo our triumph. The point is not to push on farther than is necessary. Returning to the regular order of life as soon as deliverance is achieved brings good fortune. If there are any residual matters that ought to be attended to, it should be done as quickly as possible, so that a clean sweep is made and no retardation occurs.[52]

In commenting on the Inner World Arrangement, Wilhelm suggested that the southwest represents a time of work during the agricultural year when men join together to harvest the crops. It is the end of the period when the life forces have been expanding (spring and summer). Standing just before the joy of the completed harvest, which signals the coming contraction of the life forces in fall and winter, the southwest is associated with **K'un:** "The Receptive means the earth. It takes care that all creatures are nourished. Therefore it is said: 'He causes them to serve one another in the sign of the Receptive.' "[53] To interpret the hexagram Deliverance, Wilhelm summarized the basis of the ultracode and specifically pointed out the meaning of the southwest in this context:

> Thus the cycle is closed. Like the day or the year in nature, so every life, indeed every cycle of experience, is a continuity by which old and new are linked together. In view of this we can understand why, in several of the sixty-four hexagrams, the southwest represents the period of work and fellowship, while the northeast stands for the time of solitude, when the old is brought to an end and the new is begun.[54]

● ● ● ● ●

The ultracodes represent a treatment in the **I Ching** of two concepts—time and space. More accurately they represent views of a dialectical synthesis of time and space.

The concept of space/time is made possible through the arrangement of the trigrams. What is predicated by such an arrangement is not contained in the essence of any particular trigram or even any complex of trigrams and lines. The arrangements of trigrams effect a combining of the particular parts into a whole. Through such a synthesis the concepts of time and space may be expressed. These concepts are not in any of the trigrams, but only emerge in the synthesis of all of them.

The arrangements represent the crowning achievement of the appositional mind—the synthesis of immediate percepts into a whole that in turn becomes a percept of a nature signifying itself. The existence of the arrangements shows that appositional systems can arrive at complex and intricate ideas, and at a dialectical seeing of order.

In the **I Ching** we are provided with two basic syntheses (the Primal and Inner World Arrangements) that in turn are the basis for the understanding of complex spatial and temporal dimensions. In these arrangements space and time are both derived from the **same** synthesis—they can be inferred from either of the trigram arrangements. Furthermore these syntheses are seen to be related in the following manner: "To understand fully, one must always visualize the Inner-World Arrangement as transparent, with the Primal Arrangement shining through it. Thus when we come to the trigram **Li,** we come at the same time upon the ruler **Ch'ien** who governs with his face turned to the south."[55]

These syntheses represent end points in continuums that perceptually define primordial, temporal, and spatial dimensions. The spatial continuum may be construed as an axis of discontinuous/continuous, while the temporal continuum may be described as an axis of diachronic/synchronic.

In terms of the spatial continuum we have seen already that the arrangements stand in correspondence to various types of space—celestial/terrestrial, outer/inner, and so on. The Primal Arrangement corresponds to the discontinuous end of the spatial continuum. This arrangement is composed of pairs of opposites, so that movement within the space is not preeminently linear and continuous, but takes place in forward and backward movements. Movement in this spatial arrangement represents outer, celestial space. This view of the Primal Arrangement is supported by Wilhelm's comments:

> Thus we have first a forward-moving (rising) line, in which the forces of the preceding year take effect. . . . [F]ollowing this line leads to knowledge of the past, which is present as a latent cause in the effects it produces. In the second group, named not according to the images (phenomena) but according to the attributes of the trigrams, a backward movement sets in (a jump from Li in the east back to Kên in the northwest). Along this line the forces of the coming year develop, and following it leads to knowledge of the future, which is being prepared as an effect by its causes—like seeds that, in contracting, consolidate.[56]

The continuous spatial arrangement descriptive of terrestrial space is found in the Inner World Arrangement. As one moves from Chên in the east to Kên in the northeast, a continuous cycle is described. Wilhelm stated, "Like the day or the year in nature, so every life, indeed every cycle of experience, is a **continuity** by which old and new are linked together."[57]

Turning to the temporal dimension, we find that the Primal Arrangement corresponds to synchronic time, while the Inner World Arrangement corresponds to diachronic time. The Primal Arrangement has already been associated with mythic time—an eternal "before the world" presence. On the other hand, the Inner World Arrangement has been linked with historical, or "clock," time. The Primal Arrangement represents the dialectic moment—a time when opposites unite. From the point of view of synchronic time, every moment is a unique arrangement of opposing contraries. Jung's definition of synchronicity, in his Foreword to the Wilhelm—Baynes **I Ching**, supports this idea:

> Just as causality describes the sequence of events, so synchronicity to the Chinese mind deals with the coincidence of events. The causal point of view tells us a dramatic story about how D came into existence: it took its origin from C, which existed before D, and C in its turn had a father, B, etc. The synchronistic view on the other hand tries to produce an equally meaningful picture of coincidence. How does it happen that A', B', C', D', etc., appear all in the same moment and in the same place? It happens in the first place because the physical events A' and B' are of the same quality as the psychic events C' and D' and further because all are the exponents of one and the same momentary situation. The situation is assumed to represent a legible or understandable picture.[58]

The diachronic end of the continuum is represented by the Inner World Arrangement. Here the temporal synthesis is not given in terms of a moment, but rather in terms of sequences of stages that move from one to another. Natural and cultural historical time take the place of moments as the temporal units under consideration. The year and day progress and develop, which the text of the I **Ching** metaphorically describes as "the unfolding of the divine."

The temporal dimension of diachronic/synchronic can be conceived in terms of music. To read music one must be aware of the diachronic and synchronic aspects of the situation. The notes are read diachronically in a sequence running from left to right; simultaneously they are read synchronically (up and down), revealing the harmony between distinct and contrary notes. Time in the I Ching may be likened to the synthesis required to understand music. Musical works and the I Ching are closely identified: both are examples of synthetic inquiries.

In the I Ching time can be either reversible or irreversible. This is pointed out in the Primal Arrangement, where it is stated that "counting that which is going into the past depends on the forward movement."[59]

Generally, reversible time is pictured in the Primal Arrangement and irreversible time is pictured in the Inner World Arrangement. Thus diachronic time is distributed in **both** arrangements. Such intricacies and inconsistencies in analysis are resolved if one is aware of the "transparency" existing as a basic identity of both arrangements.

These temporal and spatial features provide a wealth of materials by which a practitioner of the I Ching can generate interpretations of hexagrams and come to understand them. A given hexagram can be seen as an instance in mythic time or as an historical occurrence. If any given hexagram is an image of a situation, the competency of a practitioner on the level of the ultracodes is determined by the appropriateness of his or her decision to employ one code or the other to explain or unravel the intrigues of the particular question. In this work a practitioner might be thought of as a **bricoleur,** with a toolbox containing a variety of sign particulars, immediate sensory codes, and ultracodes.

INVARIANT FRAMES

This chapter has proceeded from a concern with perceptual particulars (the signs) to a description of relationships that provide codes for interpreting these particulars. We have observed that temporal and spatial syntheses are effected through the two arrangements of trigrams. Through the use of signs and codes a practitioner constructs views of a world with depth and an infinite variation. Yet there are other views within the practice that are more developed. These views presuppose an understanding of the variable layers and are beyond the codes and signs. The practitioner must understand both the variable layers and the layer of understanding that is invariant.

The invariant within the lines, trigrams, and hexagrams of the I Ching can be simply conceived as **change.** While Wilhelm referred to the I Ching as the **Book of Changes,** John Blofeld's version is entitled the **Book of Change,** to emphasize that we are dealing not with a multiplicity of happenings (changes) but an omnipresent structural unity—change.[60]

This passage from the Great Treatise aids in understanding the notion of change.

> The Changes have no consciousness, no action; they are quiescent and do not move. But if they are stimulated, they penetrate all situations under heaven. If they were not the most divine thing on earth, how could they do this?[61]

The reference here is to places in a hexagram where the lines are located rather than to any particular configuration of firm and yielding lines. Change is perceptually available by concentrating on the places in hexagrams. These places are invariant over the sixty-four hexagrams. Functionally, it is these places that provide a frame in which particularities (the lines) can be seen and interpreted. Every complete hexagram has six places:

> The Changes is a book
> From which one may not hold aloof.
> Its tao is forever changing—
> Alteration, movement without rest,
> Flowing through the six empty places;
> Rising and sinking without fixed laws,
> Firm and yielding transform each other.
> They cannot be confined within a rule;
> It is only change that is at work here.[62]

Though lines are constructed through the exercise of definite rules (counting the values of thrown coins or yarrow stalks), the places themselves are not produced by the exercise of a rule. Rather, they come about tacitly—through the exercise of rules to produce and transform lines. The practitioner produces not a place, but a line to occupy a place.

Suppose, for example, in throwing the coins a practitioner obtains the hexagram **Ch'ien**:

According to his calculations all the lines have a value of 7 except the third which has a value of 9. The lines with a value of 7 are regarded as fixed. However, the third line, with the value 9, is a change line. It becomes the most significant line in the hexagram for this particular throwing, for it is expected to divide into a yielding line, bringing into existence a situation described by a different hexagram,

 Lü,Treading.

Change, as a perception, is the flowing of a line into its opposite within a common place.

The wording of the text attached to the change line in the third place for the hexagram **Ch'ien** reveals the primacy of the place as the medium of change:

> Nine in the third place means:
> All day long the superior man is creatively active.
> At nightfall his mind is still beset with cares.
> Danger. No blame.[63]

It is always an extreme value in a given place (6 or 9) that indicates change. An extreme value is associated with a given place that, by its nature, is empty and invariant.

In addition to being the source of the meaning of change, the places also convey the idea of an ordinal grid through which a situation is manifested. Wilhelm wrote:

> The places occupied by the lines are differentiated as superior and inferior, according to their relative elevation. As a rule the lowest and the top lines are not taken into account, whereas the four middle lines are active within the time. Of these, the fifth place is that of the ruler, and the fourth that of the minister who is close to the ruler. The third, as the highest place of the lower trigram, holds a sort of transition position; the second is that of the official in the country, who nevertheless stands in direct connection with the prince in the fifth place. But in some situations the fourth place may represent the wife and the second the son of the man represented by the fifth place. . . . In short, while any of various designations may be given to a line in a specific place, the varying functions ascribed to the place are always analogous.[64]

In terms of the ordinal grid, each place has a respective function in the establishment of meaning for hexagrams. These functions remain invariant to the vicissitudes presented by the lines. They provide an invariant framework in which the flux of perceptual experience represented by the lines and relations can be ordered and disclosed. Thus, the frames are the means by which a situation is opened—the places provide openings through which the fluctuations of perceptual life can be made intelligible.

The fact that the lines occupy ordinal places is the basis of certain relations that exist between the lines. These relations, though instrumental in interpretation, are different from the codes which rest on the analogy between the relations of lines and certain perceptions of nature. Two such relationships derived from the ordinal structure of the hexagrams are those of **correspondence of lines** and of **holding together.** Wilhelm describes the relationship of correspondence as follows:

> Lines occupying analogous places in the lower and upper trigrams sometimes have an especially close relationship, the relationship of correspondence. As a rule, firm lines correspond with yielding lines only, and vice versa. The following lines, provided they differ in kind, correspond: the first and the fourth, the second and the fifth, the third and the top line. Of these, the most important are the two central lines in the second and fifth place, which stand in the correct relationship of official to ruler, son to father, wife to husband.[65]

Note that analogy is operative here. But the analogy is not one of the lines to natural relationships but of the lines to places in an ordinal grid. The second and fifth places are analogous because they both are in the middle of primary trigrams. They represent a case of "ordered pairs," as the basis of their relationship is the internal order of the hexagrams themselves, considered from the point of view of their invariant features. Change represents a diachronic flow of lines through the places, bringing about the manifestation of a sequence of hexagrams. Correspondence represents the synchronic harmony of opposites in analogous places in the same hexagram. In both change and correspondence we are viewing the possibilities inherent in the invariant situation of the hexagrams. Both are relationships constituted by change—the former indicates the direction in which change is operating, while the latter indicates the fortune or misfortune of change in the situation.

Another relationship based upon the places is "holding together." Wilhelm wrote: "Between two adjacent lines of different character there may occur a relationship of holding together, which is also described with respect to the lower line as 'receiving' and with respect to the upper as 'resting upon'."[66] The meaning of such a relationship was described by Wilhelm.

> [T] he relationship of holding together occurs also between the fifth and the top line. Here it pictures a ruler placing himself under a sage; in such a case it is usually a humble ruler (a weak line in the fifth place) who reveres a strong sage (a strong line above). . . . This is naturally very favorable. But when, conversely, a strong line stands in the fifth place with a weak one above it, this points rather to association with inferior elements and is undesirable.[67]

In both the relationship of correspondence and that of holding together we find the source of meaning not in the signified relationship of nature, but in the grid that constitutes the invariant frame of a hexagram. In explicating such relationships, the I Ching relies on social structural relationships (such as between ruler and minister, sage and ruler, husband and wife). The order that is posited on this layer becomes primarily a social order. It is in the relationship extant in social structure that the production of invariance can be observed. The indefinite variance observable in nature gives way to the invariance of social relationships which in turn is based on a human propensity to recognize and base existence on an essential emptiness (represented by the places). Insofar as the emptiness is being constantly filled with values (represented by the lines) culture is constructed out of perceptions. This construction involves the operation of ordinal grids that provide frames for practitioners to fill. The ordinal grid composed of the six places of a hexagram works as a "culture-producing machine." The grid produces myths of the world out of the material presented by nature. These mythic orders in turn become the reality of practitioners who work to fill the grid's emptiness. As nature throws up new problems the grid assimilates the perceptions, transforming them into versions of itself. This work becomes realized in change—for it is in such situations that the grid is perceptually outlined. Mythic orders are constructed, only to be replaced by new perceptions. The pieces are collected again and reconstructed in terms of an ordinal grid that becomes increasingly more apparent. The perceptual work on the layer of the invariant frames involves the discovery of the grid **as** the perception of change in the occupants of its ordered places.

Lévi-Strauss's analysis of South American Indian myth helps to clarify this abstract description. In analyzing specific myths by means of a grid, he discovered that they contain distinctions that occur in various myths. For example, he reported that five myths contain the distinctions edible/inedible, animal/vegetable, cultural/natural, and obtained/refused. Each of these distinctions can be assigned a value (+ or −), thus making possible the following table.

TABLE 3. A CLASSIFICATION OF INDIAN MYTHS

	M_{144} , M_{145}	M_{158}	M_{143}	M_{150} , etc.
	Origin of fish poison (timbo)	Loss of the abundance of food	Loss of the abundance of timbo	Origin of fire
Edible/inedible	−	+	−	+
Animal/vegetable	−	−	+	+
Cultural/natural	−	−	+	−
Obtained/refused	+	−	−	+

Source: Claude Lévi-Strauss, **The Raw and the Cooked: Introduction to a Science of Mythology,** vol. I, trans. John and Doreen Weightman, London: Jonathan Cape Ltd., and New York: Harper & Row, 1969, p. 269.

To understand this table one should see each myth as a version of the particular grid composed of four oppositions. These places are occupied by values created through the telling of a myth. Lévi-Strauss assigned values in accord with an established invariant frame. Myths are made by a type of thought that involves the placing of values side by side in terms of a grid, which remains tacit, but which frames the inquiry. The invariant frame may not be recognized as such by myth tellers, but it becomes observable through a structural analysis showing that various myths employ the same oppositions.

The isomorphism of the I Ching and the primitive thought described by Lévi-Strauss is apparent. In the I Ching there is a grid, of six ordered places, which corresponds to the distinctions of the Lévi-Strauss table, edible/inedible, animal/vegetable, and so on. A given hexagram is the result of assigning values to the respective places. Each hexagram differs as different values are assigned to invariant places.

Suppose, for example, that a person studying the practice of the I Ching observed five throwings and rendered a verbal accounting of the conversation that developed in framing the question with the vocabulary of the signs, codes, and framework of the I Ching. Imagine that these conversations were carried out under the constraints that, in answer to five significant questions, the five hexagrams

were observed to occur, and the researcher labeled them H_1, H_2, H_3, H_4, and H_5, respectively. He would have observed an invariance in these five throwings—the consultation of the oracle to obtain a hexagram. Such a researcher might summarize this invariance as in Table 4.

Such a structural analysis is exactly what Lévi-Strauss did in his analysis of Indian myths. He discovered that they may differ in the values assigned the pairs

TABLE 4. A CLASSIFICATION OF I CHING THROWINGS

Line	H_1	H_2, H_5	H_3	H_4
6	———	—— ——	—— ——	—— ——
5	———	—— ——	—— ——	———
4	———	—— ——	—— ——	—— ——
3	———	—— ——	———	—— ——
2	———	—— ——	—— ——	—— ——
1	———	—— ——	———	———

of oppositions, but that the same pairs of oppositions are always present, constituting an invariant framework for the telling of a story.

There are, of course, differences. Lévi-Strauss considered stories that have been told for generations and are common to a number of tribes. Any given myth, however, is apt to have differing versions, even in the same village. I Ching practitioners, on the other hand, would be more likely to constitute a group within a subculture. Yet these throwings could become aspects of a subcultural folklore, as occurrences of hexagrams in answer to particularly relevant questions that seem uncannily "appropriate" may come to be told and retold. It is in this sense that such methods—the I Ching, the Tarot, Tantra, and other synthetic inquiries—can be viewed as culture-producing machines. They essentially have the capability of providing a framework for constructing an alternative reality radically different from that of a larger culture founded on the primacy of the scientific method, of analysis, and of propositional mind.

In this chapter our orientation has been to explicate the structure of thinking in the I Ching. In this analysis, we arrived at an argument that appositional thought is the opposite of thought according to principles, for it is thought that is layered with sign particulars, codes, and an invariant frame. And it is not thought that pursues clarity and distinctness, but rather veiledness and complexity. The use of time and space, which are central to the propositional and appositional minds, are united in the mythic time symbolized in the Primal Arrangement mandala. In fact, the unity and struggle of pairs of opposites virtually permeates the I Ching. This leads us, as did the analysis of scientific inquiry, to the dialectic.

NOTES

1. Giorgio de Santillana and Hertha von Dechend, Hamlet's Mill: An Essay on Myth and the Frame of Time, Boston: Gambit, Inc., 1969, p. xiii.
2. Lévi-Strauss, The Raw and the Cooked, p. 147.
3. Ibid., p. 341.
4. Ibid., pp. 340–341.
5. Ibid., p. 341.
6. Merleau-Ponty, Phenomenology of Perception, pp. 52–53.
7. Merleau-Ponty, The Primacy of Perception, pp. 172–173.
8. Ibid., p. 42.
9. Marcel Granet, "The Tao " in Talcott Parsons, Edward Shils, Kaspar D. Naegele, Jesse R. Pitts, eds., Theories of Society: Foundations of Modern Sociological Theory, vol. 2, New York: Free Press, 1961, p. 1098, emphasis added.

10. Ibid., p. 1098.
11. Wilhelm, **op. cit.,** p. 297 footnote. If **tao** can be defined as a principle of order, then its symbolic representation as a mandala could reveal its principal components—direction, intensity, closure, and involvement (involution). A mandala is in esoteric Taoism usually represented in the form of a flower, cross, or wheel with extension in four or eight directions. The two arrangements of trigrams in Figures 18 and 19 are mandalas, and a Golden Flower mandala is shown in Figure 20:

Figure 20. A Golden Flower mandala.
Source: Richard Wilhelm and Cary F. Baynes, trans., **The Secret of the Golden Flower: A Chinese Book of Life,** New York: Harcourt Brace Jovanovich, 1962, Figure 1.

The **direction** in a mandala is its extension in form. Carl G. Jung's discussion of a taoist text reveals, in correct order, the next three components of order.

> The **Tao,** the undivided, great One, gives rise to two opposite reality principles, the dark and the light, yin and yang. These are at first thought of only as forces of nature apart from man. Later, the sexual polarities and others as well are derived from them. From yin comes K'un, the receptive feminine principle; from yang comes Ch'ien, the creative masculine principle; from yin comes ming, life; from yang, hsing, or human nature. (Carl G. Jung, in Richard Wilhelm and Cary F. Baynes, trans., **The Secret of the Golden Flower: A Chinese Book of Life,** New York: Harcourt Brace Jovanovich, 1962, p. 64.)

Jung explained:

The unity of . . . life and consciousness, is the **Tao,** whose symbol would be the central white light. This light is the image of the creative point, a point having intensity without extension, thought of as connected with the space of the 'square inch,' the symbol for that which has extension. The two together make the **Tao.** Human nature [hsing] and consciousness [hui] are expressed in light symbolism, and therefore intensity, while life [ming] would coincide with extensity. . . . The **'enclosure'** or **circumambulatio,** is expressed in our text by the idea of a 'circulation.' The 'circulation' . . . means fixation and concentration. . . . [T]ao begins to work and to take over the leadership. Action is reversed into non-action; all that is peripheral is subjected to the command of what is central. Therefore it is said: 'Movement is only another name for mastery.' Psychologically, this circulation would be the 'turning in a circle around oneself,' whereby, obviously, all sides of the personality become involved. (**Ibid.,** pp. 103–104, emphasis added.)

Here, "non-action" is used in the same way that don Juan uses "non-doing."

12. Ibid., p. 264.
13. Granet, op. cit., p. 1098.
14. Wilhelm, op. cit., p. 25.
15. Ibid., p. 25.
16. Ibid., p. 273.
17. Ibid., p. 275.
18. Granet, op. cit., p. 1098.
19. Wilhelm, op. cit., p. 357.
20. Ibid., p. 44.
21. Ibid., p. 204.
22. Ibid., pp. 208–210.
23. Ibid., p. 357.
24. Ibid., pp. 78–79.
25. Ibid., pp. 358–359.
26. Ibid., pp. 359–360.
27. Ibid., p. 237.
28. Ibid., pp. 237–238.
29. Ibid., p. 359.
30. Granet, op. cit., p. 1100.
31. Eliphas Levi, **Transcendental Magic: Its Doctrine and Ritual,** trans. Arthur Edward Waite, New York: Samuel Weiser, 1972, as cited in Sadhu, op. cit., p. 44.
32. Lévi-Strauss, **The Raw and the Cooked,** p. 240.
33. Wilhelm, op. cit., p. 264.
34. Ibid., pp. 6–7.
35. Hsü Kua, the Ninth Wing, comments on linear sequence of hexagrams 3–64, Wilhelm, op. cit.
36. Ibid., p. 266.
37. Ibid., pp. 12–13.
38. Ibid., p. 12.
39. Ibid., p. 266.
40. Ibid., p. 265.
41. Ibid., p. 338.
42. Ibid., pp. 267–268.
43. Ibid., p. 245.
44. Ibid.
45. Ibid., p. 249.
46. Ibid., pp. 249–250.
47. Granet, op. cit., p. 1098.
48. Wilhelm, op. cit., pp. 268–270.
49. Ibid., pp. 265–266.
50. Ibid., p. 268.
51. Ibid., p. 154.

52. Ibid., p. 155.
53. Ibid., p. 269.
54. Ibid., p. 271.
55. Ibid.
56. Ibid., p. 267.
57. Ibid., p. 271, emphasis added.
58. Ibid., pp. xxiv–xxv.
59. Ibid., p. 265.
60. Blofeld, op. cit.
61. Wilhelm, op. cit., p. 315.
62. Ibid., p. 348.
63. Ibid., p. 8.
64. Ibid., pp. 359–360.
65. Ibid., p. 361.
66. Ibid., p. 362.
67. Ibid., p. 363.

Chapter
9

Dialectical Bases of Inquiry

ON THE MEANING OF DIALECTIC

Up to this point the analysis of inquiry has focused on the distinction between two kinds of thought: propositional, or analytic, and appositional, or synthetic. Analytic thought, as formal logic, has also been contrasted with a method of thinking called dialectic thought. Philosopher Immanuel Kant explained that analytic logic examines and estimates the application of formal rules, which must then be tested to determine their truth or falsity in relation to a perceived object. Kant recognized that formal logic alone is insufficient to establish positive truth and produces only the semblance of objective assertions.

> For as logic teaches nothing with regard to the contents of knowledge, but lays down the formal conditions only of an agreement with the understanding, which, so far as the objects are concerned, are totally indifferent, any attempt at using it . . . in order to extend and enlarge our knowledge . . . can end in nothing but mere talk, by asserting with a certain plausibility anything one likes or, if one likes, denying it.[1]

Kant saw analytics as inadequate to unite form and content. This unity, the precondition for the establishment of empirical truth, requires collecting "trustworthy information, in order afterward to attempt its application."[2] Formal logic and abstract argument alone cannot determine objective truth. The error of dialectical semblance—the assumption that the form of understanding can establish truth—leads to the reification of knowledge. It is observed in practice as sophistry, which Kant identified as the "art of giving to one's ignorance . . . the outward appearance of truth, by imitating the accurate method which logic always requires, and by using its topic as a cloak for every empty assertion."[3]

Kant added **real** dialectics to logic as "a **critique** of dialectical semblance."[4] Dialectics is thus an effort to criticize incorrect application of analytics to objective content. It contains principles of reason beyond the edge of analytic thought.

A modern scholar whose views are close to Kant's is Lévi-Strauss, who writes:

> In my view dialectical reason is always constitutive; it is the bridge, forever extended and improved, which analytical reason throws out over an abyss: it is unable to see the further shore but knows that it is there, even should it be constantly receding. The term dialectical reason thus covers the perceptual efforts analytical reason must make . . . if it aspires to account for language, society and thought; and the distinction between **the two forms of reason** in my view rests only on the **temporary gap** separating **analytical reason** from the **understanding** of life.[5]

This metaphorical explication of the concept of dialectics is complemented by a structural analysis of dialectics by means of anthropological data. To this end, Lévi-Strauss considers so-called dual organizations, which are societies that appear to be divided into two parts. The data include Paul Radin's study of a Great Lakes Indian tribe, the Winnebago. Each Winnebago village was divided into two moieties, called **wangeregi**, or "those who are above," and **manegi**, or "those who are on earth." The populations of the two parts of the village (technically called **phratries**) were groups of exogamous clans that had reciprocal rights and duties. For example, members of each phratry held the funerals for deceased members of the opposite phratry.[6]

Radin noted a strange discrepancy in his informants' descriptions of village organization. Lévi-Strauss explains:

> They described, for the most part, a circular village plan in which the two moieties were separated by an imaginary diameter running northwest and southeast [Figure 21]. However, several informants vigorously denied that arrangement and outlined another, in which the lodges of the moiety chiefs were in the center rather than on the periphery [Figure 22]. According to Radin, the first pattern was always described by informants of the upper phratry and the second by informants of the lower phratry.[7]

Thus for some of the natives the village was circular in form and was divided into two halves, with the lodges scattered throughout the circle. For the others, there remained a twofold partition of a circular village, but with two important differences: Instead of a diameter cutting the circle, there was a small circle within a larger one; and instead of a division of the nucleated village, the inner circle represents the lodges grouped together,

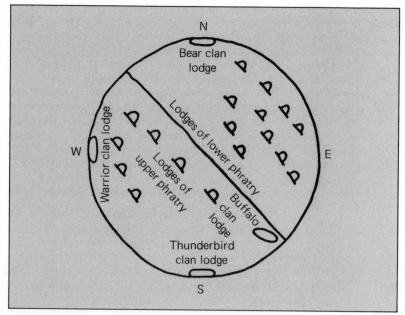

Figure 21. Plan of a Winnebago village according to members of the upper phratry.
Source: Figure 6 in Chapter 8, "Do Dual Organizations Exist?" in **Structural Anthropology** by Claude Lévi-Strauss, trans. by Claire Jacobson and Brooke Grundfest Schoepf, © 1963 by Basic Books, Inc. (After Paul Radin, **The Winnebago Tribe,** Washington, D.C.: Bureau of American Ethnology, 37th Annual Report, 1923, Figure 33.)

as against the outer circle, which represented the cleared ground and which was again differentiated from the virgin forest that surrounded the whole.[8]

The two arrangements are pictured in Figures 21 and 22.

Lévi-Strauss concludes that both descriptions correspond to real arrangements, "describing one organization too complex to be formalized by means of a single model, so that the members of each moiety would tend to conceptualize it one way rather than another, depending upon their position in the social structure."[9] Lévi-Strauss calls the two conceptions **diametric** structure for the village viewed as divided in half, and **concentric** structure for the village seen as circular. He then embarks on a structural analysis:

There is a profound difference between diametric and concentric dualism. Diametric dualism is static, that is, it cannot transcend its own limitations; its transformations merely give rise to the same sort of dualism as that from which they arose. But concentric dualism is dynamic and contains an implicit triadism. Or, strictly speaking, any attempt to move from an asymmetric triad to a symmetric dyad presupposes concentric dualism, which is dyadic like the latter but asymmetric like the former (Figure 23).
The ternary nature of concentric dualism also derives from another source. The system is not self-sufficient, and its frame of reference is al-

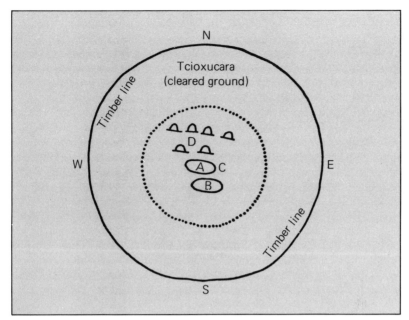

Figure 22. Plan of Winnebago village according to members of the lower phratry.
Source: Figure 7 in Chapter 8, "Do Dual Organizations Exist?" in **Structural Anthropology** by Claude Lévi-Strauss, trans. by Claire Jacobson and Brooke Grundfest Schoepf, © 1963 by Basic Books, Inc. (After Paul Radin, **The Winnebago Tribe,** Washington, D.C.: Bureau of American Ethnology, 37th Annual Report, 1923, Figure 34.)

ways the environment. The opposition between cleared ground (central circle) and waste land (peripheral circle) demands a third element, brush or forest—that is, virgin land—which circumscribes the binary whole while at the same time extending it, since cleared land is to waste land as waste land is to virgin land. In a diametric system, on the other hand, virgin land constitutes an irrelevant element; the moieties are defined by their opposition to each other, and the apparent symmetry of their structure creates the illusion of a closed system.[10]

This argument is compatible with our conceptualization of order as a whole containing distinguishable layers. What Lévi-Strauss calls diametric structure is here called the first layer of a social order; what he calls concentric structure is here called the second layer of a social order, where the center is the region of maximum intensity: In an Indian village, apart from its physical layout, the center of the society, the focal point of the production of cultural form, is found in the dwellings of the chiefs. And the physical environment both encloses and makes possible the extension of cultural form into the world. Thus we argue that a social order, like a mental order, consists of two layers enclosed in a third: the outer layer of cultural and social form, the inner layer of social structure, and an enclosing third layer, which is the sensed environment. The world, as seen by our eyes, has a three-dimensional spatiality. It has height and width, and

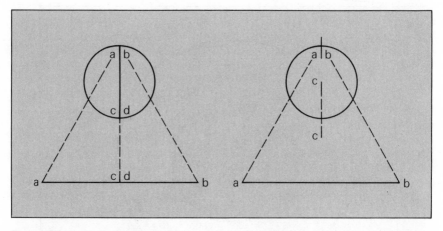

Figure 23. Left, representation on a straight line of a diametric structure; Right, representation on a straight line of a concentric structure.
Source: Figure 12 in Chapter 8, "Do Dual Organizations Exist?" in **Structural Anthropology** by Claude Lévi-Strauss, trans. by Claire Jacobson and Brooke Grundfest Schoepf, © 1963 by Basic Books, Inc.

these generate the notion of depth, of seeing into the world, of inquiring and thereby gaining knowledge of the spectacle of life before us and as us.

In neither the social order nor the mental order does the appearance of dualism imply that order can be dualistic; both the mental and the social orders are dialectical. In fact, Lévi-Strauss concludes: "The study of so-called dual organization discloses so many anomalies and contradictions . . . that we should be well advised to . . . treat the apparent manifestations of dualism as superficial distortions of structures whose real nature is quite different and vastly more complex."[11] Thus he shows that "the opposition between moieties expresses a subtle dialectic."[12]

Lévi-Strauss extends his analysis to consider symbols "used to express the antithesis of the moieties."[13] The antithesis of the moieties—which are the components of the social order—amounts to a dialectical symbolism of the society. Symbols that are the antithesis of their social order create culture that is inspired by, and mirrors, nature. Although the mind is invisible it is a task of the social order to produce in its outer layer visible symbols that mirror it. In diagramming a Winnebago village circle, Lévi-Strauss explains:

> The lower moiety contains two groups of four clans each ("earth" and "water"). The upper moiety contains one group of four clans ("sky"). The triskelion represents the possibility of marriage according to the exogamy rule of the moieties. The large circle, which coincides with the perimeter of the village, encompasses the whole, making it a residential unit.[14]

Note that the diagram (Figure 24) shows each of the three components connected both directly and indirectly. Also note that the two views of the social order, superimposed, constitute a mandala. (See note 11, Chapter 8).

• • • • •

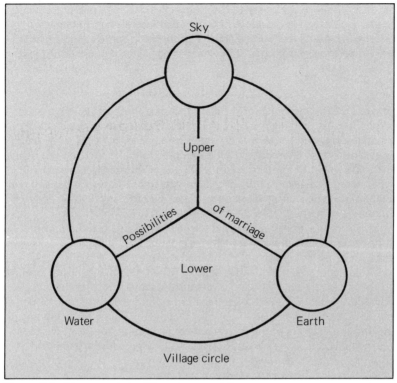

Figure 24. Diagram of the Winnebago social structure.
Source: Figure 13 in Chapter 8, "Do Dual Organizations Exist?" in **Structural Anthropology** by Claude Lévi-Strauss, trans. by Claire Jacobson and Brooke Grundfest Schoepf, © 1963 by Basic Books, Inc.

The view of dialectics as beyond the edge of analytics is implied by distinctions within the philosophy of science. Carl G. Hempel, for instance, writes:

> Broadly speaking, then, the formulation of a theory will require the specification of two kinds of principles; let us call them internal principles and bridge principles for short. The former will characterize the basic entities and processes invoked by the theory and the laws to which they are assumed to conform. The latter will indicate how the processes envisaged by the theory are related to empirical phenomena with which we are already acquainted, and which the theory may then explain, predict, or retrodict. [15]

The internal principles are the analytic systems used in the theory, including formal logic, mathematics, and natural language. The bridge principles are the ways in which propositional thought, with its capacity for abstract analysis, can be dynamically connected to objects.

Hempel's conception of bridge principles—which are dialectical—is but one view of dialectical thought. For these same bridge principles, which include laws of dialectics, are at work in the synthetic inquiries as well. The rationalities and enemies of synthetic inquiries are the opposites of the rationalities and enemies of scientific inquiries. The existence of these two kinds of inquiry implies a synthesis, an integrated and unified activity of the mind, which contains both analytic and perceptual capacities, but which is exhausted by neither of them.

● ● ● ● ●

Kant, the last great philosopher of the static, claimed that instruction in dialectics is "quite beneath the dignity of philosophy."[16] But the development of Western philosophy demanded that dialectics be pursued. It was G. W. F. Hegel who went where Kant refused to go and attempted to make a science out of the dynamic involvement of mind beyond the edge of analytics. Hegel's work remains the theory of dialectical thought; it therefore constitutes the basis of our claims that mind is dialectical and that dialectics are basic to scientific and synthetic inquiries.

In its struggle with its first enemy, science vanquished belief but at the same time banished metaphysics—which Hegel defined as "the intellect occupying itself with its own pure essence."[17] Belief was not destroyed but transformed into its opposite, disbelief. He added: "When such metaphysical shadows and such colorless self-concentration of the introspective spirit, had been brushed aside, existence seemed to be transformed into the sunny land of flowers—and, as we know, no flowers are black."[19] To see requires the non-doing of reaching into the shadows of mind, into self-concentration; into the invisible, colorless, realm within, where what is peripheral is subject to the command of what is central. Everything we look at has color: But we can see beyond looking by having vision manifested as a quality of perception.

Hegel saw philosophy as "ordered knowledge," which "cannot borrow its Method from a subordinate science, such as Mathematics, any more than it can rest satisfied with categorical assertion of pure intuition, or using reason based on external reflection."[20] These "subordinate sciences" correspond to the three layers of the mental order (ordered knowledge): Mathematics represents the propositional; pure intuition, the appositional; and external reflection, the sensory. Ordered knowledge comes about through reason. Hegel wrote:

> Reason is negative and dialectical because it dissolves into nothing the determinations of Understanding; Reason is positive because it is the source of the Universal in which the Particular is comprehended. . . . [I]n its real truth Reason is Mind—Mind which is higher than either Reason which understands, or Understanding which reasons. Mind is the negative, it . . . constitutes the quality alike of dialectical Reason and of Understanding: it negates the simple and thus posits that determinate distinction which is the work of Understanding, and just as truly it resolves this distinction, and is thus dialectical. Yet it does not abide in the negative, which thus results, but is therein just as much positive.[21]

Hegel essentially argues that the perceived world of our understanding loses its certainty, its apparent simplicity dissolves, when reason is applied to it. Since reason is mind, and reason is dialectical, it follows that mind is dialectical. In this theory the determinant of dialectical thought is identified by Hegel as "the movement of thought in Notions."[22] V. I. Lenin, in his **Philosophical Notebooks**, explained: "Human concepts are not fixed but are eternally in movement, they pass into one another, they flow into one another, otherwise they do not reflect living life. The analysis of concepts . . . demands study of the **movement** of concepts, of their interconnection, of their mutual transition."[23] The second determinant of dialectics given by Hegel is "the opposition of thought to outward appearance or sensuous Being . . . and in the objective existence we see the contradiction which it has in itself, or dialectics proper."[24] Lenin explained: "Dialectics . . . is the study of contradiction in the very essence of objects. . . . Human thought goes endlessly deeper from appearance to essence, from essence of the first order, as it were, to essence of the second order, and so on."[25] It is the study of contradiction, which means that "not only are appearances transitory, but the **essence** of things is so as well."[26]

At this point, it is helpful to refer to an analysis of dialectics presented by Mao Tse-tung.

> There are two states of motion in all things, that of relative rest and that of conspicuous change. Both are caused by the struggle between the two contradictory elements contained in a thing. . . . Things are constantly transforming themselves from the first into the second state of motion; the struggle of opposites goes on in both states but the contradiction is resolved through the second state. That is why we say that the unity of opposites is conditional, temporary and relative, while the struggle of mutually exclusive opposites is absolute. . . .
>
> The combination of conditional, relative identity and unconditional, absolute struggle constitutes the movement of opposites in all things.
>
> We Chinese often say, "Things that oppose each other also complement each other."[27] That is, things opposed to each other have identity. This saying is dialectical and contrary to metaphysics. "Oppose each other" refers to the mutual exclusion or the struggle of the contradictory aspects. "Complement each other" means that in given conditions the two contradictory aspects unite and achieve identity. Yet struggle is inherent in identity and without struggle there can be no identity.[28]

In a war, or in a game of chess, there is an absolute contradiction between the two sides. The struggle between them is unconditional and absolute and is resolved only by the defeat of one side. The unity of opposites comes about in conditional coalitions between sides that are unconditionally opposed to each other and in the moments of destruction and construction that change the situation.

Thus it can now be argued that while the neurological theory has identified two kinds of consciousness, or minds, that think independently and in opposite ways, it is also the case that these minds are not self-contained. Instead, they are the absolute contradiction in the mental order. It is hypothesized that these two minds do not stand as a duality, but are contained in the mental order. The struggle between the propositional and appositional minds is inherent in the identity of the mental order, for without this dialectical struggle there can be no mental order. Dialectical thought thus includes both propositional and appositional thought, and constitutes the basis of thought.

THE LAWS OF DIALECTICS IN INQUIRY

The next three sections explicate Hegel's laws of dialectics and attempt to demonstrate their workings in scientific and synthetic inquiries. Frederick Engels summarized Hegel's laws of dialectics as follows:

> It is . . . from the history of nature and human society that the laws of dialectics are abstracted. For they are nothing but the most general laws of the two aspects of historical development as well as thought itself. And indeed they can be reduced in the main to three:
>> The law of the transformation of quantity into quality and vice versa;
>> The law of the interpenetration of opposites;
>> The law of the negation of the negation.[29]

Quality, Quantity, and Measure

The distinction between quality and quantity in dialectics can be seen, at the most basic level, in Mao's distinction between the two states of motion.

> When the thing is in the first state of motion, it is undergoing only qualitative and not quantitative change and consequently presents the outward appearance of being at rest. When the thing is in the second state of motion, the quantitative change of the first state has already reached a culminating point and given rise to the dissolution of the thing as an entity and thereupon a qualitative change ensues, hence the appearance of a conspicuous change.[30]

A further explication of the quality–quantity distinction can be found in the work of Merleau-Ponty. He suggested that there are, in our phenomenal reality, three orders: the physical order, the vital order, and the human order. In his critique of Pavlov's theory that animal behavior can be explained by conditioned reflexes, Merleau-Ponty wrote:

> The reactions of an organism are not edifices constructed from elementary movements, but gestures gifted with an internal unity. Like that of stimulus, the notion of response separates into "geographical behavior"—the sum of the movements actually executed by the animal in their objective relation with the physical world; and behavior properly so called—these same movements considered in their internal articulation as a kinetic melody gifted with a meaning.[31]

He then wrote:

> If behavior is a "form," one cannot even designate in it that which depends on each one of the internal and external conditions taken separately, since their variations will be expressed in the form by a global and indivisible effect. Behavior would not be an effect of the physical world, either in the crude sense of productive causality or even in the sense of the relation of function to variable. The original character of a physiological field beyond the physical field—a system of directed forces—in which it has its place, of a second "system of stresses and strains" which alone determines actual behavior in a decisive manner, will have to be acknowl-

edged. Even if we take symbolic behavior and its proper characteristics fully into account there would be a reason for introducing a third field which . . . we will call mental field. . . .

It is here that the notion of form would permit a truly new solution. Equally applicable to the three fields which have just been defined, it would integrate them as three types of structures. . . . Quantity, order and value or signification, which pass respectively for the properties of matter, life and mind, would . . . be . . . the dominant characteristic in the order considered and would become universally applicable categories. Quantity is not a negation of quality, as if the equation for a circle negated circular form, of which on the contrary it attempts to be a rigorous expression. Often, the quantitative relations with which physics is concerned are only the formulae for certain distributive processes: in a soap bubble as in an organism, what happens at each point is determined by what happens at all the others. But this is the definition of order.[32]

Merleau-Ponty goes on to find fault with gestalt psychology and its assertion that order is form alone. For he contends that physical, physiological, and mental forms are not reducible to one another and, further, that physiological behavior is no passive mediator between the physical and mental orders. If this were so, then a psychology of form would reduce behavior to a sequence of mundane events (as described in stimulus-response theory).

This argument leads to the conclusion that the central property of the material order is quantity and the central property of the human order is value or signification—that is, quality. To **know** the world is thus to connect, dialectically, the orders characterized by quantity and quality. As a physiological order, the body is the bridge; by means of it, knowing is possible. Thus each of the three layers of the mental order is directed to the investigation of an order. Propositional (analytic) thought investigates itself; appositional thought investigates perception and the body—the physiological order; and the senses investigate the "material" order, the environment.

Merleau-Ponty also observed that an organism maintains equilibrium, not "by a plurality of vectors, but by a general attitude toward the world. . . . [T]he organism itself measures the action of things upon it and itself delimits its milieu by a circular process which is without analogy in the physical world."[33] He then contended that the relations between an individual and his milieu are dialectical rather than mechanistic. On the contrary, "physical stimuli act upon the organism only by eliciting a global response which will vary qualitatively when the stimuli vary quantitatively; with respect to the organism they play the role of occasions rather than of cause; the reaction depends on their vital significance rather than on the particular properties of the stimuli."[34] Thus, to argue that dialectics forms the basis of inquiry is to take a stand against the reduction of the social order or the mental order to the physical order. Inasmuch as the mental order dynamically knows the vital and physical orders, the three orders are known as a unitary reality.

● ● ● ● ●

Merleau-Ponty's argument that value, or significance, characterizes the human order contains an analytic problem that can be resolved in a manner consistent with the present theory of inquiry. For Hegel wrote:

Quality may be described as the determinate mode immediate and identical with Being—as distinguished from Quantity (to come afterwards), which, although a mode of Being, is no longer immediately identical with Being, but a mode indifferent and external to it. A Something is what it is in virtue of its quality, and losing its quality it ceases to be what it is. Quality, moreover, is completely a category only of the finite, and for that reason too it has its proper place in Nature, not in the world of Mind.[35]

Thus, "quality" is identical to "being," and yet its proper place is not in the mind. For manifestations of quality in mind are pathological. Hegel defined quality as "being-for-another," which properly belongs to language and the social order. If quality is our being for others, it is our social being, and we can make this entirely personal, being-by-self, only when we would possess another person. Hegel wrote: "[A] . . . manifestation of Quality as such, in mind even, is found in the case of besotted or morbid conditions, especially in states of passion and when the passion rises to derangement. The state of mind of a deranged person, being one mass of jealousy, fear, etc., may suitably be described as Quality."[36]

Thus we are forced to the conclusion that what Merleau-Ponty called the human order corresponds to what we call the social order, with its being-for-others, and that what he calls the vital order includes what we call the mental order, in its being-by-self; for after all there is nothing more purely subjective than ideas.[37] Thus quantity and quality do not connect matter and mind, but rather matter and value or significance—which is a distinguishing characteristic of the social order. For it is through value and significance that we generate language and symbols that mirror nature and our mental life.

Hegel provides a succinct analysis of the mediation of quality and quantity.

Each of the three spheres of the logical idea proves to be a systematic whole of thought-terms, and a phase of the Absolute. This is the case with Being, containing the three grades of quality, quantity, and measure. Quality is, in the first place, the character identical with being: so identical, that a thing ceases to be what it is, if it loses its quality. Quantity, on the contrary, is the character external to being, and does not affect the being at all. Thus e.g., a house remains what it is, whether it be greater or smaller; and red remains red, whether it be brighter or darker. **Measure, the third grade of being, which is the unity of the first two, is a qualitative quantity.** All things have their measure: i.e. the quantitative terms of their existence, their being so or so great, does not matter within certain limits; but when these limits are exceeded by an additional more or less, the things cease to be what they were.[38]

Measurement in Scientific Inquiries

Given that the unity of quality and quantity is brought about through measure, it follows immediately that this dialectical law represents measurement methodology within scientific inquiries. Engels explained:

All qualitative differences in nature rest on differences of chemical composition or on different qualities or forms of motion (energy) or, as is almost

Figure 25.
Source: Reprinted by permission of Faber and Faber Ltd., from Rudolph Arnheim, **Art and Visual Perception: A Psychology of the Creative Eye,** Berkeley: University of California Press, 1954, Figure 1.

> always the case, on both. Hence it is impossible to alter the quality of a body without addition or subtraction of matter or motion, i.e., without quantitative alteration of the body concerned. In this form, therefore, Hegel's mysterious principle appears not only quite rational but even rather obvious.[39]

In scientific inquiry the unity of quality and quantity comes about through an effort to describe the object of study as consisting of variables and relations between variables. The object of investigation, while itself fundamentally a unity, is broken down into the many, generating as much fragmentation as is necessary to describe the behavior of the object over time (its performance, as it were, or its form as its law of development). First the scientist substructs the object of his attention into parts, and then he attempts to reassemble these parts in a coherent whole. The unity of the object can be seen if the reassembly is viable, if its described form is in correspondence with the external form of the object.

When a general system of equations connecting the variables for an object being studied leads to measurable description, then the scientist can employ measurement techniques and replace the variables with constant terms, rendering the resulting particular statement capable of being adjudged as consistent or inconsistent with measure.

Hegel's theory of being views measure, where quality and quantity are in unity, as the completion of being. He wrote: "Being, as we first apprehend it, is something utterly abstract and characterless: it is the very essence of Being to characterize itself, and its complete characterization is reached in Measure."[40]

Measurement in Synthetic Inquiries
Quality and quantity are related by measure in perception. Consider an analysis of a geometric figure (Figure 25) presented by Rudolph Arnheim:

> The location of the disk could be determined and described by means of measurement. A yardstick would tell in inches the distance from the edges of the square. Thus it could be inferred that the disk lies off center.
> But this result would come as no surprise. We do not have to measure—we can see that the disk lies off center. How is this "seeing" done? Which faculty of the mind provides such information? It is not the intellect,

because the result is not obtained by means of abstract concepts. It is not emotion, for although the sight of the eccentric disk may produce discomfort in some persons and a pleasurable stir in others, this can happen only after they have spotted its location. Emotion is a consequence, rather than an instrument, of discovery.

We constantly make statements that describe things in relation to their environment. "My right hand is larger than the left." "This flagpole is not straight." "The piano is out of tune." . . . An object is seen immediately as having a certain size, that is, as lying somewhere on the scale between a grain of salt and a mountain. On the scale of brightness values, our white square lies high, our black disk low. Similarly, every object is seen as having a location. . . .

In other words, every act of seeing is a visual judgment. Judgments are sometimes thought to be a monopoly of the intellect. But visual judgments are not contributions of the intellect, added after the seeing is done. They are immediate and indispensable ingredients of the act of seeing itself. Seeing that the disk lies off center is an intrinsic part of seeing it at all.[41]

Arnheim goes on to describe such seeing as an example of "induced structure." He writes: "For example, in a picture done in central perspective the vanishing point may be established by the convergent lines even though no actual object can be seen at their meeting point. In a melody there may be 'heard' by mere induction the regular beat, from which a syncopated tone deviates, as our disk deviates from the center."[42]

●　●　●　●　●

In synthetic inquiries, the unity of quality and quantity comes about through the necessity of grasping meaning, not as a confusion of opposites, but as a synthetic whole. This is evident from Lévi-Strauss's commentary on the study of myth:

> The study of myths raises a methodological problem, in that it cannot be carried out according to the Cartesian principle of breaking down the difficulty into as many parts as may be necessary for finding the solution. There is no real end to mythological analysis, no hidden unity to be grasped once the breaking down process has been completed. Themes can be split up **ad infinitum.** Just when you think you have disentangled and separated them, you realize that they are knitting together again in response to the operation of unexpected affinities. Consequently the unity of the myth . . . is a phenomenon of the imagination, resulting from the attempt at interpretation; and its function is to endow the myth with synthetic form and to prevent its disintegration into a confusion of opposites.[43]

These remarks can be extended to synthetic inquiries in general, and the three case studies in particular. In the **Tarot** and the **I Ching**—in continuing experience with hexagrams and cards as they occur in throwings and readings, in innumerable contexts, in relation to innumerable problems and questions—the quality of thought does not decay into a rigid and lifeless accounting of semblances, coincidences, signs, and codes, but instead develops into a quality of perception constituting an order. And Castaneda, as mentioned, found that by the practice of listening carefully to sounds, and distinguishing them, he could recognize that the sounds of nature are not a random pattern, but an organized totality that must be recognized as an order. The measurement in such an inquiry does not come about from the assignment of abstract numbers to some indefinitely large collection of variables used to describe the form of an object. Instead, the problems of measurement involve recognition of pattern, in which the order reveals itself. While an order can undergo limited transformation without corresponding structural change, order perceived as a pattern produces a real knowing of an overall coherence. Scientific knowledge leads to a formal knowing of the law of development (form) of an order, which, because of form's real opposition to structure, leads to a dialectical knowing of the object. Synthetic knowledge leads to a structured knowing of order that is direct and now. Thus while formulated scientific theory provides **prediction**, vision of the future, synthetic inquiry provides vision of the now, which can include the idea for a theory.

THE UNITY AND STRUGGLE OF OPPOSITES
Hegel's second law of dialectics posits a unity between opposites. **Real** opposites are defined by their capacity for unity, or by the fact that one **implies** the other. Thus left and right, yang and yin, and so forth are opposites. Processes in the world are knowable by the "self-development," the struggle of opposing tendencies within.

In dialectics, development is not seen as a harmonious and mechanical unfolding, but as "struggle" between opposing tendencies that are inherent in objects. The forces in such development are not seen as the results of external causes, but, in Hegel's term, as "self-movement." Thus the oppositions inherent in a thing are opposed to its identity, for they contain the seeds of both transformation and structural change to a new and different order. The concept of opposition is opposed to the concept of identity, in which quality is invariant under change. Hegel argued that identity determines only simple immediacy, a static being, while the interpenetration of opposing tendencies within an object is a source of its motion; things change because they possess internal contradictions that struggle with one another. While self-identity is static, self-contradiction is dynamic.

This conceptualization is consistent with the position taken here, that oppositions, such as left and right, are contained in concepts. Thus dialectics includes the study of opposites within order. These contradictory parts are not organized **eclectically,** such that one can cast about for innumerable "independent variables" drawn from phenomena at varying levels to explain change, but **dialectically,** being so interpenetrated that one cannot exist without the other and neither is external.

Oppositions in Scientific Inquiries
Science is constructed out of visions; in this sense theory construction employs the rationalities, and possesses the enemies, of the synthetic inquiries, which are the mirror images or opposites of the rationalities and enemies of science. The scientific rationalities are directed to the conversion of these visions of structure

into form. A scientific theory that is supported by empirical evidence stands as a mirror image of the theory's object. The practice of science thus presupposes a special instance of its opposite—synthetic inquiry that has as its goal the construction of theories. Synthetic rationalities are used in theory construction; scientific rationalities are used in theory formulation.

We have seen that while the rationalities for having a special kind of vision—the idea for a theory, and for the formulation of a theory operate on opposing rationalities, they must be brought into unity. For the vision must be defied and the character of its order changed from entwined ideas at the edge of words to a linear order in which the ideas are set forth propositionally.

Kant saw that inquiry into logic "teaches nothing with regard to the content of knowledge, but lays down the formal conditions only of an agreement with the understanding, which, so far as the objects are concerned, are **totally indifferent.**" Yet, within the practice of science, it is **absolutely necessary** that events be explained by statements formally deduced from the laws of a theory. Thus sentences—which are indifferent to content—must be brought into unity with observation. To this end scientists devise abstract implements constituting methodologies[44] to evaluate whether events implied by a theory are in unity with measurement. The scientist has the problem of creating a unity between form and structure, generating statements that can, with sensory observation and methodology, be critically evaluated as to whether they are actually **about** the topic of the theory.

There is both struggle and unity of opposites in science. It is a struggle to have a vision, as don Juan tells us, and it is a struggle to unravel the vision, bringing its image into form. Thus the **struggle** of opposites in science comes at the level of theory construction; the **unity** of opposites, in contrast, comes in observation of events predicted by a theory.

Oppositions in Synthetic Inquiries

The notion of critique is basic in inquiry. While critique can be traced in any synthetic inquiry, it can be seen clearly in the teachings of don Juan. In conversations with his apprentice, don Juan's statements were not merely answers to Castaneda's rhetorical questions. Rather they can be interpreted as a persistent critique of Castaneda's attitudes. Don Juan's behavior seems to be motivated by an attempt to teach Castaneda to be a man of knowledge by creating the conditions in which an apprentice (the opposite of a man of knowledge) is induced to function in a manner equivalent to a man of knowledge. It is through don Juan's ceaseless criticism that the operation of his system is learned and **validation** of the apprentice as a practitioner of the system is established. Without such critique the practice of sorcery and the seeing it produces would eventually become reified and idiosyncratic. If sorcerers did not instruct apprentices, the practice of sorcery would come to lose all practical value.

Knowledge within the synthetic systems involves the competent seeing of "nonordinary reality." The sorcerer's problem vis-à-vis the external world is to produce this nonordinary reality. To accomplish this work it is necessary to project quality into the world. For example, what was previously seen as a nonconsequential plant contains an ally. Such a change is produced by a disciplined program in which the analytic units of don Juan's system are extended into the world. The practices necessary to effect such a change include singing to the plants, ingesting the plants in determinate ways, cueing into the psychotropic states produced by the plants (for example, **Datura** was seen to be a woman). Castaneda's personal struggle was one of being able to indwell in don Juan's analytic units, thereby seeing a different world.

● ● ● ● ●

The interpenetration of opposites can be shown in the **Tarot** and the **I Ching** as well. Again, we will focus on the **I Ching**. An essential feature of the **I Ching** is the splitting apart of a situation into contradictory parts. Hexagrams are composed of firm and yielding lines representing opposite principles. The study of the **I Ching** is an inquiry into the interrelations of opposites, in that each hexagram constitutes a distinctive relation between opposite forces occupying the six places.

The firm and yielding lines in hexagrams can either complement or combat each other; similarly, the trigrams in a hexagram can either complement or combat each other. These relations between lines and trigrams are the bases of interpretation. Favorable and unfavorable auguries are the result of unified and conflicting relations, respectively. For example, the hexagram with fire above the lake,

K'uei, Opposition,

represents a dialectical tension of opposites. Wilhelm wrote:

> In general, opposition appears as an obstruction, but when it represents polarity within a comprehensive whole, it has also its useful and important functions. The oppositions of heaven and earth, spirit and nature, man and woman, when reconciled, bring about the creation and reproduction of life. **In the world of visible things, the principle of opposites makes possible the differentiation by categories through which order is brought into the world.**[45]

The interpenetration of opposites is further expressed in the basic organization of the hexagrams. The hexagrams are ordered in a sequence in which hexagrams are adjacent to their opposites or their mirror images, and in the two cases involving opposite pairs of symmetric trigrams, in both. The hexagrams Peace and Stagnation,

and ,

are numbers 11 and 12 in the sequence, and the hexagrams After Completion and Before Completion,

and ,

are numbers 63 and 64. Of course the hexagrams that are symmetric about the vertical axis are their own mirror images. These eight hexagrams are paired with their **opposites**. For example, we have seen that the hexagrams **Ch'ien** and **K'un** are numbers 1 and 2 in the sequence, and the hexagrams the Abysmal (water) and the Clinging (fire),

are numbers 29 and 30. Thus in the sequence presented in Wilhelm's **I Ching** every hexagram that is not its own mirror image is paired with its mirror image, and every hexagram that is its own mirror image is paired with its opposite.

The sequence of hexagrams set forth by a great master of Sung Confucianism (A.D. 960–1127) Shao Yung, called the **natural order** of the hexagrams, reveals the interpenetration of opposites that can be generated from the numerical ordering of the 64 hexagrams, as shown in Figure 26. Hellmut Wilhelm explains how the natural order was obtained by Shao Yung:

> He starts with two primary lines, the light and the dark, then adds to each again a light and a dark line, thus obtaining four two-lined complexes:

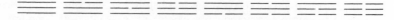

> Above each of these a light line and again, alternately, a dark line is added, so that the eight trigrams stand in the following arrangement:

> Continuing in the same way, he obtains first complexes of four, then of five, and finally of six lines, that is, the hexagrams. . . . This so-called natural order can be arranged . . . in a square of eight times eight hexagrams, in which counting begins at the lower right-hand corner and continues through to the lower left, then starts again at the right on the second line from below and continues to the left, and so on.[46]

H. Wilhelm goes on to describe a strange meeting of East and West:

> Shao Yung's schema has led to one of the most extraordinary episodes in the history of the human mind, and to this day it has never been satisfactorily cleared up. More than six hundred years after its origin, Shao's diagram fell into the hand of [G. W. von] Leibniz through the agency of Jesuit missionaries, and he recognized in it a system that had previously sprung from his own mathematical genius. To facilitate the solution of certain mathematical problems, Leibniz had thought out the so-called binary, or dyadic, numeral system, which makes use of two numbers only, instead of ten, but otherwise follows the same principle as the decimal system. The two figures are 0 and 1. The numerical sequence of the binary system would look as follows:

> 1, 10, 11, 100, 101, 110, 111, 1000, etc.

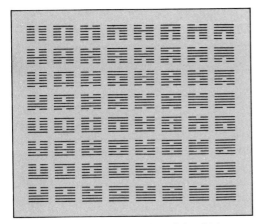

Figure 26. The natural order of the 64 hexagrams in the I Ching.
Source: Figure 2 in Hellmut Wilhelm, **Change: Eight Lectures on the I Ching**, trans. Cary F. Baynes, Bollingen Series LXII, copyright © 1960 by Bollingen Foundation, reprinted by permission of Princeton University Press.

In the sequence of Earlier Heaven Leibniz now rediscovered his own dyadic system, though he had to begin with zero for the correspondence to emerge. He took the broken line for a zero, and the unbroken for a 1. Thus the hexagram **Po** was 1, if zeros preceding 1 are disregarded, and stood in the first place in his system; the next, **Pi,** was 10, that is, our two, and so on. Leibniz placed the zero (= **K'un**) at the beginning of the sequence, and so Shao Yung's system corresponded point for point with the binary system, right up to the last hexagram, **Ch'ien** which for Leibniz was 111111, or 63. The only difference is that this correspondence is not a direct but an inverted one, that is, in order to obtain it, one must begin at the end of the series, which serves to emphasize once more the fact that parallel cultural phenomena in East and West are as Mirror images to each other![47]

As H. Wilhelm explains, the astonishing thing about the correspondence is that the two great minds started with completely different methods. "To Leibniz, the key to the problem before him was number; to Shao Yung, it was the hexagram."[48]

The law of the interpenetration of opposites in the practice of the I Ching is explicit for two methods historically used to study it. First, the **p'ang-tung** method, as H. Wilhelm notes, "consisted in the coordination of hexagrams that are opposite in structure. Two hexagrams . . . were placed side by side, and from the contrast of their total aspects conclusions were drawn for the situation as such and for the individual lines."[49] Second, in the **ch'in-kua** method, "the hexagrams were reversed. In each hexagram its inverse was seen to be latent."[50]

● ● ● ● ●

The interpenetration of opposites is manifested also on the practical level in the I Ching. Every practitioner must deal with the opposition of **chance** and **objec-**

tive necessity. A hexagram is constructed through what appears to be a nearly random procedure. When coins are thrown, the bias from which this book is written—that of scientific inquiry—suggests that the coins fall by chance. Of course, in spite of this apparent randomness, a great majority of practitioners of the I Ching (and of the Tarot) suspend belief in the proposition that the coins (and cards) fall by chance. They are open to the possibility that they are receiving a specific answer through the direct intervention of some suprahuman intelligence, sometimes referred to as an oracle. As the practice is developed, the question of chance is often a troubling one. It is a usual experience that the hexagrams come to be so dramatically applicable to the question—so much can be seen in them—that it becomes difficult to doubt the presence of an oracle. There is no consensus among practitioners of these systems. It could be that the "magic" in the consultation of the oracle is what the obtained hexagram reflexively does to the question. Since a comprehension of a hexagram at the level of seeing demands consideration of the change hexagram, the mirror-image hexagram, the opposite hexagram, and more generally the sequence of all hexagrams, it may be that the answer comes through the invariable in the method, the framing of the question in a context of the I Ching itself. If so, then the obtained hexagram can be thought of as providing one of sixty-four views, or perspectives, for framing the question.

While a hexagram might occur by chance, it is an objective necessity for using the system. A hexagram provides more than an answer to a question. It is seen as the objective image of the situation, and the pronouncements associated with a hexagram prescribe and proscribe the necessary activities demanded in the situation. The proper attitude of a practitioner is not to doubt an obtained hexagram, but rather to discover means of applying it to the world, of indwelling in the situation provided by the hexagram. Thus the throwing of the coins is a most serious act for a practitioner.

It is incumbent on practitioners to produce the conditions under which the contradiction between chance and absolute necessity is resolved. A practitioner approaching the oracle is in a state of relative necessity. Throwing the coins changes this state of relative necessity into an absolute necessity. There may be a premonition of the hexagram that will come up, but this hunch may not be borne out. The only way to attain certainty is to pick up the coins and throw them. During this process the possibilities for interpretation of the situation are reduced, and the practitioner is forced into a particular hexagram. While the practitioner needs to generate a position, the coins are indifferent to this need. Thus objective necessity is produced from an interpenetration of relative necessity and chance. A thrown hexagram is the synthesis that reconciles the oppositions of chance and necessity.

In light of this analysis—which parallels the dialectical connection of indifferent form and the object of investigation in science—Engels's summary of Hegel on this idea is useful. He wrote:

> Hegel came forward with the hitherto quite unheard-of proposition that the accidental has a cause because it is accidental, and just as much also has no cause because it is accidental; that the accidental is necessary, that necessity determines itself as chance, and, on the other hand, this chance is rather absolute necessity. . . .[51] Natural science has simply ignored these

propositions as paradoxical trifling, as self-contradictory nonsense, and, as regards theory, has persisted on the one hand in the barrenness of thought of Wolffian metaphysics, according to which a thing is either accidental **or** necessary, but not both at once; or, on the other hand, in the hardly less thoughtless mechanical determinism which by a phrase denies chance in general only to recognize it in practice in each particular case.[52]

The I Ching becomes a case specifying the basic preconditions necessary for a system of knowledge; it includes procedures in which "the accidental is necessary, that necessity determines itself as chance, and on the other hand, this chance is rather absolute necessity." The relationships of these oppositions constitute the dynamic in the practice as well as the dynamic observable in nature. All developed systems of knowledge must have, as the basis of their practicality, a procedure for the production of indifference. This operationally means a chance or random procedure that functions as the opposite of different points of view, or sides, that compose the object of the practice. Such a procedure has the purpose of changing a positioned, or biased, view of a practitioner into an article of objective (absolute) knowing.

This proposition can be shown to exist in each of the three case studies. In the **Tarot** it is seen in the procedural shuffling of the cards; in the I Ching, in throwing coins; in the sorcery of don Juan, in ingesting peyote. According to Castaneda, don Juan says that Mescalito has **no** rule (as opposed to the inflexible, invariant rules of the allies in **Datura** and **Psylocybe**). It is the teacher of the system. Having no rule must mean that what happens to a practitioner on Mescalito occurs by chance. As a teacher it determines the objective necessity of the practice in a manner analogous to the tossing of the coins or shuffling of cards, in which the resulting hexagram or array of cards teaches a practitioner.

● ● ● ● ●

In the synthetic inquiries, signs and codes, as described in the last chapter, function as metaphors in a system productive of an art form. In this connection, Lévi-Strauss sees that these metaphors, in myth, are

> based on an intuitive sense of the logical relations between one realm and other realms; metaphor reintegrates the first realm with the totality of the others, in spite of the fact that reflective thought struggles to separate them. Metaphor, far from being a decoration that is added to language, purifies it and restores it to its original nature, through momentarily obliterating one of the innumerable synecdoches that make up speech.[53]

The signs and codes running through synthetic inquiries constitute bundles of polar opposites, but the fact that endless interpretations can be given to the meaning of works of art, music, poetry, the telling of mythical stories, and the practice of sorcery or some system such as the I Ching or the Tarot does not imply that these systems have no motion-in-themselves, or that they become rigid and dead. Referring to myth, Lévi-Strauss writes:

> The mythological system is relatively autonomous when compared with the other manifestations of the life and thought of the group. Up to a

point all are interdependent, but their interdependence does not result in rigid relations which impose automatic adjustments among the various levels. It is a question rather of long-term pressures, within the limits of which the mythological system can, in a sense, argue with itself and acquire dialectical depth.[54]

THE NEGATION OF THE NEGATION

The law of the negation of the negation is central to Hegel's theory of logic, and is most closely related to the doctrine of the notion. The notion is defined as a being that passes outward into its opposite, but in so doing remains completely identical with itself. Thus while being is immediate (simple apprehension), and essence is mediation-by-another (understanding), the notion is characterized by self-mediation.

A central idea in the notion is that thought is both subjective and objective. Objectivity is seen as just as much thought as is subjectivity. But this form and content, subject and object, while distinguishable, are also identical. W. T. Stace explains Hegel's argument as follows.

> The Notion is the identity of opposites. Since its opposite is immediately identical with itself, it is, therefore, absolute identity. This unity or identity is the **universal**. . . . The Notion . . . goes into opposition to itself and this opposition is particularity. But its opposite is only itself. This identity of its opposite with itself constitutes the **negation of the negation** and so the return of the Notion into itself. For if the Notion first negates itself and becomes its opposite, this opposition is now again negated to absolute identity. . . . The return into itself of the Notion is therefore the unity of the universal and the particular. . . . Put in another way, . . . [t]he original Notion in going forth into its opposite develops a duality within itself, but this duality is again immediately annulled; and in this return into itself, . . . it is the identity of identity or difference, i.e., it is the **singular** or **individual**.[55]

Hegel's argument means that thought transcends the distinction between itself and its object. Thought is dialectic in that, at every stage of its development, it contains both the analytic and synthetic methods, and is itself the dialectical synthesis of the two modes of thought. Stace writes:

> Because it advances from the abstract universal, through further and further specification, to the concrete **singular**, it is synthetic. And because it begins with immediacy, and advances through mediation to the concrete **universal**, which contains the previous immediacy under it and within it, it is analytic.[56]

Analytic cognition deals with objects in detachment, and gives abstract meaning to them. It breaks the particular aspects of objects down into their universal aspects. For example, an object might be characterized by variables that pertain to classes of objects: mass, weight, etc. In this mode of thought, an object is a creation of the mind. Synthetic cognition, on the other side, has as its starting point the universal (a definition), and proceeds to divide objects into their partic-

ularities. In this mode of thought, objects are perceptually grasped in their particularity, interesting because they are first of all known. The analytic and synthetic modes of thought are brought into unity in the moment we make a judgment, that is, attach an abstract idea of an object to the perception of it. Hegel
wrote: "This equally synthetic and analytic moment of the Judgment, by which
the original universal determines itself out of itself to be its own Other, may
rightly be called the **dialectic** moment."[57]

Negation of the Negation in Scientific Inquiries

In science, the law of the negation of the negation comes into play in the fundamental operation of empirical testing of theories. Theories having the formal
structure of deductive argument—called hypothetico-deductive—are a reconstruc-
tion of the logic of scientific explanation. According to Carl G. Hempel and Paul
Oppenheim, such explanations consist of two components: an **explanans**—the
sentences adduced to account for a phenomena—and an **explanandum**—a linguistic description of the empirical phenomena to be explained. The statements in
the explanandum must be valid logical consequences of the statements in the
explanans; that is, the explanandum must be derived in a manner compatible
with internal principles. The explanans contains general statements, called laws,
axioms, assumptions, or postulates, and singular statements called **antecedent
conditions**; the statements in the explanandum are called **events** or **hypotheses**.[58] The statements in a theory must be internally consistent, and not contradictory.

All deductive theories are, or can be, formalized and considered in the
abstract apart from their content. All sentences in a theory, in both the explanans and the explanandum, must be declarative statements that are logically
true or false.

The laws in a theory are universally quantified, meaning that they are in
the form "all **A**'s are **B**'s," or "for every **x**, if **x** is an **A**, then **x** is a **B**." In this
statement the phrase "for every **x**" is the universal quantifier. It means that all
things of a given sort—the **x**'s constituting the objects the theory is about—either
have certain properties or stand in certain relations to other things having certain
properties. Statements with this linguistic property are defined as **universal gen-
eralizations**, or as **laws**. R. B. Braithwaite writes that a scientific law

> always includes a generalization, i.e., a proposition asserting a universal
> connection between properties. It always includes a proposition stating
> that every event or thing of a certain sort either has a certain property or
> stands in certain relations to other events, or things, having certain proper-
> ties. The generalization may assert a concomitance of properties in the
> same thing or event, that everything having the property **A** also has the
> property **B**. . . . Or it may assert that, of every two events or things of
> which the first has the property **A** and stands in the relation **R** to the sec-
> ond, the second has the property **B**. . . . Or it may make more complicated
> but similar assertions about three or four or more things. The relationship
> between the things may be a relationship holding between simultaneous
> events in the things, or it may hold between events in the same thing or in
> two or more things which are not simultaneous.[59]

It is by establishing universally applicable statements that theoretical thinking—while negative in that it dissolves certainty that the outer shell of objects we look at reflects their inner structure—is positive.

If a theory is not consistent with the events implied by it, it can be said to have false laws in it. Karl Popper argues that such a theory, containing one or more false laws, should be declared, as a whole, to be false. In this sense, theories can be proven false; but they can never be proven true, as this would involve an impossible requirement: It would be necessary to make observations at all times, everywhere.[60] However, if a theory consistently leads to observations consistent with events deduced from it, then there is no basis for rejecting it, and scientists can presume that the theory will continue to weather future attempts to find weaknesses in it.

The test of a theory, therefore, comes down to a choice:

1. Reject the theory.
2. Do not reject the theory.

The first choice means "not the theory," or "the theory is not true." The second choice means "not not the theory," or that the theory, being consistent with observed events, cannot be declared false, and therefore is, as a whole, dynamically connected to the laws of development of an object. This is the law of the negation of the negation in the methodology of theory testing, a fundamental operation in science. The methodology of theory testing constitutes a dialectic basis of scientific inquiry, and gives science its practical value. By means of establishing theories consistent with observation, science synthesizes the theory and the measurement of events that follow logically from the theory. This indeed shows that, as Hegel claimed, dialectics is the soul of scientific knowledge.

● ● ● ● ●

There is an additional use of the law of the negation of the negation in science that should be mentioned. Jean Piaget, in criticizing Lévi-Strauss's conception of dialectics as a matter of "throwing out bridges over the abyss of a human ignorance whose further shore is constantly receding," writes:

> It is often construction itself which begets the negations along with the affirmations, and the syntheses . . . whereby they are rendered coherent as well.
>
> This Hegelian or Kantian pattern is not . . . merely . . . conceptual or abstract. . . . It corresponds to a progression which is inevitable once thought turns away from false absolutes. In the realm of structure it matches a recurrent historical process well described by G. Bachelard in . . . **La Philosophie du non**. Its principle is that, given a completed structure, one negates one of its seemingly essential or at least necessary attributes. Classical algebra, for example, was commutative, but since Hamilton we have a variety of non-commutative algebras; Euclidean geometry has by "negation" (of the parallel postulate) engendered the non-Euclidean geometries; two-valued logic with its principle of excluded middle has, through Brouwer's denial of the unrestricted validity of this principle . . . become supple-

mented by multi-valued logics, and so on. In logic and mathematics, construction by negation has practically become a standard method; given a certain structure, one tries, by systematic negation of one after another attribute, to construct its complementary structure, in order later to subsume the original together with its complements in a more complex total structure.[61]

The procedure used here constitutes an instance of construction by negation. Four rationalities of science were negated, and four enemies of synthetic inquiries—and the resulting eight statements were included in the theory. A theory in which **every** law, when negated, produces another law in the theory is called a **dual** theory. The principle of duality applies to the algebra of sets, to the statement calculus in symbolic logic, to Boolean algebras in general, and to numerous substantive theories.[62] Of course, a theory that conforms to a principle of duality—such that the substitution of complementary concepts in laws generates other laws—does not mean the theory is dualistic.

Negation of the Negation in Synthetic Inquiries
Hegel argued that ideas do not flow from one into another in a predetermined harmony. Instead, they develop out of struggle. The underlying principle expresses development as struggle in the strongest terms: The negation of the negation means the defeat of the enemy. The laws of dialectics were seen by Engels to represent laws of evolution in nature as well as of thought. The laws of dialectics were seen by Marx to represent laws of social development, according to which revolutionary change in societies comes about through the progressive resolution of contradictions between opposed classes. To say that dialectics constitutes the basis of synthetic inquiries is to assert that both the scientist and the synthetic inquirer have enemies against which they must struggle. For both the scientist and the sorcerer, it is a struggle to see. But the struggle is not the seeing. It is possible to see without struggle, without being a warrior. As don Juan advises Castaneda, to see without first becoming a warrior would make him weak and indifferent. The spirit of a warrior is geared to struggle, and in his last battle the warrior attains free spirit and impeccable will. Thus we argue that to be a dialectician is, by definition, to be a warrior.

Castaneda's penetrating analysis of don Juan's teachings explicates the meaning of being a warrior.

The existence of a man of knowledge was an unceasing struggle, and the idea that he was a warrior, leading a warrior's life, provided one with the means for achieving emotional stability.[63] The idea of a man at war encompassed four concepts: (1) a man of knowledge had to have respect; (2) he had to have fear; (3) he had to be wide-awake; (4) he had to be self-confident. Hence, to be a warrior was a form of self-discipline which emphasized individual accomplishments; yet it was a stand in which personal interests were reduced to a minimum. . . .

A man of knowledge in his role of warrior was obligated to have an attitude of deferential regard for the items with which he dealt; he had to imbue everything related to his knowledge with profound respect in order to place everything in a meaningful perspective. Having respect was equiva-

lent to having assessed one's insignificant resources when facing the Unknown.

If one remained in that frame of thought, the idea of respect was logically extended to include oneself, for one was as unknown as the Unknown itself. . . .

Another necessity of a warrior's life was the need to experience and
carefully to evaluate the sensation of fear. . . .

As a warrior, a man of knowledge also needed to be wide-awake. A man
at war had to be on the alert in order to be cognizant of most of the factors pertinent to the two mandatory aspects of awareness: (1) awareness
of intent and (2) awareness of the expected flux, . . . capable of detecting
at all times the important variables involved in the relationship between
the specific purposes of every act and one's specific reason for acting. By
being aware of the expected flux one was supposed to detect the most
subtle changes. . . .

The last aspect of the idea of a warrior's behavior was the need for
self-confidence, that is, the assurance that the specific purpose of an act
one may have chosen to perform was the only plausible alternative for
one's own specific reasons for acting.[64]

Isaiah Berlin, in describing the thinkers that embraced Hegel's theory, writes:

Citing again the texts undeniably to be found in Hegel, the radicals reminded their opponents that progress was the result of tension between
opposites, which grew to a crisis and then burst into open revolution: then
and only then did the leap into the next stage occur. These were the laws
of development found equally in the obscure processes of brute nature and
in the affairs of men and societies.

The plain duty of the philosopher who carries the burdens of civilization on his shoulders is, therefore, to promote revolution by the special
technical skill which he alone commands, that is by intellectual warfare.[65]

Hegel was an intellectual warrior of the first order. He saw the development of
ideas as a struggle.

Since in this chapter, and to some extent in the entire book, attention has
been most closely directed to the I Ching, it is not difficult to note the presence
of struggle in this system. The entire text and commentary is permeated with the
topic of struggle, with transformations and changes. The attributes of the trigrams include such an interpretation: "Water and fire complement each other,
thunder and wind do not interfere with each other, and the forces of mountain
and lake are united in their action. Thus only are changes and transformations
possible, and thus only can all things come to perfection."[66]

The Book of Changes is not a theory of change, but it can be regarded as
an inquiry that enables a practitioner to see transformations and changes in
situations that obey laws yet come about through perseverance and struggle,
such that any situation can be produced from another. The conventional interpretation of such a situation is that the first (initial) hexagram represents the
starting point, and the change lines indicate the pattern of movement that develop into the "change" hexagram representing the future.

For example, suppose a throwing yields fire on the mountain, or the Wanderer, with a change line in the fourth place:

$$\overline{\underline{\quad\quad}}$$ Lü   above: **Li**, fire
              below: **Kên**, mountain

In this situation the fourth position is changing into its own negation—from a changing yang line to a nonchanging yin line. The resulting hexagram is Keeping Still (mountain):

$$\overline{\underline{\quad\quad}}$$ Kên   above: **Kên**, mountain
              below: **Kên**, mountain

The Wanderer is the present situation, which has within it the end of wandering, or keeping still. The hexagram Keeping Still, the change hexagram, can be said to represent the totality of circumstances necessary to induce a moving yang line in the fourth place to function as its own opposite, a firm yin line. For a yang line that is active in the constitution of the situation of the Wanderer to become a yin line at rest necessitates Keeping Still.

● ● ● ● ●

It has been shown that Hegel's three laws of dialectics are **present** in the **I Ching**. But this is insufficient to show that dialectics are the **basis** of the **I Ching**. One could argue, for instance, that while they are present, they may be tangential, or present only in certain contexts. Or one could argue that while dialectics is basic to science, the basis of the **I Ching** is a principle of order called **tao**. Now dialectic and order are often regarded as opposites,[67] but struggle is in the very essence of order.

Taoism, the basis of the **I Ching**, is a philosophy for developing the Mind. It is an ancient conception of dialectics. Hegel was able to develop his theory at a time when Taoist ideas were flowing, as Chang puts it, "like an invisible stream into the mind of the West, to scholars who held differing views concerning **tao** and whose insight was applied to their respective subjects."[68] Hegel was one German scholar much influenced by these ideas. Chang writes: "In 1816 . . . Hegel was lecturing learnedly at Heidelberg on Taoism, Confucianism, and the philosophy found in the **I Ching**. His information, to be sure, was derived secondhand from the translations of the Jesuits, but he was surprisingly well-informed, notably on the subject of Taoism."[69]

What is the essential content of this conception? Chang writes: "The value of **tao** lies in its power to reconcile opposites on a higher level of consciousness." Jung wrote: "If we take **tao** as the method or conscious way by which to unite what is separated, we have probably come quite close to the psychological content of the concept."[70] In both Buddhism and Taoism unity within diversity and the unity of the particular and the universal are fundamental principles. The Confucian Hsun Ching said: "If we look upon **tao** as words, we are merely being dialectic."[71] Chang notes:

Lao Tzu identifies **tao** as the One which is invisible, inaudible, unfathomable. It is the same One, past and present; it embraces form and formless alike, being as well as nonbeing. The One is therefore a unification of duality and multiplicity. It is the One without opposite, infinite and unceasing.[72]

Through analysis of apparent duality, Chang notes,

the Taoist attains a synthesis of opposites, or what Hegel calls an 'identity-in-difference.' . . . The achievement of Taoism was not merely that of the concept of unity of dualities or the identification of opposites. For the Taoist there is also a unity in multiplicity, a wholeness of parts.[73]

The law of the negation of the negation is fundamental to Taoist and Buddhist doctrines. For example, compare Hegel's three doctrines—Being, Essence, and Notion—to the well-known "Double Truth on Three Levels" propounded by the sixth-century Buddhist Chi Tsang:

The common people take all things for **yu** (being) and know nothing about **wu** (non-being). But . . . actually all things are **wu** and empty. Thus, on this level, to say that all things are **yu** is the common truth and to say that all things are **wu** is the higher sense of truth.
When we ascend to the second level, to say that all is **yu** is to look at things one-sidedly. But to say that all things are **wu** is similarly one-sided. Actually, what is **yu** is simultaneously **wu**. On this second level, then, of double truth, to say that all things are **yu** and to say that all things are **wu** are both equally common sense. One now ought to say that . . . things are neither **yu** nor **wu**. That now becomes the higher sense of truth.
But on the third level, to say that absolute truth consists of what is not one-sided, means that we are making distinctions, and all distinctions are by their nature one-sided. Therefore, on this level, to say that things are neither **yu** nor **wu** is merely common sense. The higher truth consists in saying that things are neither **yu** nor **wu**, neither not-**yu** nor not-**wu**, and that the absolute truth is neither one-sided nor not one-sided.[74]

To this Chang adds:

The absolute truth is achieved through denial of the denial. The truth of the first level is denied on the second. The truth of the second level is further denied on the third. The absolute truth [compare Hegel's "Absolute Idea"] of the third level is neither one-sided nor not one-sided, neither assertion nor nonassertion.[75]

This dialectical process is intended to describe the dynamic process of the Mind developing itself to the point where it can see order. The Taoist and Buddhist descriptions call the possible result of the struggle sudden illumination, Hegel called it the dialectic moment, and don Juan calls it the "meeting with an ally," which can be manipulated to take one into a nonordinary reality by its own inflexible rules, its invariant frame.

Chang writes:

> The understanding of **tao** is an inner experience in which distinction be-
> tween subject and object vanish. It is an intuitive, immediate awareness
> rather than a mediated, inferential, or intellectual process.[76]

This is precisely what Hegel meant by the self-mediated being that defines the
notion, and which culminates in the dialectic moment. The idea of the unity of
subject and object derives from the pre-Buddhist concept of **sympathy** in Chinese Taoism. Chang writes:

> This sympathy was primordial identification, interfusion, and unification
> of subject and object, of one and many, of man and the universe. It was
> not a product of rational intellection, but an ontological experience.[77]

It is ironic that an idea developed in ancient China may have found its way into
Hegel's mind, and by its application to the historical development of societies by
Hegel's disciples—Marx, Engels, and Lenin—found its way to Mao and thereby
found its way home.

CONCLUSIONS

We have considered two intellectual conceptions in this book constructed by
medicine men. Bogen and others write that the neurological research in which
the two brain hemispheres are divided reveals that we have two independent
spheres of consciousness, two minds. Bogen and Bogen also write that our highest mental capabilities are associated with the fibers connecting the two sides of
the brain, which are involved in thought that is simultaneously propositional and
appositional.

Don Juan, the Yaqui medicine man, argues that there are two worlds. In
Indian American culture, minds are not thought of primarily as independent
spheres of consciousness, for they emphasize that what constitutes our worlds is
shared. Don Juan says that our highest mental capabilities are associated with
thought that is neither in our everyday world, nor in the nonordinary world of
sorcery, but in the thought of a warrior able to sneak between the two worlds
and see that one is as real as the other.

Thus we find that the medicine men, whether practitioners of scientific or
synthetic inquiry, have produced isomorphic arguments. The theory presented
here contends that there are two opposite kinds of inquiry that are fundamentally complementary and share a basis in the dialectic.

Most scientists live in a world where propositional thought prevails, where
it is defined as **the** criterion for knowing, where it alone defines intelligence, and
where it is disproportionately rewarded. It is a struggle for any scientist to know
that there might exist another world, and that he has a mind that is already in it.
But it is this world that theories come from, for it is the world in which visions
are real. In creating its theories, science relies on practitioners who can sneak
between the two worlds and transform their visions into the form of words.

Science represents the historical synthesis of propositional-analytic inquiries and appositional-synthetic inquiries. In its present condition, science is a

dialectical synthesis of the two kinds of thought, propositional and appositional, or analytic and synthetic. Since—as we have seen from the study of their rationalities, enemies, and dialectics—these two modes of thought stand as real opposites, with formulated theories mirroring their object, science retains its dialectic.

While science makes use of both analytic and synthetic thought, it would be in error to conclude that inquiries into form or into structure represent underdeveloped versions of science. While the practice of science includes synthetic inquiry, it hardly includes all synthetic inquiries, and it cannot be said that science is better or that it stands alone as a method for knowing. In constructing concepts, theories, and methods, scientists necessarily employ synthetic rationalities that are essentially subjective. In the work of linguistic formulation, in the other hand, scientists employ an opposite set of rationalities that are essentially objective. To regard the practice of science as entirely objective is to ignore its unity of subjective and objective rationalities, its dialectical basis.

NOTES

1. Immanuel Kant, **Critique of Pure Reason**, trans. F. Max Muller, Garden City, N.Y.: Doubleday, 1961, p. 60.

2. Ibid.

3. Ibid.

4. Ibid.

5. Lévi-Strauss, **The Savage Mind**, p. 246, emphasis added.

6. Paul Radin, **The Winnebago Tribe**, Washington, D.C.: Bureau of American Ethnology, 37th Annual Report, 1923.

7. Ibid., p. 188.

8. Lévi-Strauss, **Structural Anthropology**, pp. 129—130.

9. Ibid., p. 130.

10. Ibid., pp. 148—149, emphasis added.

11. Ibid., p. 158.

12. Ibid., p. 150.

13. Ibid., p. 149.

14. Ibid., pp. 149—150. This analysis shows the dialectical reality of "primitive" social organizations. From the standpoint of the "civilized" nations, primitive societies are static in that they seem detached from, or left behind, history. But as the civilized world progressively exploits and exterminates the "underdeveloped" societies, they enter "history," and wage warfare according to dialectical principles with such effectiveness that their survival is possible. And if civilized societies resolve both their external and internal contradictions, they may find themselves "primitivized," finding their dialectical problems not in class struggle but in the production of culture and knowledge. It can be expected that the struggle between advanced industrial nations (with their endless need for natural resources) and the third world will become the object of a radical social science.

15. Carl G. Hempel, **Philosophy of Natural Science**, Englewood Cliffs, N.J.: Prentice-Hall, 1966, pp. 72—73.

16. Kant, op. cit., p. 60.

17. G. W. F. Hegel, **Science of Logic**, vol. 1, trans. W. H. Johnston and L. G. Strathers, London: Allen and Unwin, 1929, p. 33.

18. Ibid., p. 39.

19. Ibid. And Koestler remarks: "Among the intellectual élite, the rapid advance of science created a rather shallow optimistic belief in the infallibility of Reason, in a clear, bright, crystalline world with a transparent structure, with no room for shadows, twilights, and myths." See Koestler, **The Ghost in the Machine**, p. 256.

20. Ibid., p. 36.

21. Ibid., emphasis deleted.

22. Ibid., p. 240.

23. V. I. Lenin, **Collected Works,** vol. 38, Moscow: Foreign Languages Publishing House, 1961, p. 254, cited in Howard Selsam and Harry Martel, **Reader in Marxist Philosophy: From the Writings of Marx, Engels, and Lenin,** New York: International Publishers, 1963, p. 355.

24. Hegel, op. cit., p. 240.

25. Lenin, op. cit., cited in Selsam and Martel, op. cit.

26. Ibid.

27. Mao remarks that this saying appeared in the work of Pan Ku, a noted historian in the first century **A.D.** Cited in Mao Tse-tung, **On Contradiction,** Peking: Foreign Languages Press, 1967, p. 57f.

28. Ibid., pp. 45–46, emphasis added.

29. Frederick Engels, **Dialectics of Nature,** trans. and ed. Clemens Duft, New York: International Publishers, 1940, p. 26.

30. Mao, op. cit., p. 45.

31. Merleau-Ponty, **Structure of Behavior,** p. 130.

32. Ibid., pp. 130–131.

33. Ibid., p. 148.

34. Ibid., p. 161.

35. G. W. F. Hegel, **The Encyclopaedia of the Philosophical Sciences,** trans. William Wallace, 2nd ed., Oxford: Clarendon, 1892, pp. 170–171.

36. Ibid., p. 171.

37. In this sense Husserl was quite right when he defined his treatise on ideas as "Pure Phenomenology." See Husserl, **Ideas: General Introduction to Pure Phenomenology.**

38. Hegel, **Encyclopaedia,** p. 157, emphasis added.

39. Engels, op. cit., p. 27, cited in Selsam and Martel, op. cit., p. 124.

40. Hegel, **Encyclopaedia,** p. 201.

41. Rudolph Arnheim, **Art and Visual Perception: A Psychology of the Creative Eye,** Berkeley: University of California Press, 1954, pp. 1–2.

42. Ibid., p. 2.

43. Lévi-Strauss, **The Raw and the Cooked,** p. 5.

44. In synthetic inquiries the "toolbox," consisting of **concrete** implements, plays a role similar to that of methodology.

45. R. Wilhelm, op. cit., p. 148, emphasis added.

46. Hellmut Wilhelm, **Change: Eight Lectures on the I Ching,** trans. Cary F. Baynes, Princeton, N.J.: Princeton University Press, Bollingen Series LXII, 1960, pp. 89–90.

47. Ibid., pp. 90–91.

48. Ibid., p. 91.

49. Ibid., pp. 84–85.

50. Ibid., p. 85.

51. See Hegel, **Encyclopaedia,** pp. 257–277, for his discussion of Actuality, Possibility, Contingency, and Necessity.

52. Engles, op. cit., pp. 233–234, cited in Selsam and Martel, op. cit., pp. 121–122.

53. Lévi-Strauss, **The Raw and the Cooked,** p. 339.

54. Ibid., p. 332.

55. W. T. Stace, **The Philosophy of Hegel: A Systematic Exposition,** London: Dover, 1955, pp. 227–228.

56. Ibid., p. 288.

57. Hegel, **Science of Logic, II,** p. 473.

58. Carl G. Hempel and Paul Oppenheim, "Studies in the Logic of Explanation," **Philosophy of Science,** 15, 1948, pp. 135–175. Explanations with this form are called "deductive-nomological."

59. R. B. Braithwaite, **Scientific Explanation: A Study of the Function of Theory, Probability and Law in Science,** New York: Harper & Row, 1960, p. 9.

60. Karl R. Popper, **Logic of Scientific Discovery,** London: Hutchinson, 1959.

61. Jean Piaget, **Structuralism,** New York: Harper & Row, 1970, pp. 123–124.

62. In the algebra of sets, for example, the terms $\cup$ and $\cap$, for "or" and "and," and the sets W and ϕ, containing all or no elements, are real opposites. Thus the law, $A \cup \phi = A$, meaning "the collection of elements in set **A**, which is not empty, or, in set ϕ, which is empty, equals the collection of elements in A." The "dual" law becomes: $A \cap W = A$. See, e.g., Robert R.

Stoll, Sets, Logic, and Axiomatic Theories, New York: Freeman, 1961, pp. 18–20. A Boolean algebra is one in which the dual commutative law holds. This is true in set theory, but
not in ordinary algebra, where A · (B + C) = A · B + A · C does not imply its dual,
A + (B · C) = (A + B) · (A + C). Conclusion: Multiplication and addition are not "real opposites."

  For one example of a dual theory, see Frank Harary, Robert Z. Norman, and Dorwin
Cartwright, Structural Models, New York: Wiley, 1965.

  Statements in a dual theory may be self-dual, if they contain no terms that have real
opposites. For other terms, the principle of duality holds that "(a) the dual of a dual statement is the original statement; (b) the dual of a true statement is true." See ibid., p. 38.

63. The idea that the highest levels of human thought are dialectic implies the obverse, that
thought which is fragmented and dualistic is pathological. Also, thought that is excessively
one-sided can become pathological. If the propositional mind suppresses and dominates the
other to an excessive degree, the result can be an increasing rigidity and obsessive compulsiveness. If the appositional mind suppresses and dominates the propositional mind, the
result can be hysteria and a reduced capacity to analyze.

64. Castaneda, The Teachings of Don Juan, pp. 209–211.

65. Isaiah Berlin, Karl Marx: His Life and Environment, 3rd ed., London: Oxford University Press, 1963, p. 65.

66. R. Wilhelm, The I Ching, p. 272.

67. For example, John Horton contrasts order models of society and conflict models of
society. "Contemporary sociological theories of deviation are adaptations of two fundamental models of analysis rooted in nineteenth-century history and social thought. These
are order and conflict models of society. 'Order models' imply an anomy theory of societal
discontents and an adjustment definition of deviation. Conflict models imply an alienation
theory of discontent and a growth definition of deviation." (John Horton, "Order and Conflict Theories of Social Problems as Competing Ideologies," American Journal of Sociology,
vol. 71, 1966, p. 704.) Horton notes that the Parsonian model, whereas the Marxian theory
is a conflict theory. Dialectics is clearly the basis of Marxian theory, but not of Parsonian
theory. But, as mentioned at the outset of Chapter 4, there is a difference between a system
and an order, and a system theory is not the same as an order theory: An order theory
would require a basis in dialectics.

68. Chang, Creativity and Taoism, p. 9.

69. Ibid., pp. 3–4.

70. Jung, in Secret of the Golden Flower, pp. 95–96.

71. See Hsün-tzu, The Works of Hsün-tzu, trans. Homer H. Bubs, London: A. Probsthain,
1928, Book XXI, cited in Chang, op. cit., p. 26.

72. Chang, ibid., p. 31.

73. Ibid., pp. 32–33.

74. Yu-lan Feng, A History of Chinese Philosophy, trans. Derk Bodde, Princeton: Princeton
University Press, 1952, cited in Chang, ibid., p. 116.

75. Chang, op. cit., p. 116.

76. Ibid., p. 19.

77. Ibid., p. 21.

References

Alexander, Christopher, **Notes on the Synthesis of Form,** Cambridge: Harvard University Press, 1964.

Anderson, A. Lloyd, "The Effect of Laterality Localization of Focal Brain Lesions on the Wechsler-Bellevue Subtests," **Journal of Clinical Psychology,** vol. 7, 1951, pp. 149–153.

Arnheim, Rudolph, **Art and Visual Perception: A Psychology of the Creative Eye,** Berkeley: University of California Press, 1954.

Bakan, Paul, "The Eyes Have It," **Psychology Today,** vol. 4, 1971, pp. 64–67 and p. 97.

Balthazar, E. E., et al., "Visuo-Constructive and Verbal Responses in Chronic Brain Damaged Patients and Familial Retardates," **Journal of Clinical Psychology,** vol. 17, 1961, pp. 293–296.

Basser, L. S., "Hemiplegia at Early Onset and the Faculty of Speech with Special Reference to the Effects of Hemispherectomy," **Brain,** vol. 85, 1962, pp. 427–460.

Benton, A. L., "Differential Behavioral Effects in Frontal Lobe Disease," **Neuropsychologia,** vol. 6, 1968, pp. 53–60.

Berlin, Isaiah, **Karl Marx: His Life and Environment,** 3rd ed., London: Oxford University Press, 1963.

Bharati, Agehananda, **The Tantric Tradition,** Garden City, N.Y.: Doubleday, 1965.

Black Elk, recorded and edited by Jose Epes Brown, **The Sacred Pipe: Black Elk's Account of the Seven Rites of the Oglala Sioux,** Norman, Okla.: University of Oklahoma Press, 1953.

Blofeld, John, trans. and ed., **I Ching: The Book of Change,** New York: Dutton, 1968.

Bogen, Joseph E., "The Other Side of the Brain I: Dysgraphia and Dyscopia Following Cerebral Commissurotomy," **Bulletin of the Los Angeles Neurological Societies,** vol. 1, 1969, pp. 73–105.

Bogen, Joseph E., "The Other Side of the Brain II: An Appositional Mind," **Bulletin of the Los Angeles Neurological Societies,** vol. 34, 1969, pp. 135–161.

Bogen, Joseph E. and Glenda M. Bogen, "The Other Side of the Brain III: The Corpus Callosum and Creativity," **Bulletin of the Los Angeles Neurological Societies,** vol. 34, 1969, references 98a–107, pp. 206–207.

Bogen, Joseph E., R. DeZure, W. D. TenHouten, and J. F. Marsh, "The Other Side of the Brain IV: The AP Ratio," **Bulletin of the Los Angeles Neurological Societies,** vol. 37, 1972, pp. 49–61.

Braithwaite, R. B., Scientific Explanation: A Study of the Function of Theory, Probability and Law in Science, New York: Harper & Row, 1960.

Bruner, Jerome S., **On Knowing: Essays for the Left Hand,** Cambridge: Harvard University Press, 1963.

Carnap, Rudolf, "On Inductive Logic," **Philosophy of Science,** vol. 7, 1945, pp. 72–97.

Carroll, John B., ed., **Language, Thought and Reality: Selected Writings of Benjamin Lee Whorf,** Cambridge, Mass.: MIT Press, 1965.

Case, Paul Foster, **The Tarot: A Key to the Wisdom of the Ages,** Richmond, Va.: Macoy Publishing Company, 1947.

Castaneda, Carlos, **The Teachings of Don Juan: A Yaqui Way of Knowledge,** New York: Ballantine, 1968.

Castaneda, Carlos, A Separate Reality: Further Conversations with Don Juan, New York: Simon and Schuster, 1971.

Castaneda, Carlos, Journey to Ixtlan: The Lessons of Don Juan, New York: Simon and Schuster, 1972.

Chang, Chung-yuan, **Creativity and Taoism: A Study of Chinese Philosophy, Art, and Poetry,** New York: Harper & Row, 1963.

Chisholm, Roderick M., **Theory of Knowledge,** Englewood Cliffs, N.J.: Prentice-Hall, 1966.

Corballis, Michael C. and Ivan L. Beale, "On Telling Left from Right," **Scientific American,** vol. 224, March 1971, pp. 96–104.

Costa, L. D. and H. G. Vaughn, "Performance of Patients with Lateralized Cerebral Lesions: 1. Verbal and Perceptual Tests," **Journal of Nervous and Mental Disorders,** vol. 134, 1962, pp. 162–168.

Creeley, Robert, ed., **Selected Writings of Charles Olson,** New York: New Directions, 1951.

Critchley, Macdonald, **The Parietal Lobes,** New York: Hafner, 1966.

Day, Merle E., "An Eye-Movement Indicator of Individual Differences in the Physiological Organization of Attentional Processes and Anxiety," **Journal of Psychology,** vol. 66, 1967, pp. 51–62.

DeRenzi, E., P. Faglioni, and H. Spinnler, "The Performance of Patients with Unilateral Brain Damage on Face Recognition Tasks," **Cortex,** vol. 4, 1968, pp. 17–34.

DeRenzi, E., and H. Spinnler, "Visual Recognition in Patients with Unilateral Cerebral Disease," **Journal of Nervous and Mental Disorders,** vol. 142, 1966, pp. 515–525.

Domhoff, G. William, "But Why Did They Sit on The King's Right Hand in the First Place?" **Psychoanalytic Review,** vol. 56, 1970, pp. 586–596.

Engels, Frederick, **Dialectics of Nature,** trans. and ed., Clemens Duft, New York: International Publishers, 1940.

Eriksen, C. W., "Discrimination and Learning Without Awareness: A Methodological Survey and Evaluation," **Psychological Review,** vol. 67, 1960, pp. 279–300.

Eriksen, C. W. and J. L. Kuethe, "Avoidance Conditioning of Verbal Behavior Without Awareness: A Paradigm of Repression," **Journal of Abnormal and Social Psychology,** vol. 53, 1956, pp. 203–209.

Feng, Yu-lan, **A History of Chinese Philosophy,** trans., Derk Boddé, Princeton, N.J.: Princeton University Press, 1952.

Fenichel, Otto, **The Psychoanalytic Theory of Neurosis,** New York: Norton, 1945.

Frankel, Charles, **The Love of Anxieties and Other Essays,** New York: Dell, 1967.

Freud, Sigmund, **On Aphasia,** trans. E. Stengel, New York: International Universities, 1953.

Frolov, Y. P., **Pavlov and His School,** trans. C. P. Dutt, New York: Oxford University Press, 1937.

Gardner, Martin, **Fads and Fallacies in the Name of Science,** New York: Dover, 1957.

Gardner, Martin, **The Ambidextrous Universe,** New York: Basic Books, 1964.

Garfinkel, Harold, **Studies in Ethnomethodology,** Englewood Cliffs, N.J.: Prentice-Hall, 1967.

Gazzaniga, M. S. and Roger W. Sperry, "Simultaneous Double Discrimination Response Following Brain Bisection," **Psychoanalytic Science,** vol. 4, 1966, pp. 261–262.

Gazzaniga, M. S. and E. D. Young, "Effects of Commissurotomy on the Processing of Increasing Visual Information," **Experimental Brain Research,** vol. 3, 1967, pp. 368–371.

Ghiselin, Brewster, ed., **The Creative Process: A Symposium,** New York: New American Library, 1952.

Glees, P., **Experimental Neurology,** London: Oxford University Press, 1961.

Gödel, Kurt, "Üder Formal Unentscherdbare Sätze der Principia Mathematica und Verwandter Systeme I," **Monastsnefe für Mathematik und Physic,** vol. 38, 1931, pp. 1173–1198.

Goodman, Leo A., "Simple Statistical Methods for Scalogram Analysis," **Psychometrika,** vol. 24, 1959, pp. 29–43.

Granet, Marcel, "The Tao," **Theories of Society: Foundations of Modern Sociological Theory,** vol. 2, Talcott Parsons, Edward Shibs, Kaspar D. Naegele and Jesse R. Pitts, (eds.), New York: Free Press, 1961.

Gray, Eden, **The Tarot Revealed,** New York: Bell, 1970.

Guttman, Louis, "The Cornell Technique for Scale and Intensity Analysis,"

Education and Psychological Measurement, vol. 7, 1947, pp. 247–279.

Guttman, Louis, "The Principal Components of Scale Analysis," in Samuel A. Stouffer, et al., **Studies in Social Psychology in World War II,** vol. IV, **Measurement and Prediction,** New York: Wiley, 1950, pp. 312–361.

Guttman, Louis, "The Principal Components of Scalable Attitudes," in Paul L. Lazarsfeld, ed., **Mathematical Thinking in the Social Sciences,** New York: Free Press, 1954.

Harary, Frank, Robert Z. Norman, and Dorwin Cartwright, **Structural Models,** New York: Wiley, 1965.

Hartnack, Justus, **Wittgenstein and Modern Philosophy,** Garden City, N.Y.: Doubleday, 1965.

Hays, William L., **Statistics for Psychologists,** New York: Holt, Rinehart & Winston, 1963.

Head, Henry, **Aphasia and Kindred Disorders of Speech,** vol. 1, London: Cambridge University Press, 1926.

Hécaen, Henri, "Clinical Symptomatology in Right and Left Hemisphere Lesions," **Interhemispheric Relations and Cerebral Dominance,** ed. V. B. Mountcastle, Baltimore: Johns Hopkins Press, 1962.

Hécaen, Henri Hyacinthe Octave, and R. Angelergues, **La Cecito Psychique: Etude Critique de la Notion d'Agnosie,** Paris: Masson, 1963.

Hegel, G. W. F., **The Encyclopedia of the Philosophical Sciences,** trans. William Wallace, 2nd ed., Oxford: Clarendon, 1892.

Hegel, G. W. F., **Science of Logic,** vols. 1 & 2, trans. W. H. Johnston and L. G. Strathers, London: Allen and Unwin, 1929.

Hempel, Carl G., **Philosophy of Natural Science,** Englewood Cliffs, N.J.: Prentice-Hall, 1966.

Hempel, Carl G. and Paul Oppenheim, "Studies in the Logic of Explanation," **Philosophy of Science,** 15, 1948, p. 135.

Henschen, S. E., "On the Function of the Right Hemisphere of the Brain in Relation to the Left in Speech, Music, and Calculation," **Brain,** vol. 49, 1926, pp. 110–123.

Hertz, Robert, **Death and the Right Hand,** trans. Rodney and Claudia Needham, New York: Free Press, 1960.

Hilbert, David and Paul Bernays, **Grundlager der Mathematik,** 2 vols., Berlin: Springer, 1934.

Hilbert, David and Wilhelm Ackerman, **Grundzüg der Theorischen Logik,** Berlin: Springer, 1928.

Horton, John, "Order and Conflict Theories of Social Problems as Competing Ideologies," **American Journal of Sociology,** vol. 71, 1966, pp. 701–713.

Hsün-tzu, The Works of Hsün-tzu, trans. Homer H. Bubs, London: A. Probsthain, 1928.

Husserl, Edmund, **Ideas: General Introduction to Pure Phenomenology,** trans. W. R. Gibson, London: Collier-Macmillan, 1962.

Kant, Immanuel, **Critique of Pure Reason,** trans. F. Max Muller, Garden City, N.Y.: Doubleday, 1961.

Kimura, Doreen, "Left-Right Differences in the Perception of Melodies," **Quarterly Journal of Experimental Psychology,** vol. 16, 1964, pp. 355–358.

Köhler, Wolfgang, **Die Physischen Gestalten, in Ruhe und im Stationaren Zustand,** Erlangen: Braunschweig, 1920.

Koestler, Arthur, **The Ghost in the Machine,** New York: MacMillan, 1968.

Krashen, Stephen, "Language and the Left Hemisphere," **Working Papers in Phonetics,** UCLA, No. 24, October 1972, p. 43.

Kuhn, Thomas S., "Historical Structure of Scientific Discovery," **Science,** vol. 136, 1962, pp. 760–764.

Kuhn, Thomas S., **The Structure of Scientific Revolutions,** vol. 2, number 2, **International Encyclopedia of Unified Science,** Chicago: University of Chicago Press, 1962.

Landsdell, H., "Effect of Extent of Temporal Lobe Ablations on Two Lateralized Deficits," **Physiology and Behavior,** vol. 3, 1968, pp. 271–273.

Lao-Tze, Tao Teh King, trans. Archie J. Bahm, New York: Ungar, 1958.

Lazarsfeld, Paul F., ed., **Mathematical Thinking in the Social Sciences,** New York: Free Press, 1954.

Lazarus, R. S. and R. A. McCleary, "Autonomic Discrimination Without Awareness: An Interim Report," **Journal of Personality,** vol. 18, 1949, pp. 171–179.

Lazarus, R. S. and R. A. McCleary, "Autonomic Discrimination Without Awareness: A Study of Subception," **Psychological Review,** vol. 58, 1951, pp. 113–122.

Legge, James, trans., **I Ching: Book of Changes,** New York: Dover, 1963.

Lenin, V. I., **Collected Works,** trans. Clemens Dutt, ed. Stewart Smith, vol. 38, Moscow: Foreign Languages Publishing House, 1961.

Lévi-Strauss, Claude, **Structural Anthropology,** trans. Claire Jacobson and Brooke Grundfest Schoepf, New York: Basic, 1963.

Lévi-Strauss, Claude, **The Savage Mind,** Chicago: University of Chicago Press, 1966.

Lévi-Strauss, Claude, **The Raw and the Cooked: Introduction to a Science of Mythology,** vol 1, trans. John and Doreen Weightman, London: Jonathan Cape Ltd., and New York: Harper & Row, 1969.

Levy, Eliphus, **Transcendental Magic: Its Doctrine and Ritual,** trans., Arthur Edward Waite, New York: Samuel Weiser, 1972.

Levy-Agresti, J. and R. W. Sperry, "Differential Perceptual Capacities in Major and Minor Hemispheres," **Proceedings of the National Academy of Sciences,** vol. 61, 1968, p. 1151.

Luriia, Aleksandr Romanovich, **Human Brain and Psychological Processes,** trans., Basil Haigh, New York: Harper & Row, 1966.

Mao Tse-tung, On Contradiction, Peking: Foreign Languages Press, 1967.

Mead, George Herbert, **Mind, Self and Society,** Chicago: University of Chicago Press, 1934.

Meikel, T. H., J. A. Sechzer, and Eliot Stellar, "Interhemispheric Transfer of Tactile Conditioned Responses in Corpus Callosum-Sectioned Cats," **Journal of Neurophysiology,** vol. 25, 1962, pp. 530–543.

Merleau-Ponty, Maurice, **The Structure of Behavior,** trans. Alden L. Fisher, Boston: Beacon, 1963.

Merleau-Ponty, Maurice, **The Primacy of Perception,** ed. with intro. by James M. Edie, Evanston, Ill.: Northwestern University Press, 1964.

Merleau-Ponty, Maurice, **Signs,** trans. Richard C. McCleary, Evanston, Ill.: Northwestern University Press, 1964.

Metzner, Ralph, **Maps of Consciousness: I Ching, Tantra, Alchemy, Astrology, Actualism,** New York: Collier, 1971.

Milner, Brenda, "Visual Recognition and Recall After Right Temporal-Lobe Excision in Man," **Neuropsychologia,** vol. 6, 1968, pp. 191–209.

Milner, Brenda, "Interhemispheric Differences in the Localization of Psychological Processes in Man," **British Medical Bulletin,** vol. 27, 1971, pp. 272–277.

Miller, George A., "Professionals in Bureaucracy: Alienation Among Industrial Scientists and Engineers," **American Sociological Review,** vol. 32, 1967, pp. 755–768.

Morris, Charles, **Signification and Significance: A Study of the Relations of Signs and Values,** Cambridge, Mass.: MIT Press, 1964.

Mountcastle, V. B., ed., **Interhemispheric Relations and Cerebral Dominance,** Baltimore: Johns Hopkins Press, 1962.

Myers, Ronald E., "Discussion" in **Interhemispheric Relations and Cerebral Dominance,** ed. by V. B. Mountcastle, Baltimore: Johns Hopkins Press, 1958.

Nagel, Ernest and James R. Newman, **Gödel's Proof,** New York: New York University Press, 1958.

Neilson, J. M., "Unilateral Cerebral Dominance as Related to Mind Blindness: Minimal Lesion Capable of Causing Visual Agnosia for Objects," **Archives of Neurology and Psychiatry,** vol. 38, 1937, pp. 108–135.

Neilson, J. M., "Dominance of the Right Occipital Lobe," **Bulletin of the Los Angeles Neurological Societies,** vol. 5, 1940, pp. 135–145.

Noble, John, "Paradoxical Interocular Transfer of Mirror-Image Discriminations in the Optic Chiasm Sectioned Monkey," **Brain Research,** vol. 10, 1968, pp. 127–151.

Novak, Michael, **The Experience of Nothingness,** New York: Harper & Row, 1970.

Olson, Charles, "Human Universe," in Robert Creely, ed., **Selected Writings of Charles Olson,** New York: New Directions, 1951.

Papus (M. Gerard Encausse), **The Tarot of the Bohemians,** trans. A. P. Morton, North Hollywood, Calif.: Wilshire, 1971.

Parsons, Talcott, **The Structure of Social Action,** New York: McGraw-Hill, 1937.

Parsons, Talcott, **The Social System,** New York: Free Press, 1951.

Parsons, Talcott, Robert F. Bales, and Edward A. Shils, **Working Papers in the Theory of Action,** New York: Free Press, 1953.

Parsons, Talcott, Edward Shils, Kaspar D. Naegele, and Jesse R. Pitts, eds., **Theories of Society: Foundations of Modern Sociological Theory,** vol. 2, New York: Free Press, 1961.

Piaget, Jean, **Structuralism,** New York: Harper & Row, 1970.

Piercy, Malcolm, "The Effects of Cerebral Lesions on Intellectual Functions: A Review of Current Research Trends," **British Journal of Psychiatry,** vol. 110, 1964, pp. 310–352.

Polanyi, Michael, **Personal Knowledge: Toward a Post-Critical Philosophy,** Chicago: University of Chicago Press, 1958.

Polanyi, Michael, **The Tacit Dimension,** Garden City, N.Y.: Anchor Books, 1967.

Popper, Karl R., **Logic of Scientific Discovery,** London: Hutchinson, 1959.

Popper, Karl R., **The Poverty of Historicism,** New York: Harper & Row, 1964.

Quarton, G. C., T. Melnechuck and O. Schmitt, ed., **The Neurosciences: A Study Program,** New York: Rockefeller University Press, 1967.

Radin, Paul, **The Winnebago Tribe,** Washington, D.C.: Bureau of American Ethnology, 37th Annual Report, 1923.

Radnitzky, Gerard, **Anglo-Saxon Schools of Metascience,** vol. 1, Göteborg, Sweden: Berlingska Baktrgcheriet Land, 1968.

Ramon y Cajal, S., "Anatomical and Physiological Considerations About the Brain," in G. Von Bonen, trans., **Some Papers on the Cerebral Cortex,** Springfield, Ill.: C. C. Thomas, 1960.

Roszak, Theodore, **The Making of a Counter-Culture,** New York: McGraw-Hill, 1969.

Rudner, Richard S., **Philosophy of Social Science,** Englewood Cliffs, N.J.: Prentice-Hall, 1966.

Russell, Bertrand and Whitehead, Alfred North, **Principia Mathematica,** London: Cambridge University Press, 1925.

Sadhu, Mouni, **The Tarot: A Contemporary Course of the Quintessence of Hermetic Occultism,** North Hollywood, California: Wilshire Book Company, 1970.

Santillana, Giorgio de, and Hertha von Dechend, **Hamlet's Mill: An Essay on Myth and the Frame of Time,** Boston: Gambit Inc., 1969.

Sapir, Edward, **Language,** New York: Harcourt, Brace, Jovanovich, 1921.

Saussure, Ferdinand de, **Course in General Linguistics,** eds. Charles Bally and Albert Sechebaye in collaboration with Albert Reidtinger, trans., with introduction and notes by Wade Baskin, New York: McGraw-Hill, 1966.

Schopenhauer, Arthur, **The World as Will and Idea,** vol. 1, trans. R. B. Haldane and J. Kemp, London: Routledge & Kegan Paul, 1957.

Selsam, Howard and Harry Martel, **Reader in Marxist Philosophy: From the Writings of Marx, Engels, and Lenin,** New York: International Publishers, 1963.

Sherrington, Charles, **The Integrative Action of the Nervous System,** London: Cambridge University Press, 1947.

Siu, R. S. H., **The Men of Many Qualities: A Legacy of the I Ching,** Cambridge, Mass.: MIT Press, 1968.

Smith, Aaron, "Speech and Other Functions After Left (Dominant) Hemispherectomy," **Journal of Neurology, Neurosurgery and Psychiatry,** vol. 29, 1966, pp. 467–471.

Smith, C. U. M., **The Brain: Toward an Understanding,** New York: Capricorn, 1970.

Smith, I. Macfarlane, **Spatial Ability: Its Educational and Social Significance,** San Diego: Robert K. Knapp, 1964.

Snow, Sir Charles Percy, **The Two Cultures and Scientific Revolution,** New York: Cambridge University Press, 1960.

Snyder, Gary, **Earth House Hold,** New York: New Directions, 1957.

Solla Price, Derek J. de, **Little Science, Big Science,** New York: Columbia University Press, 1963.

Spearman, C., **Psychology Down the Ages,** Vol. I, London: Macmillan, 1937.

Spearman, C. and L. Wynn Jones, **Human Abilities,** London: Macmillan, 1950.

Spender, Stephen, "The Making of a Poem," in **The Creative Process: A Symposium,** ed. Brewster Ghiselin, New York: New America Library, 1952.

Sperry, R. W., "Problems Outstanding in the Evolution of Brain Function," James Arthur Lecture, American Museum of Natural History, New York, 1964.

Sperry, R. W., "Split-Brain Approaches to Learning Problems," in **The Neurosciences: A Study Program,** eds. G. C. Quarton, T. Melnechuch, and O. Schmitt, New York: Rockefeller University Press, 1967, pp. 714–722.

Sperry, R. W., M. S. Gazzaniga, and J. E. Bogen, "Interhemispheric Relations: The Neocortical Commissures; Syndrome of Hemisphere Disconnection," ed. P. J. Vinken and G. W. Brugm, **Handbook of Clinical Neurology,** vol. 4, ch. 14, Amsterdam: North Holland Publishers, 1969, pp. 273–290.

Sperry, R. W., M. S. Gazzaniga, and J. E. Bogen, "Role of the Neocortical Commissures," in P. J. Vinken and G. W. Brugm, eds., **Handbook of Clinical Neurology,** vol. 4, Amsterdam: North Holland Publishers, 1969.

Spier, Leslie, ed., **Language, Culture, and Personality: Essays in Memory of Edward Sapir,** Menasha, Wisconsin: Sapir Memorial Publications Fund, 1941.

Stace, W. T., **The Philosophy of Hegel: A Systematic Exposition,** London: Dover, 1955.

The Standard Edition of the Complete Psychological Works of Sigmund Freud, vol. 5, trans. James Strachey, London: Hogarth, 1953.

Stevens, S. S., **Handbook of Experimental Psychology,** New York: Wiley, 1951.

Stoll, Robert R., **Sets, Logic & Axiomatic Theories,** New York: Freeman, 1961.

Stouffer, Samuel A., et al., **Studies in Social Psychology in World War II,** vol. IV, **Measurement and Predictions,** New York: Wiley, 1950.

Street, Roy F., **A Gestalt Completion Test: A Study of a Cross Section of Intellect,** New York: Teachers College, 1931.

Taylor, James, ed., **Selected Writings of John Hughlings Jackson,** vol. 2, New York: Basic Books, 1958.

TenHouten, Warren D., "Scale Gradient Analysis: A Statistical Method for Constructing and Evaluating Guttman Scales," **Sociometry,** vol. 32, 1962, pp. 80–98.

TenHouten, Warren D., **Cognitive Styles and the Social Order,** Final Report, part II, OEO Study B00-5135, "Thought, Race, and Opportunity," Los Angeles, Calif., 1971.

Vinken, P. J. and G. W. Brugm, eds., **Handbook of Clinical Neurology,** vol. 4, Amsterdam: North Holland Publishers, 1969.

Waite, Arthur Edward, **The Pictorial Key to the Tarot,** New Hyde Park, New York: University Books, 1959.

Warrington, Elizabeth K. and Merle James, "An Experimental Investigation of Facial Recognition in Patients with Unilateral Cerebral Lesions," **Cortex,** vol. 3, 1967, pp. 317–326.

Wechsler, David, **The Measurement of Adult Intelligence,** 2nd ed., Baltimore: Williams & Wilkins, 1952.

Weisenburg, Theodore and Katherine McBride, **Aphasia: A Clinical and Psychological Study,** New York: Commonwealth Fund, 1936.

Wertheimer, Max, **Productive Thinking,** enlarged edition, ed. Michael Wertheimer, New York: Harper & Row, 1959.

White, Harry Houston, "Cerebral Hemispherectomy in the Treatment of Infantile Hemiplegia," **Confinia Neurologica,** vol. 21, pp. 1–50.

White, Morton, **The Age of Analysis: 20th Century Philosophers,** Boston: Houghton Mifflin, 1955.

Whorf, B. L., "The Punctual and Segmentative Aspects of Verbs in Hopi," **Language,** vol. 12, 1936, pp. 127—131.

Whorf, Benjamin Lee, "Some Verbal Categories of Hopi," **Language,** vol. 14, 1938, pp. 275—286.

Whorf, Benjamin Lee, "Science and Linguistics," **Technology Review,** vol. 42, 1940, pp. 229—231.

Whorf, Benjamin Lee, "The Relation of Habitual Thought and Behavior to Language," in **Language, Culture and Personality: Essays in Memory of Edward Sapir,** ed. Leslie Spier, et al., Menasha, Wisconsin: Sapir Memorial Publications Fund, 1941, pp. 75—93.

Whorf, Benjamin Lee, "Linguistic Factors in the Terminology of Hopi Architecture," **International Journal of American Linguistics,** vol. 19, 1943, pp. 141—145.

Whorf, Benjamin Lee, "An American Indian Model of the Universe," **International Journal of Linguistics,** vol. 16, 1950, pp. 62—72.

Whorf, Benjamin Lee, "Discussion of Hopi Linguistics," in **Language, Thought and Reality: Selected Writings of Benjamin Lee Whorf,** ed. John B. Carroll, Cambridge, Mass.: MIT Press, 1965.

Wigan, A. L., **The Duality of the Mind,** London: Longman, 1844.

Wilhelm, Hellmut, **Change: Eight Lectures on the I Ching,** trans. Cary F. Baynes, Princeton, N.J.: Princeton University Press (Bollinger Series LXII), 1960.

Wilhelm, Richard and Cary F. Baynes, trans., **The Secret of the Golden Flower: A Chinese Book of Life,** New York: Harcourt, Brace, Jovanovich, 1962.

Wilhelm, Richard and Cary F. Baynes, trans., **The I Ching, or Book of Changes,** Princeton, N.J.: Princeton University Press, Bollinger Series, 1967.

Wittgenstein, Ludwig, **Tractatus Logico-Philosophicus,** New York: Harcourt Brace Jovanovich, 1922.

Wittgenstein, Ludwig, **Philosophical Investigations,** trans. G. E. M. Anscombe, Oxford: Blackwell, 1963.

Wooldridge, Dean E., **The Machinery of the Brain,** New York: McGraw-Hill, 1963.

Index of Names

Alexander, Christopher, 85–86
Anderson, A. Lloyd, 15
Angelergues, R., 16
Arnheim, Rudolph, 205–206

Bahm, Archie J., 61–62, 117
Bakan, Paul, 24–25, 77
Baynes, Cary F., 45, 163, 183
Beale, Ivan L., 16–17, 22, 23
Berlin, Isaiah, 218
Bharati, Agehananda, 130, 131
Black Elk, 52
Blofeld, John, 122, 135, 184
Bogen, Glenda, 40, 49, 221
Bogen, Joseph E., 4, 12, 13, 19, 40, 49, 77, 221
Braithwaite, R. B., 215
Bruner, Jerome S., 25–26

Case, Paul F., 36, 37–38
Castaneda, Carlos, 5, 51–59, 126, 135, 144–145, 207, 208–209, 213, 217–218
Chang Chung-yuan, 141, 219–221
Chi Tsang, 220
Chisholm, Roderick, 151–152
Chou, Duke of, 43
Chou Hsin, 43
Cleary, R. A., 21
Confucius, 44, 171–172
Corballis, Michael C., 16–17, 22, 23
Costa, L. D., 16
Critchley, Macdonald, 15–16

Day, Merle E., 24
De Santillana Giorgio, 158
De Solla Price, Derek J., 154
Dechend, Hertha von, 158
DeRenzi, E., 27
Domhoff, G. William, 24

Encausse, M. Gerard (Papus), 36, 136–137
Engels, Friedrich, 6, 202, 204–205, 212–213, 217, 221
Eriksen, C. W., 21

Fenichel, Otto, 13
Frankel, Charles, 145
Freud, Sigmund, 13, 16

Frolov, Y. P., 24
Fu Hsi, 180

Gardner, Martin, 22–23, 152–153
Garfinkel, Harold, 5, 113–115, 140
Gazzaniga, M. S., 17, 77, 79
Gödel, Kurt, 149–152
Granet, Marcel, 161–162, 165, 172–173
Gray, Eden, 33, 37, 38, 41
Guttman, Louis, 66, 67, 69, 71–76, 80

Hartnack, Justus, 104–105, 132
Hécaen, Henri, 16
Hegel, G. W. F., 6, 200–205, 207, 212–216, 218–221
Hempel, Carl G., 199, 215
Henschen, S. E., 19
Hermes Trismegistus, 33
Hertz, Robert, 23
Hilbert, David, 148
Horton, John, 224
Hsun Ching, 219
Husserl, Edmund, 136, 223

Isis, 33

Jackson, John Hughlings, 12–13
Jones, Wynn, 14
Jung, Carl G., 137–138, 139, 183, 190–191, 219

Kant, Immanuel, 194–195, 200, 208
Kimura, Doreen, 20
Koestler, Arthur, 145
Köhler, Wolfgang, 67
Krashen, Stephen, 103
Kuethe, J. L., 21
Kuhn, Thomas S., 153–154

Lao Tzu, 44, 117–118, 219
Lazarus, R. S., 21
Legge, James, 122
Leibniz, G. W. von, 210–211
Lenin, V. I., 6, 201, 221
Lévi-Strauss, Claude, 80–85, 100, 101–102, 105–106, 116, 124, 159–160, 174, 187–189, 195–198, 206, 213–214, 216

Levy, Eliphus, 61
Levy-Agresti, J., 13
Luriia, Aleksandr R., 13

McBride, Katharine E., 15
Mao Tse-tung, 201, 202
Marx, Karl, 6, 217, 221, 224
Matus, Juan, 5, 32, 51–59, 60, 126, 134–
    135, 140, 144–145, 208–209, 213,
    217–218, 221
Mead, George Herbert, 124
Meikel, T. H., 79
Merleau-Ponty, Maurice, 59–60, 67, 102,
    103, 105, 119, 123, 124, 129, 132,
    160, 161, 168, 202–203, 204
Metzner, Ralph, 44, 130
Milner, Brenda, 16, 20
Morris, Charles, 124
Myers, Ronald E., 17

Nagel, Ernest, 149–151
Newman, James R., 149–151
Noble, John, 17
Novak, Michael, 145–146

Olson, Charles, 129
Oppenheim, Paul, 215
Osiris, King, 33

Pan Ku, 223
Papus (M. Gerard Encausse), 36, 136–137
Parsons, Talcott, 67, 113, 224
Pavlov, Ivan P., 13, 22, 24, 202
Piaget, Jean, 216–217
Piercy, Malcolm, 16
Polanyi, Michael, 3–4, 21, 139
Popper, Karl R., 4, 153, 216

Radin, Paul, 195
Ramon y Cajal, S., 77
Rudner, Richard, 148
Russell, Bertrand, 103, 149–150

Sadhu, Mouni, 33, 34, 38, 39, 40, 125–126,
    134, 136, 173–174
Sapir, Edward, 103
Schopenhauer, Arthur, 7
Shao Yung, 210–211
Sherrington, Charles, 77–78
Siu, R. G. H., 139
Smith, Aaron, 19
Smith, C. U. M., 7
Smith, I. Macfarlane, 13, 25
Snow, C. P., 25
Snyder, Gary, 52–53
Spearman, C., 13–14
Spender, Steven, 26
Sperry, Roger W., 13, 77, 79
Spinnler, H., 27
Sraffa, Piero, 132
Stace, W. T., 214

Vaughn, H. G., 16

Waite, Arthur E., 61, 124, 126, 137
Wechsler, David, 15
Weisenburg, Theodore, 15
Wên, King, 43, 180
Wertheimer, Max, 20
Whitehead, Alfred North, 103, 149–150
Whorf, Benjamin Lee, 90–95, 97–101, 102,
    107, 119
Wigan, A. L., 17, 77
Wilhelm, Hellmut, 211
Wilhelm, Richard, 45–49, 51, 82–85, 117,
    122, 134, 135, 138, 163, 168–172,
    176, 178–183, 184, 186–187, 209–
    210
Wittgenstein, Ludwig, 87, 104–106, 132–
    133, 148
Wooldridge, Dean E., 3

Young, E. D., 17

Index of Subjects

Absolute necessity, 208, 211–213
Agnosia, 16
Ally, 54–55, 208–209, 213, 220
Alpha waves, 25
Ambiguity, 170–171
Analytic a priori, 151
Analytic thought, 13–14, 147–152, 194–195, 199–200, 214. See also Propositional thought
Aphasia, 15, 19
Appositional thought, 4–5, 14–22, 99–100, 103–105, 142, 158–189, 194, 200–201, 203, 224
Apprentice, 51–59, 208–209
Apraxia, 15
Arcana, 33–43, 82
Art, 22–23, 213
Attendance, 91–94

Being, 55, 201, 204–205, 219–220
Belief, 145–146, 200
Body, 67, 80, 126–135
Bricoleur, 105–106, 169
Brain, 3–4, 12–20
Buddhism, 219–222

Cerebral commissures, 16–17
Cerebral commissurotomy, 17–19, 49–50, 77–80, 87
Cerebrum, 12
Chance, 211–213
Change, 184–189
Character, 55
Clarity, 55, 103–104, 126, 146–152
Closure, 13, 76, 78, 82, 103, 191
Codes
  extended ultracodes, 173–184
  immediate sensory codes, 166–173
Commonsense, 112–113
Complementarity, 201. See also Dialectics
Complexity, 116–127
Confucianism, 5, 44
Conjugate lateral eye movements, 24–25
Consciousness, 3–4, 6, 78–80, 201, 219
Construction, 161, 201
Constructional apraxia, 16
Contradiction, 201, 207, 209, 212, 216–217

Corpus callosum, 16–18, 79–80
Correspondence, 186–187
Creativity, 39–40, 49–50
Critique, 195, 198, 208–209
Cryptotype, 98–99, 123
Culture, 22–24, 80–85, 91–92, 99–100

Datura inoxia, 52–53, 63, 213
Dialectic moment, 215, 220–221
Dialectics
  and dual organizations, 195–199
  laws of, 203–219
    interpenetrating opposites, 207–214
    quality-quantity, 203–207
    negation of the negation, 214–219
  in scientific inquiry, 6, 204–205, 207–208, 214–217
  in synthetic inquiry
    in I Ching, 44, 173, 178–179, 182, 184, 206–213, 218–219
    in Tarot, 32, 39–40, 206–207
    in vision quest, 58–59, 207–209, 217–219
  in Taoism, 190–191, 219–222
Direction, 76–103, 106–107, 191, 198
Disbelief, 145–146, 200
Disciplines in inquiry, 32–33
Distinctness, 114–115
Divination
  in I Ching, 50–51, 117, 163, 170–172, 211–213
  in Tarot 40–43, 212
  in vision quest, 54–55, 213
Dual organizations. See Dialectics
Duality, 6, 77–80, 196–199, 201, 206, 214, 217, 220
Dyscopia, 19
Dysgraphia, 19

Easy, 47
Enemies, 217
  in scientific inquiry, 144–156, 215–216
  in synthetic inquiry, 55–56, 144–145, 147–148, 152, 217–218
English language. See Language
Enstasy, 130
Environment, 67, 85–86, 198–199
Epilepsy, 16

Eventuations, 93
Extended ultracodes. See Codes

Fear, 55–56, 144–145, 217–218
Form
  and ally, 60, 118
  and behavior, 129, 201–203
  and dialectics, 194–200, 202–203
  and logic, 148–151, 194–195
  and mental order, 78
  of objects, 60
  and structure, 60, 67, 80, 82, 85–86
  synthetic, 206
  and tools, 129
  and a warrior, 58
Fortune telling. See Divination
Frame of reference, 196–197. See also In-
    variant frame

Geographic behavior, 202
Gestalt, 13, 25, 170
Gestalt psychology, 67, 203
Gestalt-synthetic thought, 13
Gödel's proof, 149–151
Grasping, 13–14, 60, 78, 82, 128–129, 206

Handedness, 16, 23–26
Hemispherectomy, 17
Hemispheres of brain, 12–15
Hexagrams, 45–51, 62, 82, 121–123, 133–
    134, 139–140, 163–172, 175–189,
    208–212
Holding together, 186–187
Hopi language. See Language
Horizon, 161, 168, 173
Hypermediation, 79, 81–82, 100–103, 124–
    125
Hysteria, 224

I Ching, 5, 43–50, 116–117, 121–123, 137–
    140, 162–189, 206, 209–213, 218–
    219
Idealism, 2, 6–7
Identity, 201, 207–214, 220
Image, 82–83, 121–123, 160–164
  in I Ching, 46
Immaturity, 154–156
Immediate sensory codes. See Codes
Inquiry
  scientific, xi-xiii, 5–6, 25–26, 32–33,
    104–105, 113–114, 144–155, 204–
    205, 207–208, 214–217
  synthetic, xii–xiii, 5–6, 25–26, 32–33, 60,
    82, 104–105, 115–140, 158–189,
    205–208, 214–219
Intelligence, 142, 221
  appositional, 14, 16, 27, 142, 221
  general, 14
  and intuition, 136–137

propositional, 14, 16, 27
Intensity, 76, 78–79, 81–82, 101, 103,
    106–107, 190, 198
Interenvelopment, 129–131
Intuition, 25–26, 134–140
Invariant frame, 59, 184–189
Involution, 76, 78, 100, 191
Involvement. See Involution

Jimson weed. See Datura inoxia
Judgment
  in dialectics, 215
  in I Ching, 46
  visual, 206

Laws, 102, 215–216, 223
Language
  and brain, 12–15, 20, 103
  English, 90–100
  games, 105
  Hopi, 90–103
  in inquiry, 82, 104, 113–114, 117–126
  as overlaid function, 103
  and perception, 100, 104
Layers
  as components of order, 71
  in ensemble, 85
  of structural perception, 115, 126–135
Left-movers, 24–25
Lines in I Ching, 43–44, 48, 50–51, 209
Locators, 92
Logic, 114, 146–152, 194
Logical-analytic thought, 13
Logical empiricism, 7, 104
Looking, 57, 60, 127–128, 140
Lophophora williamsii, 52–53

Magic, 34, 58–59
Manifested, 99
Manipulatory techniques
  in I Ching, 50–51
  in Tarot, 40–43
  in vision quest, 52–55
Mantra, 131
Materialism, 2–3, 6
Measurement, 67–76, 204–207
  category, 68
  interval, 68–69
  and order, 67–76
  ordinal, 68–76
  and perception, 67, 205
  quality and quantity, 202–207
Mechanism, 3–4, 203
Mediation, 81. See also Hypermediation
Mental order, 77–80, 103, 198, 201, 203
Mescaline, 59–60. See also Psylocybe mexi-
    cana
Metaphor, 25–26, 213
Mind, 2–3, 6, 40, 77–80, 103, 161

Chinese, 161–162
as dialectical, 200–204
and mental order, 77, 103
neurological model of, 3
Mirror image, xii, 13, 17–18, 22–23, 146
evidence and theory, 207–208
kinds of inquiry, xii
language and nature, 105
Music
and language, 81–82, 100–103
and myth, 102
and right hemisphere, 19–21, 81–82
Myth, 80–85, 100–103, 106, 158–161, 187–189, 206, 213–214

Nature, 22–24, 99–100, 117, 213
and culture, 80–85
Negation, 56–60, 85–86, 200, 215–221
Negation of the negation, 215–221
Nothingness, 146, 220
Notion, 214, 220

Objectivity, 59
in dialectics, 221–222
and Hopi language, 99
myth of, 145–146
Obsessive compulsiveness, 224
Old age, 56
Opposites, 178–179, 201, 220
unity and struggle of, 207–214
Optic chiasm, 17–18
Oracle, 50, 212. See also Divination
Order, 59–60, 66–67, 85
and dialectics, 209, 219, 224
and form, 67, 85, 203
of hexagrams. See Sequence of hexagrams
as layered, 71, 198
and measurement, 67–76
in perception, 59
social, 198, 203
and structure, 85
and system, 67

Perception
of depth, 160
and horizon, 161
immanence and transcendence, 119, 141
and language, 99–100, 103–104
and right hemisphere, 13, 78
in scientific inquiry, 103
synaesthetic, 58
in synthetic inquiry, 102, 120, 135–140, 160, 165–172, 187
and Tao, 117–119
thresholds, 67
Perfect scale, 71
Pointing, 128
Power, 46, 54–55, 58
Primary process thought, 13

Primitive thought, 105. See also Appositional thought
Principal components, 71–77, 86. See also Measurement
Propositional thought, 4–5, 13, 27, 78, 100, 103–104, 194, 200–201, 203, 224
Psychotropic plants, 52–55, 208–209
Psylocybe mexicana, 52–54, 63, 213

Quality, 202–207, 209
Quantity, 202–207

Rationalities, 113
scientific, 5–6, 26, 113–115
synthetic, 5–6, 26, 102, 115–141
Reading **Tarot** cards, 40–43. See also Divination
Reductionism, 2–4, 203
Relative necessity, 211–212
Revolution, 217–218
Right-movers, 24–25

Scales, 69–71
Science, 5, 221–222. See also Rationalities
development of, 153–154, 158
and language, 90–91
myth of objectivity, 45–46
Scientific inquiry. See Inquiry
Scientific rationalities. See Rationalities
Secondary process thought, 13
Sequence of hexagrams, 45, 209–211
Sign subception, 21–22
Sign particulars, 21–22, 161–166
Signals, 162, 165
Signs, 162–166
Simple, 47
Social order. See Order
Sorcery, 53–54
Space, 172–173, 182–184
in English and Hopi, 99–102
and hypermediation, 100–103
in **I Ching**, 46–48
and right hemisphere, 13–16
and time, 106–107
Spatial ability, 13–14, 16. See also Intelligence
Spatial agnosia, 16
Speech, 132. See also Talking
Split-brain operation. See Cerebral commissurotomy
Split representation, 22
Structural perception, 126–135
Structure, 102, 151, 203, 206
and form, 67, 80
as layers in order, 80, 160
and mental order, 78
in synthetic inquiry, 187–189
Struggle, 48, 54, 58, 201, 207–214, 217
Subception. See Sign subception

Subjectivity, 59–60, 107, 220, 222
  in Hopi language, 99–101
Symbols, 124–125, 165–166
Symmetry, 22–24
Synaesthetic perception. See Perception
Synchronic time. See Time
Synthetic a priori, 151–152
Synthetic form. See Form
Synthetic inquiry. See Inquiry
Synthetic rationalities. See Rationalities
Synthetic thought. See Appositional
  thought
System, 67, 85–86, 196–197

Tacit knowing, 21–22
Talking, 56–57, 79, 98, 104, 120, 122–123,
  213
Tantra, 132–133
Tao, 116–119, 121, 162, 190–191, 219–
  221
Taoism, 5, 44
Tarot, 5, 32–43, 116, 123–126, 134, 136–
  137
Temporals, 93
Theory, 67, 146–147, 152–156, 164, 199,
  207–208, 215–217, 221, 223
Throwing, 132–133
Throwing I Ching coins, 50–51, 212–213.
  See also Divination
Time, 172–173, 175–176, 182–184

diachronic and synchronic, 82, 183–184
in English and Hopi, 99–102
in I Ching, 45–46, 82, 175–177, 180, 184
and language, 93–94, 106
and left hemisphere, 13
and music, 82
principal components of, 107–108
and space. See Space
Tools, 25, 105–106, 184
Touching, 128–129
Trigrams, 44–45, 165, 169–170, 174–182

Unmanifested, 98–99

Veiledness, 37–39, 98, 116–127, 146–152
Verbal intelligence, 14–16. See also Intelligence
Vision quest, 51–60, 118, 126, 134–135,
  140, 144–145

Warrior, 54–58, 217–218
Weakness, 152–154, 216
Whorf hypothesis, 101–102
Will, 35–37, 54, 140

Yab, 131
Yang, 44
Yin, 44
Yum, 131